A Vision of Holiness

A
VISION
OF HOLINESS

THE FUTURE OF
REFORM JUDAISM

RICHARD N. LEVY

URJ Press   ✦   New York

To Carol Levy

Library of Congress Cataloging-in-Publication Data

Levy, Richard N.
   A vision of holiness: the future of Reform Judaism / Richard N. Levy.
      p. cm.
   Includes the text of Statement of principles for Reform Judaism : the Pittsburgh
Principles.
   ISBN 0-8074-0941-3 (pbk. : alk. paper)
     1. Reform Judaism—Doctrines. 2. Central Conference of American Rabbis.
     Statement of principles for Reform Judaism. 3. Reform Judaism—United
     States—History. 4. Holiness—Judaism. I. Central Conference of American
     Rabbis. Statement of principles for Reform Judaism. II. Title.

BM197.L45 2005
296.8'341—dc22   2005048528

Look! Today I have set before you life and harmony and death and chaos, in that today I tell you commandingly how important it is to Me that you love *YHVH* your God, walk in God's ways, and keep the Eternal's mitzvot and statutes and judgments, that you may live and multiply and bless *YHVH* your God in the land whither you have come to inherit.

—Deuteronomy 30:15–16, Torah portion for Yom Kippur
morning in Reform liturgy (translation by R. N. Levy)

In all these ways and more, [God, Torah, and Israel] give meaning and purpose to our lives.

—"A Statement of Principles for Reform Judaism,"
conclusion of each major section

Contents

Preface: Shapers of a Vision

Two biblical texts about vision (*chazon* in Hebrew) are instructive for our times:

> And as a child Samuel ministered to *Adonai* before Eli, and the word of the Eternal was rare in those days; there was no widespread vision.
>
> — I Samuel 3:1

> Without vision the people are at loose ends, but the one who observes Torah is happy.
>
> — Proverbs 29:18

Perceiving, as the twenty-first century was about to dawn, that the Reform Movement lacked a "widespread vision" that could encompass the changes the movement had undergone since the 1970s, the Central Conference of American Rabbis (CCAR) undertook to write a new statement of its principles that could help guide the largest community of Jews in North America at the start of the new century. "A Statement of Principles for Reform Judaism," often referred to as the Pittsburgh Principles because of the city in which it was approved in 1999, is the result. Holiness is a major theme of this document; more and more Reform Jews are restless that "the word of the Eternal [is] rare" in our days. The preamble to the Pittsburgh Principles states that "we hope to transform our lives through *kedushah*, holiness." The "means by which we make our lives holy" are mitzvot, also defined as "sacred obligations." The "Statement of Principles" itself could be called "a vision of holiness."

This book is an explication of the Pittsburgh Principles' vision. In a sense, it is a personal reflection of a communal vision, an attempt to explore the implications of the 1999 document for Reform belief and practice from the perspective of a rabbi who has served congregations and Hillel foundations, has been on the editorial committee of both *Gates of Prayer* and *Mishkan T'filah*, was president of the CCAR while this document was being conceived and passed, and is now director of the rabbinic school at the Los Angeles campus of the Hebrew Union College. While Reform Jews will differ in their views of the interpretations in this volume, my hope is that its pages will challenge all of its Jewish readers, Reform or not, to reflect on the nature of their religious lives and deepen their relationships with God, their absorption in Torah, and their critical commitment to the destiny of the Jewish people and the Jewish state. For non-Jews who are considering conversion or are merely interested in the nature of this religious movement, I hope the book will illumine the manner in which this vibrant group of Jews envisions its purpose in the world.

What does "vision" mean? The citation from the Book of Proverbs seems to regard "vision" as parallel with "Torah." In *Parashat R'eih*, Deuteronomy 13:2–4 seeks to insure that the visions we pursue are in consonance with Torah. One could ask, therefore, "Why does a Jew need a vision if its content is already included in the Torah?" The answer seems to be that the *experience* of Revelation as well as the *text* of it are necessary for Torah to be authoritative in our lives. In keeping with this view, the Pittsburgh Principles describes mitzvah as part of both the (experiential) dialogue with God and the (textual) dialogue with Torah. The people need a vision to awaken them to the life of holiness lying dormant in a scroll.

The Statement of Principles itself and this book that resulted from it owe their existence to a number of visionaries. It was my eminent good fortune to become vice president of the CCAR when Rabbi Paul Menitoff was coming into office as the CCAR's executive vice president.

Together with the new president, Rabbi Simeon (Shim) Maslin, Paul grasped the opportunity to reinvent the CCAR. He was determined to turn it into an organization that would meet the many different needs of Reform rabbis and would play a leading role in the guidance of the Reform Movement, a task in which he was strongly assisted by the CCAR's administrative director, Shelley Limmer, and by his administrative assistant Dale Panoff, both of whom were of great support to me during this period. Paul's strategic wisdom, based on an innate understanding of the nature and concerns of our colleagues, was crucial to the passage of the Pittsburgh Principles. Working with him was one of the great experiences of my life.

Colleagues who served on the board of the CCAR during the two years of my presidency initially looked warily at the idea of a new statement of principles, though they supported the process of discussion and revision that ultimately led to its approval. Their caution made their eventual endorsement of bringing the draft document to a vote in Pittsburgh all the more heartening. At the suggestion of Rabbi Lee Bycel, Rabbi Charles A. Kroloff, vice president of the CCAR at the time, chaired the convention during the actual vote on the Pittsburgh Principles, and he handled the discussion with masterful skill, ease, and humor. Rabbi Elliot Stevens, now associate executive director of the CCAR, lent his enormous experience, insight, and wit to the conduct of the floor discussion of the Statement of Principles, inspiring immense confidence as we waded through the jungle of Robert's Rules. While he did not play a major role in the creation of the Pittsburgh Principles, Rabbi Arnold Sher, director of placement of the CCAR, provided to colleagues wrestling with the implications of the Pittsburgh Principles an underlying trust that whatever direction the movement might take, their own professional futures were in good hands.

Aron Hirt-Manheimer, editor of *Reform Judaism* and an old friend from our days at UCLA Hillel, performed an invaluable service in bringing the statement to the attention of the Reform Movement by his courageous decision to make it the cover story of the Winter 1998 issue of *Reform Judaism* (see chapter 1). His gracious agreement to edit the draft before it was submitted to the CCAR brought his remarkable involvement in this process full circle.

Acknowledgment is also in order for some of my colleagues at the Hebrew Union College–Jewish Institute of Religion (HUC-JIR). Rabbi David Ellenson, who had just been named president of HUC-JIR, argued for the book's acceptance by the editorial board of the (now) URJ Press. My old friend and HUC classmate Rabbi Lewis Barth, dean of the Los Angeles campus, has inspired an atmosphere of high standards both of academic integrity and of a community all of whose members care about each other. Both of these concerns are supported by Dr. Norman Cohen, the provost, who has presided over major changes in the College that have been introduced with widespread support and enthusiasm. I first worked with Norman in the early days of the Reform Leadership Council, when the lay and professional heads of the CCAR, HUC-JIR, and the Union for Reform Judaism (URJ) were laying the groundwork for an unprecedented collegial shaping of the Reform Movement as a whole. Major contributors to that effort were Rabbi Eric Yoffie, president of the URJ, and another old friend, Rabbi Lennard Thal, URJ senior vice president. While Eric preferred to change the movement one initiative at a time rather than issue an overall statement of purpose, once the Pittsburgh Principles passed he instructed various departments of the URJ to provide study guides and other instruments to insure its widespread distribution.

Indispensable for the shaping of this volume has been Rabbi Hara Person, editor in chief of URJ Press, an impressively patient, persistent, and perceptive editor, whose enthusiasm for this project has been crucial to its completion. Her probing editorial eye uncovered holes in arguments and impediments to a comprehensible text. She has been a wonderful partner in this book. I am also grateful to Michael Goldberg for his remarkable blend of flexibility in response to my idiosyncracies and his firmness in regard to standards of language and design. It has been inspiring to work with them both. Many others at URJ Press gave critical support to this book, including Ron Ghatan, Debra Corman, Lauren Dubin, Dahlia Schoenberg, and Victor Ney.

This book is not only about the Pittsburgh Principles, but about the life that more and more Reform Jews would like to lead as they become increasingly aware of the *k'dushah* that is possible for them to build into their lives. Two of the best exemplars of this struggle are Mark and

Peachy Levy (no relation), who are increasingly known for the depth of their philanthropy in the name of Peachy's late parents, Red and Lee Kalsman. But before they became philanthropists, we knew them as Jews in search of a more accessible vision of the word of God. They wore *tallitot* and *kippot* when such garb was frowned upon in Reform synagogues, kashered their house when few other Reform Jews were doing so, and expressed their frustration with what they perceived as the slow pace of the Reform Movement to make serious Jews like them feel at home. Both of them have spent significant time in Israel, they traveled to the Soviet Union to help refuseniks, and Peachy rode donkeys down the mountains to Gondar Province to bring sustenance to the Jews of Ethiopia. Mark has worked unstintingly as an officer and consultant with the URJ to strengthen the Reform synagogue and has chaired the board of MAZON: A Jewish Response to Hunger. Peachy has made notable contributions to the practice of *hidur mitzvah* (beautifying the commandment) through her creation of embroidered pieces that adorn many homes and institutions of the Movement. There is hardly a chapter in this book nor a topic in the Pittsburgh Principles in which the two of them have not left their footprint. If you wish to see what Reform Jews of the twenty-first century can look like, talk to Mark and Peachy Levy.

Finally, there is another Levy without whose strong and inspiriting presence neither this book nor most other things I have put my hand to in almost thirty-five years could have been accomplished. My wife, Carol Levy, is a unique creation of God, with a piercing intelligence, a profound sense of the importance of Jews and Judaism in the world, a restless spirituality, and a wise, funny, and nurturing soul that has let her rise to the heights of lay and professional Jewish community leadership accompanied by the love and admiration of her peers in both worlds. She is a beloved teacher of young and old, who sets audiences on fire with her insights into Jewish texts and ideas, and regularly brings her students to tears of both empathy and laughter in the course of a single lecture. With her deep, rich voice she has also been an actress, a singer, a song leader, a director, a radio broadcaster—and, of course, the mother of two wise, multitalented, beautiful, and affectionate young women, our daughters, Sarah and Elizabeth. She is the best person I know to spend time with, and she electrifies the most ordinary environment merely by her presence. Throughout the creation and passage of the Pittsburgh Principles, she was at my side, reading, critiquing, consoling, and cajoling, and she sat in the back of the room at the Pittsburgh convention cheering me on with her big dark eyes and her mouth that needd no words to be expressive. It goes without saying that I have dedicated this book to her.

It is my hope that you who hold this book in your hands will be inspired to take your place as a person of vision for the Jewish future.

A Statement of Principles for Reform Judaism: The Pittsburgh Principles (1999)

Preamble

On three occasions during the last century and a half, the Reform rabbinate has adopted comprehensive statements to help guide the thought and practice of our movement. In 1885, fifteen rabbis issued the Pittsburgh Platform, a set of guidelines that defined Reform Judaism for the next fifty years. A revised statement of principles, the Columbus Platform, was adopted by the Central Conference of American Rabbis in 1937. A third set of rabbinic guidelines, the Centenary Perspective, appeared in 1976 on the occasion of the centenary of the Union of American Hebrew Congregations and the Hebrew Union College–Jewish Institute of Religion. Today, when so many individuals are striving for religious meaning, moral purpose and a sense of community, we believe it is our obligation as rabbis once again to state a set of principles that define Reform Judaism in our own time.

Throughout our history, we Jews have remained firmly rooted in Jewish tradition, even as we have learned much from our encounters with other cultures. The great contribution of Reform Judaism is that it has enabled the Jewish people to introduce innovation while preserving tradition, to embrace diversity while asserting commonality, to affirm beliefs without rejecting those who doubt, and to bring faith to sacred texts without sacrificing critical scholarship.

This "Statement of Principles" affirms the central tenets of Judaism—God, Torah and Israel—even as it acknowledges the diversity of Reform Jewish beliefs and practices. It also invites all Reform Jews to engage in a dialogue with the sources of our tradition, responding out of our knowledge, our experience and our faith. Thus we hope to transform our lives through קְדֻשָּׁה (*kedushah*), holiness.

GOD

We affirm the reality and oneness of God, even as we may differ in our understanding of the Divine presence.

We affirm that the Jewish people is bound to God by an eternal בְּרִית (*b'rit*), covenant, as reflected in our varied understandings of Creation, Revelation and Redemption.

We affirm that every human being is created בְּצֶלֶם אֱלֹהִים (*b'tzelem Elohim*), in the image of God, and that therefore every human life is sacred.

We regard with reverence all of God's creation and recognize our human responsibility for its preservation and protection.

We encounter God's presence in moments of awe and wonder, in acts of justice and compassion, in loving relationships and in the experiences of everyday life.

We respond to God daily: through public and private prayer, through study and through the performance of other מִצְוֹת (*mitzvot*), sacred obligations—בֵּין אָדָם לַמָּקוֹם (*bein adam la-Makom*), to God, and בֵּין אָדָם לַחֲבֵרוֹ (*bein adam la-chaveiro*), to other human beings.

We strive for a faith that fortifies us through the vicissitudes of our lives—illness and healing, transgression and repentance, bereavement and consolation, despair and hope.

We continue to have faith that, in spite of the unspeakable evils committed against our people and the sufferings endured by others, the partnership of God and humanity will ultimately prevail.

We trust in our tradition's promise that, although God created us as finite beings, the spirit within us is eternal.

**In all these ways and more, God gives meaning and
purpose to our lives.**

TORAH

We affirm that Torah is the foundation of Jewish life.

We cherish the truths revealed in Torah, God's ongoing revelation to our people and the record of our people's ongoing relationship with God.

We affirm that Torah is a manifestation of אַהֲבַת עוֹלָם (*ahavat olam*), God's eternal love for the Jewish people and for all humanity.

We affirm the importance of studying Hebrew, the language of Torah and Jewish liturgy, that we may draw closer to our people's sacred texts.

We are called by Torah to lifelong study in the home, in the synagogue and in every place where Jews gather to learn and teach. Through Torah study we are called to מִצְווֹת (*mitzvot*), the means by which we make our lives holy.

We are committed to the ongoing study of the whole array of מִצְווֹת (*mitzvot*) and to the fulfillment of those that address us as individuals and as a community. Some of these מִצְווֹת (*mitzvot*), sacred obligations, have long been observed by Reform Jews; others, both ancient and modern, demand renewed attention as the result of the unique context of our own times.

We bring Torah into the world when we seek to sanctify the times and places of our lives through regular home and congregational observance. Shabbat calls us to bring the highest moral values to our daily labor and to culminate the workweek with קְדֻשָּׁה (*kedushah*), holiness, מְנוּחָה (*menuchah*), rest and עֹנֶג (*oneg*), joy. The High Holy Days call us to account for our deeds. The Festivals enable us to celebrate with joy our people's religious journey in the context of the changing seasons. The days of remembrance remind us of the tragedies and the triumphs that have shaped our people's historical experience both in ancient and modern times. And we mark the milestones of our personal journeys with traditional and creative rites that reveal the holiness in each stage of life.

We bring Torah into the world when we strive to fulfill the highest ethical mandates in our relationships with others and with all of God's creation. Partners with God in תִּקּוּן עוֹלָם (*tikkun olam*), repairing the world, we are called to help bring nearer the messianic age. We seek dialogue and joint action with people of other faiths in the hope that together we can bring peace, freedom and justice to our world. We are obligated to pursue צֶדֶק (*tzedek*), justice and righteousness, and to narrow the gap between the affluent and the poor, to act against discrimination and oppression, to pursue peace, to welcome the stranger, to protect the earth's biodiversity and natural resources, and to redeem those in physical, economic and spiritual bondage. In so doing, we reaffirm social action and social justice as a central prophetic focus of traditional Reform Jewish belief and practice. We affirm the מִצְוָה (*mitzvah*) of צְדָקָה (*tzedakah*), setting aside portions of our earnings and our time to provide for those in need. These acts bring us closer to fulfilling the prophetic call to translate the words of Torah into the works of our hands.

In all these ways and more, Torah gives meaning and purpose to our lives.

ISRAEL

We are Israel, a people aspiring to holiness, singled out through our ancient covenant and our unique history among the nations to be witnesses to God's presence. We are linked by that covenant and that history to all Jews in every age and place.

We are committed to the מִצְוָה (*mitzvah*) of אַהֲבַת יִשְׂרָאֵל (*ahavat Yisrael*), love for the Jewish people, and to כְּלַל יִשְׂרָאֵל (*k'lal Yisrael*), the entirety of the community of Israel. Recognizing that כָּל יִשְׂרָאֵל עֲרֵבִים זֶה בָּזֶה (*kol Yisrael arevim zeh ba-zeh*), all Jews are responsible for one another, we reach out to all Jews across ideological and geographical boundaries.

We embrace religious and cultural pluralism as an expression of the vitality of Jewish communal life in Israel and the Diaspora.

We pledge to fulfill Reform Judaism's historic commitment to the complete equality of women and men in Jewish life.

We are an inclusive community, opening doors to Jewish life to people of all ages, to varied kinds of families, to all regardless of their sexual orientation, to גֵּרִים (*gerim*), those who have converted to Judaism, and to all individuals and families, including the intermarried, who strive to create a Jewish home.

We believe that we must not only open doors for those ready to enter our faith, but also to actively encourage those who are seeking a spiritual home to find it in Judaism.

We are committed to strengthening the people Israel by supporting individuals and families in the creation of homes rich in Jewish learning and observance.

We are committed to strengthening the people Israel by making the synagogue central to Jewish communal life, so that it may elevate the spiritual, intellectual and cultural quality of our lives.

We are committed to מְדִינַת יִשְׂרָאֵל (*Medinat Yisrael*), the State of Israel, and rejoice in its accomplishments. We affirm the unique qualities of living in אֶרֶץ יִשְׂרָאֵל (*Eretz Yisrael*), the land of Israel, and encourage עֲלִיָּה (*aliyah*), immigration to Israel.

We are committed to a vision of the State of Israel that promotes full civil, human and religious rights for all its inhabitants and that strives for a lasting peace between Israel and its neighbors.

We are committed to promoting and strengthening Progressive Judaism in Israel, which will enrich the spiritual life of the Jewish state and its people.

We affirm that both Israeli and Diaspora Jewry should remain vibrant and interdependent communities. As we urge Jews who reside outside Israel to learn Hebrew as a living language and to make periodic visits to Israel in order to study and to deepen their relationship to the Land and its people, so do we affirm that Israeli Jews have much to learn from the religious life of Diaspora Jewish communities.

We are committed to furthering Progressive Judaism throughout the world as a meaningful religious way of life for the Jewish people.

In all these ways and more, Israel gives meaning and purpose to our lives.

בָּרוּךְ שֶׁאָמַר וְהָיָה הָעוֹלָם.
(Baruch she-amar ve-haya ha-olam.)
Praised be the One through whose word all things came to be.
May our words find expression in holy actions.
May they raise us up to a life of meaning devoted to God's service
And to the redemption of our world.

I

Preamble: The Pittsburgh Principles and the Ways of Reform Judaism

On three occasions during the last century and a half, the Reform rabbinate has adopted comprehensive statements to help guide the thought and practice of our movement. In 1885, fifteen rabbis issued the Pittsburgh Platform, a set of guidelines that defined Reform Judaism for the next fifty years. A revised statement of principles, the Columbus Platform, was adopted by the Central Conference of American Rabbis in 1937. A third set of rabbinic guidelines, the Centenary Perspective, appeared in 1976 on the occasion of the centenary of the Union of American Hebrew Congregations and the Hebrew Union College–Jewish Institute of Religion. Today, when so many individuals are striving for religious meaning, moral purpose and a sense of community, we believe it is our obligation as rabbis once again to state a set of principles that define Reform Judaism in our own time.

Throughout our history, we Jews have remained firmly rooted in Jewish tradition, even as we have learned much from our encounters with other cultures. The great contribution of Reform Judaism is that it has enabled the Jewish people to introduce innovation while preserving tradition, to embrace diversity while asserting commonality, to affirm beliefs without rejecting those who doubt, and to bring faith to sacred texts without sacrificing critical scholarship.

This "Statement of Principles" affirms the central tenets of Judaism—God, Torah and Israel—even as it acknowledges the diversity of Reform Jewish beliefs and practices. It also invites all

Reform Jews to engage in a dialogue with the sources of our tradition, responding out of our knowledge, our experience and our faith. Thus, we hope to transform our lives through *kedushah*, holiness.

—Statement of Principles, "Preamble"

Return to Pittsburgh

Shortly after the Jewish people gathered in the month of Sivan 5759 to celebrate Shavuot, the anniversary of the giving of the Torah, the Central Conference of American Rabbis (CCAR) gathered in Pittsburgh to receive another sort of document: "A Statement of Principles for Reform Judaism." There was no apparent connection between these two events—how could anything compare with the giving of the Torah?—and yet there was a very strong connection. In the city where fifteen Reform rabbis had gathered in 1885 to proclaim that only the Torah's moral laws were binding, that laws regarding diet and dress "obstruct . . . modern spiritual elevation," in that very city 114 years later some four hundred Reform rabbis met to vote on a document that said, "We are committed to the ongoing study of the whole array of *mitzvot* and to the fulfillment of those that address us as individuals and as a community. Some of these *mitzvot*, sacred obligations, have long been observed by Reform Jews; others, both ancient and modern, demand renewed attention as the result of the unique context of our own times." On Wednesday, May 26, 1999, the CCAR voted 324 to 68 that Reform Jews can be open to responding to all the mitzvot—in all the diverse ways individual Reform Jews will respond.

Pittsburgh 1999 marked the fourth time that North American Reform rabbis had come together to articulate the direction of Reform Judaism. Each of the previous formulations was occasioned by a perceived crisis in American Judaism. Most of the fifteen rabbis who originally met in Pittsburgh felt an overwhelming desire to make a clear distinction between themselves and the growing Conservative Movement on one side, and the growth on the other of Ethical Culture, a humanist

---

The initial sections of this chapter originally appeared in somewhat different form in "The Challenge of the 'Principles,'" *CCAR Journal,* Winter 2000, pp. 7–11.

movement almost all of whose members were Jews. While Isaac Mayer Wise of Cincinnati had hoped to draw all American Jews together, avoiding polarizing theological stands and writing a very traditional prayer book in Hebrew with English translation, Kaufmann Kohler and the other more radical Reformers on the East Coast preferred a theology that staked out their differences from other Jews, as well as a prayer book written primarily in English. The promulgation of the Pittsburgh Platform in 1885, which Wise called a "Declaration of Independence," contributed to the separation of Reform and Conservative Judaism. While the framers of the 1937 Columbus Platform and the 1976 Centenary Perspective intended their documents to supercede the 1885 Pittsburgh Platform, the condemnation of Torah laws dealing with diet, purity, and dress continued for over one hundred years to convey the belief that some observances were "off limits" to Reform Jews.

The major elements of the 1885 Pittsburgh text that led fifty years later to the need for a new document were its rejection of "a return to Palestine," its celebration of "the modern era of universal culture of heart and intellect," its preference for the phrase "God-idea" in place of "God," and the absence of any positive mention of specific Jewish observances. By 1937, the immigration of more traditional Jews from eastern Europe had overwhelmed the more acculturated German Jews, changing the face of Reform Judaism and Reform Jewish practice. With the rise of Nazism and with the political necessity of a Jewish homeland more and more apparent, the CCAR (which had come into being six years after the Pittsburgh Platform) created in the 1937 Columbus Platform—written largely by Samuel S. Cohon, a faculty member at the Hebrew Union College—a document that addressed many of the lacunae in the 1885 statement. As controversy would surround the creation of the Pittsburgh Principles in 1999, so did it engulf the CCAR in 1937. Two different platform drafts competed for the CCAR's favor, and a vote as to whether to pass a document at all ended in a tie, resolved only by the intervention of Rabbi Felix Levy, the president of the CCAR, who resolved the tie in favor of considering a platform. The subsequent vote on Dr. Cohon's document was overwhelmingly in favor, 155 to 8.[1]

In 1973 with the Second World War a memory but the effects of the Holocaust still palpable to Jews around the world, the CCAR leadership felt a need to address the drastically changed conditions of the latter part of the twentieth century. The relief over the outcome of the Six-Day War of 1967 had been shattered by the insecurity following the 1973 Yom Kippur War, fueling fears for world Jewry's future, particularly considering the steeply rising rate of intermarriage. The CCAR itself was wracked by a polarizing debate on whether to call on rabbis not to officiate at such ceremonies. After an abortive attempt to create a platform based on papers written by a sampling of colleagues, Robert Kahn, president of the CCAR, asked Professor Eugene Borowitz of the New York School of the Hebrew Union College–Jewish Institute of Religion to write a paper on the occasion of the one hundredth anniversary of the founding of the Union of American Hebrew Congregations (UAHC) in 1873 (now the Union for Reform Judaism [URJ]) and the Hebrew Union College in 1875. Reflecting its time, the Centenary Perspective emphasized the need to secure the survival of the Jewish people, but it confidently outlined what the Reform Movement had taught the Jewish world in its hundred years and called on Reform Jews to confront the diverse claims of Jewish tradition by "exercising their individual autonomy, choosing and creating on the basis of commitment and knowledge." It led to the phrase "informed choice," which, along with "autonomy," became a watchword of Reform Judaism.

Why a New Statement?

The onset of the twenty-first century suggested to the leaders of the CCAR that a new statement of principles would be appropriate. The entire demographic of the Reform Movement had been changing for some time as a result of the continued rise in intermarriage and the resultant passage in 1983 of a CCAR resolution publicly proclaiming what had long been a quiet Reform policy: declaring Jewish those children of either a Jewish mother or a Jewish father who were raised as Jews and had celebrated "public and formal acts of identification with the Jewish faith and people."[2] This validation of intermarried families striving to establish Jewish homes sparked a growing desire for increased learning, spiritual expression, and guidelines for Reform ideology. Women's increased influence in the movement (the number of women rabbis ordained by the Reform Movement had grown from 3 in 1976 to over 300 in 2001) had changed much of the language and approach of Reform, and the movement had pioneered the opening of doors of Jewish life (including ordination) to gay and lesbian Jews. Hebrew had greatly increased in Reform worship, more Reform Jews were adopting traditional rituals, and opportunities for increased Jewish learning were being sought and provided by synagogues, other Jewish institutions, and the UAHC's popular summer *kallot*, which increasingly tended to include present and future leaders of the movement.

Despite all these changes, rejection of many observances by the 1885 Pittsburgh Platform continued to provoke tension between the Reform Jews who agreed with that statement and those who wished to practice the rejected rites. The patrilineal decision had also increased tensions between Reform Jews and Jews in other movements, as well as between American Reform Jews and those in Israel and other countries, who felt that Reform had been callous to the practices of *k'lal Yisrael*, the community of the Jewish people as a whole. Concern was also growing about the future of Reform Judaism in an Israel that seemed much more secure at century's end (the Second Intifada had not yet broken out) than it did at the time of the Centenary Perspective.

Faced by all these factors, in the fall of 1997 the CCAR began a two-year process of discussion and consultation with its entire membership and significant numbers of laypeople to create a new statement of principles. While earlier drafts focused the statement around ten principles, the version finally adopted was organized around the themes of God, Torah, and Israel, similar to the Columbus Platform and the Centenary Perspective. Pittsburgh was chosen as the site for the vote in the hope that the name "Pittsburgh" would now be permanently associated with a document that showed how much the movement had changed since 1885.

The 1999 Pittsburgh Principles describes Reform Judaism as an ongoing dialogue with tradition and innovation, with affirmation and doubt, with faith and critical scholarship. It invites Reform Jews "to engage in a dialogue with the sources of our tradition, responding out of our knowledge, our experience and our faith." Among other differences from past proclamations, this document affirms the importance of mitzvah for Reform Jews and encourages us to let Judaism transform our lives into a state of *k'dushah*, holiness. It affirms the relationship between beliefs about God and care for the environment. It affirms our struggle for a faith that "fortifies us through [all] the vicissitudes of our lives." It affirms that "Torah is the foundation of Jewish life." It stresses our commitment to the study of Hebrew, both as the language of Torah and Jewish liturgy and as the language that binds us to the Jewish people and the State of Israel, and the document includes many Hebrew words and phrases that help define who we are. The Pittsburgh Principles reaffirms our commitment to *tikkun olam,* repairing the world, as part of our mission to "bring Torah into the world." It affirms the value of *k'lal Yisrael* and *ahavat Yisrael*, the love of the people Israel, and it spells out the extent of our Reform devotion to inclusiveness. It affirms our commitment to reach out to Jews "across ideological . . . boundaries," to work with people of all faiths to better the world, and to encourage non-Jewish religious seekers to find a home with us. It affirms our commitment to build Progressive Judaism not only in Israel but around the globe. And the document ends with a prayer, a reminder that it is not a platform at all, but an aspiration that affirms how important prayer is to Reform Jews, as part of our life with God, with Torah, and with Israel.

Words and Pictures

What is remarkable about this document is not only what it says but how it was created. After hearing opinions from numerous rabbinical focus groups in 1995–96 that the rabbinate had neglected to exercise appropriate leadership in the Reform Movement, we reminded ourselves that the way in which Reform rabbis had historically helped define Reform Judaism was through the writing of "platforms," or guiding principles. We began with brainstorming sessions, first involving a group of rabbis at the fall 1997 President's *Kallah,* and then with the CCAR board, both of which I chaired as the new president of the CCAR. From these discussions we created twelve questions (see appendix 5) that regional CCAR gatherings considered and reported on,[3] which formed the basis for the first draft of the Statement of Principles, completed in March 1998. Meeting in London with Progressive rabbis from around the world, the CCAR board critiqued that first draft in an atmosphere where British and Israeli rabbis were sharing their newly crafted Statements of Purpose as well (see chapter 16).

The comments of the board and of a Southern California group of lay leaders helped create the second draft, which was discussed by some fifty colleagues at the CCAR's convention in Anaheim, California, in June 1998. This colloquy in turn produced the third draft, which was shared in the September 1998 *CCAR Newsletter* and the Winter 1998 issue of *Reform Judaism* magazine, published by the UAHC (see appendix 6). The editor of the magazine, Aron Hirt-Manheimer, decided to make the discussion of the third draft his cover story, featuring what turned out to be a provocative picture of me in a reflective pose, with *kippah* and *tallit* (though not, as many people thought, *t'fillin*) touching the *tzitzit* to my lips—a stance taken by many Reform Jews who wear a *tallit* when called to the Torah. For many other Reform Jews, though, it looked like a picture of a Judaism they or their parents had once rejected, which now seemed to be taking over Reform.

The controversial treatment in the magazine opened a coast-to-coast debate on the Statement of Principles, fueled by sermons, discussion groups, synagogue bulletin pieces, Internet postings, and articles in local and national newspapers, some of which continues to this very day. Rabbi Paul Menitoff, executive vice president of the CCAR, and I spoke with faculty at the three American campuses of HUC, receiving a different reception at each one, and with the executive board of the UAHC, which, until our appearance, had taken a negative stand toward the document, though many commented that the small group discussions of the third draft in the afternoon of their meeting provided one of the most stimulating executive board meetings they had attended.

During the time that those discussions were producing a fourth draft, we decided to bring more people into the drafting process, and so we named a fourteen member advisory task force of Reform rabbis from across the ideological spectrum, two HUC faculty members, a rabbinic student, and three prominent national Reform lay leaders active in the UAHC but not representing it.[4] The task force met in January 1999 for twenty-five hours at the UAHC's Camp Kutz in Warwick, New York,[5] and the resultant fifth draft was more concise and straightforward, but contained ideas very similar to those in earlier versions. The draft was published in the *CCAR Newsletter*, and Rabbi Menitoff and I traveled around the country to share it with conventions of all the CCAR regions, Hillel rabbis, and hospital chaplains, incorporating their suggestions into one revision of the original after another. Each new revision required a new conference call with the members of the task force to see how the alterations fit with their conception of the document as a whole. Virtually every decision made by the task force was made by consensus—sometimes thanks to a felicitous word suggested by Judge Davidson, a professional mediator. The level of participation and goodwill during those calls made the process a memorable one for all the members of the task force, and a tribute to the level of commitment of rabbis, professors, and lay leaders alike. Finally a revised draft was ready to be sent to the CCAR board, which in turn approved a motion to bring it to a vote at the Pittsburgh convention.

Several significant changes were made on the floor of the convention. In the section on bringing Torah into the world through societal action, additional references to pursuing justice were added (the word "justice" now occurs three times in that paragraph), and a phrase was inserted calling on the Reform Movement "to protect the earth's biodiversity." Though the last sentence in the social justice paragraph already spoke of "the prophetic call to translate the words of Torah into the works of our hands," the convention voted to add an additional mention of prophetic Judaism: "we reaffirm social action and social justice as a central prophetic focus of traditional Reform Jewish belief and practice." Those who proposed and voted for these additions seemed to want to balance the emphasis on increased observance in other parts of the document.

Also added on the floor was the exhortation "to actively encourage those who are seeking a spiritual home to find it in Judaism." Language was also refined to reflect greater mutuality between Israel and the Diaspora: "*As* we urge Jews who reside outside Israel to learn Hebrew as a living language and to make periodic visits to Israel in order to study and to deepen their relationship to the Land and its people, *so do we affirm that Israeli Jews have much to learn from the religious life of Diaspora Jewish communities*" (emphasis added).

The process leading to the final vote was by far the most comprehensive, involving far more rabbis and laypeople than any statement of principles the CCAR has ever issued. The vote on the final draft took place in Rodeph Shalom Congregation in Pittsburgh, which had helped to host the Pittsburgh Conference of 1885. The 1999 final draft won widespread support from rabbis and from laypeople, leading to its over-whelming approval in Pittsburgh. When the vote was announced, some members broke out in spontaneous choruses of *siman tov umazal tov*, and the last speakers at both the "pro" and "con" microphones were invited up to the *bimah* of Rodeph Shalom to link arms with the leadership of the CCAR and join all those in attendance in singing Debbie Friedman's "Shehecheyanu," thanking God for allowing us to partici-pate in this historic moment.

Issues in Dispute

Despite the final vote, some criticism of the document continued. One point of contention was on the role of reason in Reform ideology. All the platforms were influenced by philosophers of their respective ages— Hegel, Kant and the Jewish Kantian Hermann Cohen, Mordecai Kaplan, Eugene Borowitz, Franz Rosenzweig. For some critics, the absence of the word "reason" from the Pittsburgh Principles was a cause to claim that the document rejected that essential criterion for a Reform statement of beliefs. Yet the preamble states clearly that among the great contributions of Reform Judaism is that "it has enabled the Jewish people to . . . bring faith to sacred texts without sacrificing critical scholarship." The section on God states that one of the ways of respond-ing to God is "through study"—reflecting Maimonides' belief that study enables human beings to exercise our reason, which puts us in as close touch as human beings can come with the mind of God. That we possess reason is how Maimonides understands our creation *b'tzelem Elohim*, in the image of God. The Torah section affirms that "we cherish the truths revealed in Torah," the plural reflecting the traditional Reform conviction that not all of the Torah may comport with what dif-ferent ages understand as truth. As the Columbus Platform put it, "Being products of historical processes, certain of its laws have lost their binding force; . . . yet the people of Israel, through its prophets and sages, achieved unique insight in the realm of religious truth." Reason is a major vehicle to help us understand what is true, but, as the preamble to the Pittsburgh Principles concludes, "our experience and our faith" are important vehicles as well.

Another criticism was the Pittsburgh Principles' rejection of autonomy and "informed choice." While this is discussed at length in chapter 2, my colleagues Lance Sussman and Robert Seltzer are correct that these two ideas were explicitly voted down through a "considered decision of the convention" in 1999.[6] Another colleague proposed that language affirming these ideas be inserted, but a clear majority rejected it. The rabbinate wanted to indicate that while "critical scholarship" and the search for truth continue to enlighten us, we had come to understand that the process of religious decision making was much more complex than a personal decision to do *a* rather than *b*; factors outside our own conscious minds may be acting on us as well. We voted to step away from what many Reform rabbis now perceive as an immodest assertion that the only decisor in our religious lives is our own reason—and that "reason" guides all thinking people to the same conclusion.

Related to these objections is Rabbis Sussman and Seltzer's assertion that "the priority of ethics is disastrously weakened in the Principles."[7] This point is addressed in chapter 4, but a word is in order here. If Reform and other Jews seek to live a life of holiness in the presence of God, as the Pittsburgh Principles affirms, the doing of mitzvot is the way to achieve that. Mitzvot, which regulate holy relations between human beings and God, have both ethical and spiritual dimensions. By describing the observance of sacred time and the doing of ethical action as ways to "bring Torah into the world," we are saying that we do not wish to second-guess the Torah as to which aspects are more important than others. Rabbis Sussman and Seltzer claim that by placing "ethical" actions at the end of the Torah section, "the discussion of ethics is relegated to the final plank in the section."[8] This placement, however, allowed the section on Torah to culminate with its ethical imperatives, in a paragraph longer than any of its predecessors in previous statements except the Columbus Platform.

As for the charge that the Torah would not recognize some of the ethics we would practice—particularly in the areas of gender equality and sexual orientation—we understand our dialogue with Torah to include not only Rosenzweig's "Yes" and "Not Yet," but "No" as well (see chapter 9). This, of course, is why the Pittsburgh Principles speaks of "ongoing revelation." The Columbus Platform stated that "Revelation is a continuous process." The nineteenth century Reformers spoke of "progressive revelation." The issue is how different ages help us understand the meaning of Torah for those ages; the notion that the understanding of Torah in one age represents progress over the understanding of a previous age is a very subjective claim.

Criticism was voiced not only about the content of the Pittsburgh Principles but also about the process by which the document was written and passed. Despite the extent of discussions with colleagues and laypeople over the course of twenty months—a longer process than any of the previous platforms underwent—some people felt, as Rabbis Sussman and Seltzer stated, that "there was a rush to premature ratification."9 Some colleagues felt that proposing new language from the floor of the convention was a sign of a hasty, unconsidered approach to the Pittsburgh Principles, but since colleagues had been discussing the language for months, one could also view the intensity of the floor discussion as evidence of the vitality of the discussion and the engagement of the rabbinate. The CCAR leadership had ruled that no amendments could be raised from the floor, but members kept voting to suspend the rules so that new language could be inserted. While some might consider this process unruly, I for one saw it as impressively inclusive and democratic.

For decades Reform rabbis had argued about how they should exercise authority. The discussions of the Pittsburgh Principles demonstrated that the floor of the CCAR was the place where the will of the spiritual leadership of the Reform Movement was expressed. Proposals were offered and the members responded (first on the Internet, where other Reform professionals could also weigh in, then at regional CCAR gatherings, and then on the floor of the convention). The decision on same-gender marriage was made in the same fashion.

Another issue that arose periodically during the years of discussion was the nature of the "we" who were the subjects of the opening sentences in each of the paragraphs of the Pittsburgh Principles: "we affirm, we regard, we encounter," etc. Was it the task force? Was it those who voted for the Pittsburgh Principles? Was it the CCAR? The task force intended that the "we" referred to the Reform Movement as a whole, lay and clergy together. The CCAR felt it had enough of the sense of the movement to articulate its sentiments, knowing that not every Reform Jew would affirm all of them, nor was required to, but could read the Pittsburgh Principles and say, "While I may not agree with all of these statements, I agree with enough of them to recognize that this is the movement with which I wish to cast my lot." The CCAR thus presumed to speak for the direction in which it believed the Reform Movement was heading and wanted it to head. As the preamble states, "We believe it is our obligation as rabbis once again to state a set of principles that define Reform Judaism in our own time."

Finally, a number of opponents argued that the literary quality of the Pittsburgh Principles compared unfavorably with its predecessors. Some colleagues felt it paled beside the much-debated third draft (see appendix 6), despite the fact that many of them disagreed with that version. Colleagues knew that the third draft was the work of a single individual, while the fifth draft was the work of a task force; some people are convinced that committees are by definition unable to compose a coherent document. In any case, judgments on literary quality can be very subjective. But whatever the merits of the third draft, the discussion about it in the winter of 1998–99 indicated that it could never have passed in Pittsburgh. If it was important to approve a statement reflecting the current state of Reform Judaism and suggesting its future course—as I fervently believe it was—the third draft needed to be replaced by a document that could gain broader support.

What the Principles Accomplished

Despite the deletion of references to autonomy, the Pittsburgh Principles has gained broad support. As the source of individual religious decisions, "autonomy" has been replaced by "dialogue." Does the absence of the word "autonomy" mean that Reform Jews have lost their freedom? Quite the contrary. The Pittsburgh Platform of 1885 limited our freedom—it ruled that many mitzvot were off-limits to Reform Jews. The new document, by affirming our commitment to study all the mitzvot, frees each of us to respond to each mitzvah as it calls to us. In that sense, we may rightly call the 1999 Pittsburgh Principles a declaration of religious freedom for Reform Jews.

The document has also played a role in calling a truce in some of the verbal battles between Reform Jews and those of other movements. The national publicity given the discussion of the third and final drafts led many Conservative and Orthodox rabbis to understand that, despite such major differences as patrilineal descent, they had more in common with us than they had thought and that, contrary to some of their perceptions of us, we were a movement that thought seriously about its beliefs and practices. Some Orthodox Jews had not even been aware that Reform Jews believed in mitzvot. Internally, the national discussion did much to erase the tendency of some Reform Jews to use the phrase "I'm very Reform" to mean "I don't engage in many Jewish practices." It also helped Reform Jews understand that the observance of many mitzvot was not "Orthodox" but deeply rooted in Reform ideology as well. In the course of these discussions, some Reform Jews realized the inconsistency of decrying intra-Jewish hostility on the one hand and on the other voicing suspicions when non-Reform Jews praised our growing commonality.

As the new century takes shape, I believe that the Pittsburgh Principles will prove to be an important force shaping the Reform Movement's perception of itself and other people's understanding of us. I also hope that it will prove to be a guide to assist Reform Jews and others who wish to lead serious religious lives to resist the trends in the common culture that so often degrade us and rise instead to lives called by the nature of God, the mitzvot of the Torah, and the destiny of the Land of Israel and the Jewish people. It is my belief that Reform Jews— and serious Jews of all movements—wish to live not merely successful lives, but holy ones. The Pittsburgh Principles attempts to set forth ways to fulfill the injunction of Leviticus 19:2: "You shall be holy, for I, *Adonai* your God, am holy." It is my hope that this book will begin an exploration of the many ways in which, guided by the Pittsburgh Principles, Reform Jews can inspire the Jewish people as a whole to transform our lives into vessels for the holiness of God.

The
Reform Jew
in Dialogue
with God

2

Voices from the Ash Tree:
The Reality of God

We affirm the reality and oneness of God, even as we may differ in our understanding of the Divine presence.

We affirm that the Jewish people is bound to God by an eternal *b'rit*, covenant, as reflected in our varied understandings of Creation, Revelation and Redemption.

—Statement of Principles, "God," paragraphs 1–2

From God-idea to Dialogue with God

Is it possible for a human being to be in dialogue with God?

The language of dialogue, anchored in Jewish thought by Martin Buber and Franz Rosenzweig, is based on the confidence that a human being and God can have some sort of communication with each other. Dialogue assumes that God is real and the human being is real, and these two realities provide the basis for a mutual awareness of each other's presence, which—at least from the human side—can take the form of words.

While the Pittsburgh Principles' image of dialogue is a different description of our relationship with God than is used in other Reform statements of belief, it does not contradict them; in a sense the Pittsburgh Principles of 1999 carries them to their ultimate expression—from the 1885 philosophical language of "God-idea" to the current religious language of "God-experience." The authors of the 1885 Pittsburgh Platform took the term "God-idea" from the school of German Idealist philosophy. Nineteenth-century Reform thought was heavily influenced by Immanuel Kant, who in his *Foundations of the Metaphysics of Morals* asked, "Whence do we have the concept of God as the highest good? Solely from the Idea of moral perfection which reason formulates a priori,"[1] that is, independent of human experience. As the Pittsburgh Platform puts it:

> We hold that Judaism presents the highest conception of the God-idea as taught in our Holy Scriptures and developed and spiritualized by the Jewish teachers, in accordance with the moral and philosophical progress of their respective ages. . . .
> We recognize in Judaism a progressive religion, ever striving to be in accord with the postulates of reason.

The Columbus Platform expanded the definition of God from the rationalist language of Kant to the early twentieth-century God-ideas of Mordecai Kaplan, the founder of the Reconstructionist Movement, who believed that God was a power making itself felt in those forces in life that helped human beings fulfill their potential:

> The heart of Judaism and its chief contribution to religion is the doctrine of the One, living God, who rules the world through law and love. In Him all existence has its creative source and mankind its ideal of conduct. Though transcending time and space, He is the indwelling Presence of the world. We worship Him as the Lord of the universe and our merciful Father.

In the aftermath of the Holocaust and the establishment of the State of Israel, the Centenary Perspective moved away from definitions of God to affirmations based on events in Jewish history:

> The affirmation of God has always been essential to our people's will to survive. In our struggle through the centuries to preserve our faith we have experienced and conceived of God in many ways. The trials of our own time and the challenges of modern culture have made steady belief and clear understanding difficult for some. Nevertheless, we ground our lives, personally and communally, on God's reality and remain open to new experiences and conceptions of the Divine.

The author of the Centenary Perspective, Eugene Borowitz, explained in his commentary on the document, *Reform Judaism Today*, why he preferred the word "reality" to the word "existence":

> The *Perspective* does not use the term *God's existence* but rather speaks of *God's reality*. . . . The existence we know is of things—but we surely do not mean to imply that God is another thing, just a bigger and better one. So some thinkers have urged us to talk about God as the basis or ground of all existence. That is an elegant point, but the drafters of the *Perspective* had something much simpler in mind: we wanted to say that God was not an illusion, not merely something we imagined, not just a wish of ours. Our God is real, so real that we base our lives on God's reality.[2]

This choice is echoed in the Pittsburgh Principles as well. But the section on God in the Pittsburgh Principles is longer than in any of the other Reform statements, perhaps reflecting a change in the religious climate from the mid-1970s, when post-Holocaust awareness and secular culture had "made steady belief and clear understanding [of God] difficult for some." By the dawn of the twenty-first century, after new and ugly wars, growing cynicism about secular governments, and a steady tilt of popular culture toward more and more violence and other kinds of verbal and physical degradation, more and more North Americans longed for a different reality, one that would lift them above the brutal banality of daily life. If God's reality was a philosophical concept for the first three platforms, by the end of the twentieth century it had become a longed-for alternative to the reality that Jews and all sensitive Americans were experiencing.

Originally, the framers of the Pittsburgh Principles wrote a very concise opening sentence: "We affirm the reality of God." But discussions with other rabbis uncovered the need to affirm specifically that Reform was a movement that embraced a wide variety of beliefs. (The 1976 statement contained a similar affirmation, in contrast to the Columbus Platform, which spelled out how it thought Reform Jews should conceive of God.) As the draft was read by more colleagues, a concern began to grow that this definition could be affirmed by members of other religions as well, particularly by Christians who affirm the divinity of the Trinity, and so "oneness" was added to insure that there would be no compromise of Judaism's traditional monotheism ("Hear, Israel, *Adonai* our God, *Adonai* is One").

All this concern for correct doctrine is very much in keeping with earlier platforms, but it is only a prologue to the dialogic thrust of Pittsburgh 1999. The reality of both partners must be a given in a dialogue, else at least one party is talking to oneself. In the Torah, because God has spoken the words that created human beings, God knows that humans are real, and because individuals and the whole people have heard God speaking, they know God is real. The Jewish version of Descartes' "proof" of God's existence is: *I speak, therefore I am.* Dialogue is the means by which God and the Jewish people affirm their own and each other's reality.

Is this really true for Reform Jews? While statements of God's speech in the Bible may not be "proofs" for us, they do provide parameters for the content of divine speech because Jewish tradition has based its understanding of the content of God's message on the words the Bible tells us God spoke. Thus, while we may not have independent proof of the content of God's speech, we know what the Jewish people has understood God to say.

Who is this God who is speaking? If we "differ in our understanding of the Divine presence" who is speaking, how can we be sure that while this God may be real, it is also One—that the God we hear in diverse ways is still the same God? What can we know of God's nature?

The Names of God

One answer to this question can be found in the names by which the Torah sees God wanting to be called. For a name is not only evidence of a being's reality, it is the beginning of a dialogue. Becoming aware of God's presence or wishing to encounter God's presence, we speak the name of God. Names of God abound in the Bible and in rabbinic literature, each one, to paraphrase the Pittsburgh Principles, reflecting different understandings of God's nature. That God has a name itself reflects that God is real—as the climax of each act of Creation, God gives it a name ("And God called the light day and the darkness night" [Genesis 1:5]), and animals await Adam's bestowing of a name before they are fully realized ("And [God] brought them to the Human to see what he would call it and whatever the Human would call the living creature, that was its name" [Genesis 2:19]). When Abraham and Moses are called to their destiny, they are called by name (Genesis 22:1, Exodus 3:4). When God addresses Moses from the Burning Bush and Moses asks God's name (because, he says, the people will want to know), God replies, "*Ehyeh asher Ehyeh*," or simplified, "Tell the Israelites, '*Ehyeh* sent me to you'" (Exodus 3:13–14). *Ehyeh* is the first person singular of the Hebrew root *h-y-h*, meaning "to be," which, in the imperfect tense, signifies uncompleted ongoing action. God instructs Moses, "Tell the Israelites, 'I-Am-Eternally has sent me to you.'" In Exodus 6:2 the name is rendered in the third person imperfect as *YHVH*, "The One Who Is Eternally." Translated according to the Centenary Perspective and the Pittsburgh Principles, *YHVH* might be rendered, "The One Who Is Eternally Real."[3]

Long before Spinoza and the Protestant Bible critics of the nineteenth century noticed that beside *YHVH* there is another name of God (*Elohim*), sometimes used in what appear to be different accounts of the same story, the Rabbis suggested that the variation reflects different aspects of the one God. Wrestling with why both names were used, the Rabbis resolved the dilemma with an ingenious midrash: Since *Elohim*, usually translated "God," also means "judges," that name presents God in the form of *Din*, "Judgment," while *YHVH* suggests the opposite, *Rachamim*, "Compassion" (because *YHVH* is joined to *rachum v'chanun*, "compassionate and loving," in Exodus 34:6). Thus when *Elohim* is used, it could signify God acting out of the attribute of Judgment, while the use of *YHVH* could suggest actions out of the attribute of Compassion. The strictness implied in *Elohim* is somewhat mitigated by adding *-nu* to it, as in *Eloheinu*, "our God." Therefore, even when God executes justice upon Israel rather than compassion, it is meted out lovingly; the Yiddish translation of *Eloheinu* brings this out in just the intimate sound of it—*Gottenyu*. There is also a feminine aspect to the Rabbis' interpretation of *YHVH*: the root of the Hebrew word for "compassion," *rachamim*, is *r-ch-m*, whose noun derivative *rechem* means "womb." In *Birkat HaMazon*, *YHVH* is often referred to as *HaRachaman*, "the Compassionate One," or perhaps, "Womb of the world," appropriate to the root meaning of *YHVH* as eternal being.

There are other biblical names for God as well. As Moses learns in Exodus 6, his ancestors called God *El Shaddai*, combining the name of the Canaanite god *El*, with implications of power, to the name *Shaddai*. *Shaddai* is usually translated "Almighty," but there is evidence that it may derive from the Hebrew root *sh-d*, which means "breast." The Hebrew name thus combines *El*, a masculine deity in the Canaanite pantheon, with a name suggesting feminine nurture, pointing to a God who embodies both genders and transcends them. *YHVH* and *Elohim* appear together as well (e.g., in the Creation story beginning in Genesis 2:4), suggesting the same teaching. *Shaddai* is most familiar to us as the name inscribed on the mezuzah parchment, where the Rabbis suggested it is an acronym for *Shomer Daltot Yisrael*, "Guardian of the Doorposts of Israel."

These three biblical names alone suggest different experiences and conceptions of God. *YHVH*, in its biblical derivations, suggests the God of Aristotle and Maimonides: eternal, existing before the Creation and ever after. But it also suggests God's immanence, in a way that such disparate philosophers as Plato, Spinoza, and more recently, Mordecai Kaplan and Abraham Joshua Heschel could endorse, a God present in every aspect of existence, forming it, guiding it (though Kaplan might demur from these two), and accessible within it. It also has room for Lurianic Kabbalah, with its notion of holy sparks of the primeval light created on the first day embedded in each part of the material world.

Elohim, the name of God who creates merely through the word, also suggests the Aristotelian and Maimonidean God, judging the world rather than, in the rabbinic idea of *YHVH*, empathizing with it. The distant God, the clockmaker God who sets the world in motion and then steps aside, is also suggested by *Elohim*. Some Jews see the God of Genesis 1, who looked at each part of Creation and called it *tov* (usually translated "good") as a "limited" God—one who is only associated with the good. Everything that these believers perceive as not good is relegated to the realm of human actions, human free will, reflecting the decision of Adam and Eve to eat the fruit, guaranteeing that we could know—and by extension act on—good and its opposite. This idea of a "limited God" frees the Divine from being responsible for suffering, but also raises the question, how can we seek relief from God for our suffering if God has no role in our pain? Names like *El Shaddai* and *YHVH Elohim*, which conflate opposing qualities, may also be seen as evidence against a limited God: they demonstrate the unity of differing aspects of God, indicating that while names may symbolize God's reality, they do not limit it. Unlike philosophers, the Bible does not draw strict lines around the nature of God, preferring to picture God in the diverse ways revealed through changing human experience and dialogue. The very metaphor of dialogue suggests continuing variations in our experience of God.

The Rabbis added other names to the short biblical list. They called God *HaKadosh Baruch Hu*, "the Blessed Holy One," suggesting such transcendent conceptions of God's holiness as Isaiah's vision of the angels surrounding the divine throne (Isaiah 6:3), but also such immanent encounters as Moses hearing God speaking from the Burning Bush ("the place on which you stand is *admat kodesh* [holy ground]" [Exodus 3:5]) and the rabbinic *b'rachah shel mitzvah*, the blessing upon doing a mitzvah: "Praised are You *Adonai Eloheinu*, ruler of time and space, who has *kid'shanu* ["made us holy," "sanctified us," or better, "shared Your holiness with us"] through Your mitzvot, in commanding us regarding the mitzvah of. . . . " The Rabbis continued to blend the transcendent and the immanent in such names as *Ribono shel olam*, "Master of time and space," by appending the Aramaism *o* to *Ribon*, "Master," thus tying the "Master" intimately to the *olam*, "world." When it is pronounced in Yiddish, *RibbOIneh-shel-OIlem*, a paradox occurs: the name becomes very intimate, and while the words point to a transcendent idea of God, the sound is one of immanence. Even the majestic rabbinic use of *HaMakom*, "The Place," defined as "God is the place of the world, but the world is not God's place" (*B'reishit Rabbah* 68), acquires an immanent aspect from the context in which the word appears in the Bible, as the place Jacob encounters when he dreams of the ladder connecting earth and heaven, and the place where Moses stands at the Burning Bush. Maimonides and other medieval thinkers use the Hebrew root *m-tz-h* (*matzui*), literally "found," to speak of God's experienced reality. The kabbalists also took the rabbinic name *Shechinah*, meaning God's indwelling presence, and suggested it might refer to the feminine side of God. If we Reform Jews "differ in our understanding of the Divine presence," precedents have long been set in biblical, rabbinic, and medieval times, not to mention our own.

God as Connectedness

But how about Reform Jews who claim they do not believe in God—or who see themselves as agnostics, not ready to argue for or against God's reality? What does "we affirm the reality and oneness of God" mean for them?

I think that there are really very few people who do not believe in God. Those who deny their belief usually will agree that there are connections in the world—between them and other people, between them and nature. All of us feel connected to something—whether to friends or relatives, to the ocean as we watch its waves, to the mountains as the sun sets or rises over them—and we know that we are all made up of atoms and molecules that are all connected to each other. Not to believe in the interconnectedness of the universe flies in the face of what we know about science. The next step is to acknowledge that there is a sum of all the connections in the world and that another name for the sum of all those connections is God. The rabbinic name *HaMakom* itself suggests this view. Interestingly, the term the Rabbis used for a nonbeliever was *apikoros*, probably derived from the Greek philosopher Epicurus, who believed there were no connections between the isolated particles in the universe. One of the reasons the Pittsburgh Principles "affirm[s] the reality and the oneness of God" rests on our belief that most people who examine their understanding of the universe will acknowledge both connection and a source of those connections. By whatever name or conception we call it, belief in God is probably almost universal among Reform Jews.

Despite this broad definition of God, there will always be some people who will not wish to be acknowledged as God-believers. Given the Pittsburgh Principles' affirmation of God's reality, can such individuals still consider themselves Reform Jews? The answer is yes, on two grounds. The first is that they wish to be considered Reform Jews, affiliated with a Reform institution and affirming many, perhaps most, of the statements included in the Pittsburgh Principles. Not all Reform

Jews will affirm all of them. As the preamble section notes, the Pittsburgh Principles expresses the nature of belief of the preponderance of Reform rabbis and their congregants at the dawn of the twenty-first century. Some will see the Pittsburgh Principles as a goal for themselves to accept, others will maintain a "loyal opposition" to aspects of it, and all of us can feel that such internal dialogue is in keeping with a dynamic movement. But another reason for including such people in the movement is that if we hold that their beliefs can also manifest the presence of God, it does not matter whether they consider themselves God-believers or not.

If we can mostly agree on the reality of God, despite our different understandings, can we agree on the reality of dialogue? Biblical figures were confident that they could identify the voice of God, but the Rabbis were surely not. The most they might acknowledge was a *bat kol,* literally the "daughter of a voice," a divine voice once removed, and when it came to judging halachic matters, they ruled it out of order.[4] The Rabbis, who believed prophecy ended with the death of the prophet Malachi, relied heavily on the view in Deuteronomy 13:2–6 that a prophet (or anyone else) who claims to hear the voice of God commanding something contrary to what is written in the Torah is not to be believed—God speaks no new revelation to us. So what can dialogue mean in our times?

If the reality of God is suggested by "I speak, therefore I am," the Bible's confidence that God does speak and humans are able to respond is a challenge for all who seek to lead a religious life. How does God speak to us today?

I believe we hear God's voice in many ways. When we pour out our hearts in prayer and sit back in silence, one day a thought will come to us. We have to take up that thought, cradle it, ask how it responds to the prayers, the questions, that have been flooding our minds. Where did that thought come from? It never came into our heads before! To acknowledge that that thought might be a response from God is to affirm that God's reality comes to us through voiced or unvoiced speech. Part of the truth of the belief that all parts of the universe are interconnected is to see each thing that happens to us as though it were a piece of the universal jigsaw puzzle, looking for its mate. The jigsaw puzzle that is Life comes to us without a picture on the box showing how the pieces fit together. "Why is this happening now?" is a question that will help us explore the relationships between the seemingly random events in our lives and open us to the possibility that the Source of connections in the world is connecting our modest life to a wider purpose. Is it arrogance on our part to presume that our lives matter enough in the scheme of the universe that our thoughts or experiences might be messages from God? On the contrary—I believe it would be arrogant *not* to believe that, arrogant to assume that the details of our lives are outside the realm of God, outside the jigsaw puzzle that is God's vision of how the parts of existence fit together as a unified whole. Do we believe that God is One, or do we not?

The mainstream Jewish view has been that God speaks through Torah—that by learning Torah we discover what God asks of us, and it is our duty to respond. While we shall deal with Torah as a source of revelation in the next section of this book, a few words here are in order.

God as Covenant: Creation, Revelation, Redemption

No sooner has God been introduced to Moses as *YHVH*, formerly known as *El Shaddai*, than God announces the establishment of a *b'rit*, a covenant (Exodus 3:15–17). The *b'rit* announced to Moses only concerns God's promises to the people Israel—to take them out of Egypt and give them the land of Canaan, evidence that God has heard their cries. The last of these four promises, celebrated every year in the four cups of wine drunk at the seder table, is this one: "I will take you as a people for Me, and I will be as God for you, that you may know that I *Adonai* am your God who brought you out from under the burdens of Egypt" (Exodus 6:7). Not until God has fulfilled the promises of redeeming them from Egypt and has brought them to Mount Sinai does God indicate what it means for Israel to be God's people: "I adjure you to hearken thoroughly to My voice and obey My *b'rit*, becoming a treasure to Me from among all the peoples, for all the earth is Mine" (Exodus 19:5).[5] When God gives the Ten Commandments and the rest of the mitzvot to Moses, the manner in which Israel is to respond obediently to God's voice becomes clear. The reality of God's existence in the shape of *YHVH* and *Elohim* requires Israel to accept the Torah (called *Sefer HaB'rit*, "the Book of the Covenant"), which we did: "All that *YHVH* has spoken we shall do" (Exodus 19:8) and "All that *YHVH* has spoken we shall do and obey" (Exodus 24:7).

What is this Torah? Biblical scholars understand *Sefer HaB'rit* to refer just to the laws in Exodus 21–24, or *Parashat Mishpatim*. The traditional understanding, though, is that it is a synonym for the whole of the Written and Oral Torah, which includes more than the substance of the Revelation at Sinai. God asks obedience to this Revelation in response to God's decision to redeem the people and take them as God's treasure, a legitimate action because God is the Creator of all peoples and the earth on which they dwell. The *b'rit* between God and Israel thus brings together the three critical elements of the dialogue between God and Israel: Creation, Revelation, and Redemption. These three elements reflect the belief that God is *Melech haolam,* the Sovereign of time and space interwoven in a single dimension. Creation is the beginning of time, Redemption the end, making Revelation the middle, the point at which everything preceding it can be understood as the unfolding purpose of God, and everything after it as mitzvot that enable people to fulfill the will of God. Understood as dimensions of space, Creation brings space into being, Revelation sees the physical world as endlessly unfolding opportunities for mitzvot, while Redemption transforms the physical world from endless opportunities for oppression into endless expressions of liberation. Creation, Revelation, and Redemption are the instruments through which the voice of God's reality is heard.

Prayers of the Covenant

This threefold understanding of the reality of God in dialogue with the Jewish people is reenacted every morning and evening in the *Shacharit* and *Maariv* services. The first major section of the services, *Sh'ma Uvirchoteha*, the *Sh'ma* and Its Blessings, reflects the importance of these three themes to the *Sh'ma,* the affirmation of God's oneness. To be able to say the *Sh'ma* earnestly is a great challenge to anyone immersed in the tempestuous sea of modern culture. So many disparate forces clamor for our attention, so many powerful influences pull us this way and that, so many fractious ideas, seductive people and objects—how can we possibly mean it when we say, "God is One"? The ritual of closing our eyes in offering the *Sh'ma* is an attempt to act out a resolve to close our eyes to all those disparate forces and see the world whole. But of course this vision is only momentary; we must eventually open our eyes again, reminding ourselves that the real challenge is not to close ourselves off from the world but to see its interrelationships, to see how its fragments connect, to integrate its fractious pieces into a picture that is coherent. One of the benefits of the covenant is the ability to see the same Creation that is perceived as the universal handiwork of God as a particular gift from God to each of the members of the *b'rit*. To prepare ourselves for the *Sh'ma*, then, we need to see the world not as a cacophony of beauty here, ugliness there, danger behind us, majesty before us, but as a place where we may offer wholeheartedly the following Reform interpretations of the evening *Maariv Aravim* and the morning *Yotzer* prayers:

> How manifold are Thy works, O Lord! In wisdom Thou hast made them all. The heavens declare Thy glory, the earth reveals Thy creative power. Thou formest light and darkness, ordainest good out of evil, bringest harmony into nature and peace to the human heart.
>
> *Union Prayer Book*, part I (New York: CCAR, 1940), p. 118

> There lives a God:
> Your presence is the grandeur pervading the world.
> There lives a God:
> Heaven and earth alike reveal Your power and Your glory.
> Day and night, mountain, meadow and lake;
> Spring and autumn, growth and decay;
> Time and eternity, stars in their courses;
> All are witness to Your creative will.
>
> *Gates of Prayer* (New York: CCAR, 1975), p. 223

> In the beginning, even then
> A new light was sown for the righteous:
> A promise that Your light would become
> The catalyst, first for creation, and then for deliverance.
>
> Author of language and light,
> Help us to use words as You have

To cast light into dark waters,
To understand darkness
As a curtain that reveals the light.
> *Mishkan T'filah*, pilot ed. (New York: CCAR, 2004), p. 335

Both *Gates of Prayer* and the forthcoming *Mishkan T'filah* include another prayer that casts light on the covenantal aspect of Creation: *V'shamru*, from Exodus 31:16, which despite its theology appears in full in both Hebrew and English. The passage (*Gates of Prayer*, p. 198, and *Mishkan T'filah*, 2004 pilot ed., p. 56) commands the Israelites to keep Shabbat as a *b'rit olam*, an eternal covenant, as a sign that "in six days the Eternal God made heaven and earth and on the seventh day, God rested and was refreshed." In six days God made heaven and earth? Do Reform Jews not believe in a universe that has evolved over billions of years? How can we affirm this?

The *b'rit* gives us a gift. It allows us to experience Creation as though it took place not over billions of unimaginable years, but in six accessible days. Through Shabbat, it gives us words and rituals to celebrate the culmination of Creation every week. The billion-year Creation is the product of the searching, scientific mind, essential if we are to understand the inner, molecular nature of the universe. But the six-day Creation is a gift of God, a revelation for the soul. The texts of *Maariv Aravim* and *Yotzer* and the text of *V'shamru* help us through our words to celebrate the reality of the Jewish belief that God is the Creator of the world and of all the connecting pieces that make it up. These prayers and the daily *Birchot HaNehenin*, which we shall discuss in chapter 3, are ways to participate in the dialogue with the One God, who speaks through the created universe, and by our actions to be partners with the Holy One in making Creation complete. Unless we are scientists, as true as the theory of evolution may be, a billion-year Creation overwhelms us, confuses us; it reduces us to trying to understand little isolated pieces of the physical world, which, as soon as we think we've grasped them, are reinterpreted by a new generation of scientists. But a Creation that can be experienced in the humanly manageable form of six-days-plus-Shabbat of every week gives us hope that we really can be partners with God in shaping Creation. If we keep at it, our study of the pieces of the natural world may one day fall into place. In some ways, Shabbat as the culmination of a six-day Creation *is* the picture on the puzzle box. It is also a twenty-four-hour reminder that all the infinite intricacies of the Creation were formed by the One whose unity we praise in the first prayer preceding the *Sh'ma*.

The next prayer preparing us for the *Sh'ma* is *Ahavah Rabbah* (*Ahavat Olam* in the evening), which tries to help us unify the disparate world through the Torah that God revealed to us as an act of love. For Reform Jews to affirm this prayer is a reminder that despite the ambivalence about the binding quality of the Torah, as expressed in the 1885 Pittsburgh Platform, the Reform Movement believes that Revelation, like Creation, helps us see the overarching unity of a fractious world:[6]

> By laws and commandments, statutes and ordinances hast Thou led us in the way of righteousness and brought us to the light of truth.
>
> *Union Prayer Book* I, 1940, p. 12

> And how unyielding is the will of our people Israel! After the long nights, after the days and years when our ashes blackened the sky, Israel endures, heart still turned to love, soul turning still to life. So day and night, early and late, we will rejoice in the study of Torah, we will walk by the light of Mitzvot: they are our life and the length of our days.
>
> *Gates of Prayer*, 1975, p. 209

> Flood us with light,
> let Torah seize our hearts,
> and unite us to revere Your name.
> Infuse our deeds with holiness,
> radiant with passion for life.
> May Your mercy ever sustain us
> with the wisdom of Torah.
> O Holy One, we bless You
> for Your blessed gift of love.
>
> *Mishkan T'filah*, pilot ed., 2004, p. 337

Inspired by the presence of God ruling over Creation and the guidance of God's revealed Torah that helps us see the unifying principles of Creation, we are deemed sufficiently prepared to offer the *Sh'ma*.

After we have done so, the third aspect of the *b'rit*, Redemption, remains to put the themes of God's oneness in a broader context. Redemption (*g'ulah* in Hebrew) originally referred to a person's obligation to redeem a relative from bondage or redeem property for the true owner at the time of the Jubilee after it had been sold to others (Leviticus 25:24–25). The Torah came to see God as the ultimate *Go-eil* (Redeemer), who freed God's people Israel from Egyptian bondage and returned us to our land, after it had been inhabited by others. As the *Union Prayer Book* proclaimed in its version of this prayer:

> Eternal truth it is that Thou alone art God and there is none else.
> And through Thy power alone has Israel been redeemed from the
> hand of oppressors.
>
> *Union Prayer Book* I, 1940, p.14

It is God's oneness that makes Redemption possible, for there is no power great enough to challenge the Divine. But then, why has this people suffered so? If God redeemed the Jewish people from Egypt, why has the ultimate Redemption not yet come? Unlike the traditional siddur, which restricts the *G'ulah* prayer to a praise of God at the redemption from Egypt, Reform liturgy seeks to understand the reasons for the delay in the ultimate redemption, using the current state of the world to urge on the Jewish people to act on their belief in God's oneness by assisting God's redemptive work to bring unity to the fractious nations:

> And now that we live in a land of freedom, may we continue to be
> faithful to Thee and Thy word. . . .
> May Thy law rule the hearts of all Thy children and Thy truth unite
> their hearts in fellowship. . . .
> As Thou hast redeemed Israel and saved him from arms stronger
> than his own, so mayest Thou redeem all who are oppressed
> and persecuted.
>
> *Union Prayer Book* I, 1940, pp. 14, 16

> May the time not be distant, O God, when Thy name shall be worshiped in all the earth, when unbelief shall disappear and error be no more.
>
> *Union Prayer Book* I, 1940, Adoration, p. 71

> In a world torn by violence and pain, a world far from wholeness and
> peace, a world waiting still to be redeemed, give us, Lord, the
> courage to say: There is One God in heaven and earth. . . .
> It has been our glory to bear witness to our God, and to keep alive
> in dark ages the vision of a world redeemed.

> May this vision never fade; let us continue to work for the day when nations will be one and at peace. Then shall we sing with one accord, as Israel sang at the shores of the sea.
>
> *Gates of Prayer*, 1975, pp. 149–150;
> *Mishkan T'filah*, pilot ed., 2004, p. 221, slightly revised

A Reform reading of the redemption theme calls us to demonstrate the reality of God by the manner in which we put the divine word into practice in the world. The true issue in dialogue, Reform Judaism suggests, is not so much whether—and how—God responds to us, but how we respond to God.

Knowing how to respond is never easy. The voices that come to us from Creation, Revelation, and Redemption are only occasionally harmonious. Often they call us with different priorities. God is real, we affirm, but never simple. Participating in the dialogue, even when we must converse with conflicting voices in the tradition at the same time, is the way to see how the pieces fit together.

A true story: In our yard there once grew a magnificent ash tree, its graceful branches bearing delicate green leaves that in the summer would catch the sun and diffuse its rays across our yard. In autumn the leaves turned gold, brilliant against the deep blue sky, accented by the red blossoms of our climbing bougainvillea. The tree shed its beauty on our neighbor's yard as well, its colors as generous to him as to us. I used to pray outside some days, and looking at the summer or autumn leaves on the ash tree helped me feel quite powerfully the presence of the God, who had created the green and the gold and the blue and the red—and me, and the ones I loved. But one day our neighbor came by, complaining that the roots of the ash tree had been digging up his driveway and making cracks in the wall we shared, and he asked us to cut it down. Cut down this majestic tree, I anguished, this noble gift of God? Can't we pay to have his driveway repaved, our wall repaired? But we knew the roots would only tear them up again. The tree had become like a *shor nagach*, an ox that keeps finding other animals to gore. No matter that it is a living creature, the Bible says it must be destroyed. God speaks in the sweep of an ash tree's leaves, but also in the spread of its voracious roots, and the biblical principle (Exodus 21:36) is clear. Where was our covenant with our neighbor: in the gift of the soaring ash tree we thought we were giving him, or the responsibility to protect his driveway, if that was the important thing to him? If God is real, we must listen not only to the beauty in the world that sings God's praises, but also to the commanding voice of Torah that sometimes asks us to do very hard things.

It has been months since we had the ash tree chopped down, and the yard still feels empty. Sometimes I stumble over a dip in the ground where the roots had been, and while the deep blue sky is there and the red bougainvillea, the green and the gold are gone. God speaks through nature and through Torah, and also through the absence of harmony between two people on either side of a wall for whom the time is still distant when they can agree on whether the true redemptive value of a house is in its tree or its driveway. In what we hear and what we do not yet hear, God's voice is very real.

3

In the Way
of God's Presence

We affirm that every human being is created *b'tzelem Elohim*, in the image of God, and that therefore every human life is sacred.

We regard with reverence all of God's creation and recognize our human responsibility for its preservation and protection.

We encounter God's presence in moments of awe and wonder, in acts of justice and compassion, in loving relationships and in the experiences of everyday life.

—Statement of Principles, "God," paragraphs 3–5

The World Reflects God's Presence

We do not always look at nature as "God's creation." Too often when we admire a tree or a sunset or a morning lake, we do not connect the beauty with its Creator. The CCAR's *On the Doorposts of Your House* includes the texts of *Birchot HaNehenin*, the prayers over things enjoyed, which provide words with which to connect a flowering tree or a gorgeous sunset to God. One of them reads: *Baruch atah Adonai Eloheinu Melech haolam, oseh maaseih v'reishit,* "Praised are You, *Adonai* our God, Majesty of the universe, who keeps on doing the deed of Creation." These blessings help us transform a mere appreciation of nature into a dialogue with the Creator of nature. God begins the conversation by presenting a flaming sunset to us, much as God began the dialogue with Moses by enabling the bush to burn unconsumed (Exodus 3:1–4). We respond, as he did, by observing the flames and by speaking. But Moses, on a higher spiritual plane than we, knew what to say: "Let me turn aside and see this great sight; why does the bush not burn up?" And when God sees that Moses has responded by turning (Martin Buber's phrase for dialogue) to the bush, God calls out his name. For us the order is different: it is when we feel personally addressed by the flaming sunset or the flowering tree that we speak the words of the blessing, acknowledging the presence of God in the flames and the flower. While Moses knew how to respond to the conversation, we often do not, which is why we have a script: *Baruch atah Adonai. . . . Birchot HaNehenin* give us words with which to uphold our part of the conversation. And then we fix our gaze, as the golden sun and the lavender clouds continue God's message until it is dark: "The heavens are telling the glory of God" (Psalm 19:2). But does God have a mission for us, as for Moses? We shall see.

The texts of the various *Birchot HaNehenin* remind us that it is not only beauty for which we praise God. The *b'rachah* cited above is also one of the appropriate blessings to be said during an earthquake. How is an earthquake an opportunity to praise God, "who keeps on doing the deed of Creation"? To ask the question helps us transform a moment of personal terror by connecting it to the history of the earth we live upon. Earthquakes are a sign that the tectonic plates of the planet are continuing to adjust their relationship to each other and, in so doing, continue the process of bringing order to the original chaos of the universe. But praising God in this moment also transforms the cosmic into the immediate. This *b'rachah* is another example of taking Creation out of the realm of billions of scientific years into the immediacy of a six-day journey: "Thank you, God," we say a bit shakily, "for enabling us to be present at the ongoing Creation of the world."

When my family awoke terrified on the morning of the 1994 Northridge, California, earthquake, we huddled together in the dark, and when we had gotten some perspective on the event, we offered one of the *Birchot HaNehenin*, but not *oseh maaseih v'reishit*. I had learned the tradition of offering instead a praise of God *shekocho ug'vurato malei olam*, "whose power and might fill the world." What is the difference between "who keeps on doing the deed of Creation" and "whose power and might fill the world"? I think the blessing we said acknowledges the terror people feel during an earthquake—and tries to reassure us by acknowledging God's presence in the noise and the shaking. In some ways this experience was the opposite of Elijah's on Mount Horeb, another name for Sinai: "A great and mighty wind tore the mountains in pieces, shattering the rocks before *Adonai*—but *Adonai* was not in the wind; and after the wind, an earthquake—but *Adonai* was not in the earthquake" (I Kings 19:11). God wanted Elijah to feel God's presence in the *kol d'mamah dakah* that followed these pyrotechnics, a hushed, broken voice. But we are much more used to experiencing God's presence in the hushed voices of the synagogue than in the clamor of natural phenomena, and so we are urged to utter prayers that enable the dialogue with God to continue even in an earthquake and help us understand it as part of the ongoing process of Creation. Have you ever stood at the shore in a hurricane and watched the waves crash against the rocks? It is a sight filled with *yirah*, "awe," a word that connotes the stirring grandeur of God's creative power (like the days set aside to appreciate that power, the Yamim Noraim, the High Holy Days). The dark side of *yirah*, however, is the knowledge that a hurricane can shatter houses, can drag humans risking the waves out to sea in a cruel and pounding death. How could such a majestic sight be so destructive? It is because, tragically, humans have gotten in the way—however unintentionally—of God's necessary, ongoing work of Creation.

Can we imagine that light and water and seas and dry land were created without violent upheavals? The difference between that primeval time and our experience of the Creation is that there were as yet no animals and humans to get in the way of the turbulent formation of our world. Part of the message of Shabbat, perhaps, is that the aim and purpose of Creation is the harmony and peacefulness of the Seventh Day— but until Creation is totally completed, the upheavals will continue, and sometimes the life that moves upon the earth will suffer. But why did God not wait to create moving beings until the Creation was all done? The answer is clear: God wanted us to be partners in Creation, to help in its formation, and to do that, God took the risk that sometimes our free will would put us dangerously, destructively, "in the way."

We can be "in the way" in an immature fashion—tempting the Creator by taking a boat out in a hurricane, or even by building homes too close to the shore or in the flood plain of a river that overflows its banks in the spring. "Come and get us!" we shout to the chaotic waters. Too often, though, we get in the way by being the ones who "come and get" the Creation itself. God instructed humanity in Genesis 2:15 *l'avdah ul'shamrah*, to work (or serve) the earth and to guard it. If human beings are created *b'tzelem Elohim*, we are also children of the *adamah*, the humus (in Arthur Waskow's felicitous translation) from which *adam*, humanity, was shaped. To serve our bodily parent, the earth is to recognize that God shaped us from its material, and to help safeguard our planet is a metaphorical extension of the fifth commandment, to honor our parents that our days may be long upon the earth God gave us (Exodus 20:12). To cooperate with our community's recycling program may seem like a trivial civic habit, but it can be as much a celebration of God's role in the material world as it may have been for the priests when they took out the trash from the previous day's *korbanot* (offerings)—the trash brought them *karov* (close) to God, too. These simple acts of recycling can lead us through the more complicated ideals of *bal tashchit,* "do not destroy." Taking inventory of how much paper we waste, how much unrecyclable plastic we use instead of biodegradable products, can grow into a discipline as respectful of God's creation as kashrut—a way to regard with reverence all of God's creation. It is a means of walking in the ways of the Creator (Deuteronomy 8:6) rather than getting in the way.

Human Beings Reflect God's Presence

To recognize our connection to God's good earth is of a piece with our recognition of the image of God in human beings. Respect for nature and respect for humanity are both a tribute to the way in which God made us—a recognition of our mortality (to the earth we shall return) and our immortality (the soul that is God's image within us is immortal).

Just as it is easier for us to recognize God's presence in beautiful sights than in troubling ones, so it is easier to see the *tzelem Elohim* in righteous people than in dangerous ones. Earlier we referred to "people who commit odious acts" rather than "odious people." The great

Talmudic sage Beruria reminded her husband Rabbi Meir that the Torah says that God will remove sins from the earth, not sinners (*B'rachot* 10a). This is an affirmation that people are not the sum of their acts, but constitute an essence, a *n'shamah*, a soul, that is independent of those acts. Before God placed in us the conflicting inclinations to advance harmony (the *yetzer hatov*) and to impede it (the *yetzer hara*), God created us as an image of the Divine, as we read in Psalm 8:5: "You made us a little less than the angels." This seems to mean that one of the ways in which we get to know God is by looking for the presence of God in other human beings.

We are not used to doing that. We divide people into those who are nice to us or who are mean, those who are needy or who meet our needs; we do not usually see them as vessels for the presence of God. What the Pittsburgh Principles suggests is that we err when we think we shall find God only in the synagogue, only when we pray. One of the tests of the quality of our religious lives is whether we can also perceive the presence of God in ordinary human beings—the nice ones as well as the mean ones. To show how far we have come from belief in merely a "God-idea," we need to train ourselves to look for God in our neighbor, our beloved, the person tailgating us on a busy expressway—and even worse.

How do we locate a person's *tzelem Elohim*? As we learn from the priests whose holy tasks included the ordinary labor of taking out the garbage, we can also learn from the ordinary phenomenon of their clothing. The High Priest was to wear a band of gold across his forehead on which was engraved *Kodesh l'Adonai,* "Holy to God" (Exodus 28:36). Why was this necessary? Aaron, and the High Priests who followed him, must have looked like ordinary people; if he was dressed in jeans and a T-shirt, we would never recognize him as the chief personage who would help us draw close to God by helping make the proper offerings in the Tabernacle and later in the Temple. If we encountered him in his white robes, we might merely be scared, intimidated, or repelled by his formidable presence. But that would be contrary to his mission, which was to bring us near to God. Perhaps that is why he wore this gold band on his forehead—to remind us to take the opportunity of being in his presence to draw closer to the holiness of God. "Holy to God" invites us to consider each person as though he or she were as wide an entryway to the unique aspects of God's nearness as the High Priest himself.

The early Reform Movement was very much drawn to the image of the priest as a model of purity. For the early Reformers this was not a matter of ritual purity, but purity of character, in keeping with their stress on the observance of the moral laws rather than the ritual ones. But they also took literally the promise in Exodus 19:6 that the Jewish people was to be a *mamlechet kohanim v'goy kadosh*, "a realm of priests and a holy people." The mission of the people Israel was to be a priestly people bringing the world close to the service of God. Each Jew was therefore to act as though he or she were the High Priest, representing the holiness of God in our bearing and actions.

But we need not relegate the band inscribed "Holy to God" only to a long-vanished hierarch. What if we could see those words inscribed upon the foreheads of all people—our neighbors and our partners and the people whose purpose in the world seems mainly to be getting in *our* way? What would that mean?

When my neighbor asked us to cut down our ash tree, if I had remembered that this man is also holy to God, I would have seen him as more than a person threatening a treasured part of nature. I would have remembered that ultimately nature was created in order to make possible the life of human beings (see Genesis 2:8–10, 19), and so we are to take care of the creations in nature. I would have remembered that I had failed to take the steps necessary to ensure that the tree would not be a threat to our neighbor's property. I would have remembered that our neighbor plays a much larger role than merely the threatener of our ash tree. He too is concerned about his little piece of Creation; he too has a family. The neat manner in which he tends his property also sets off our house in an attractive way. The little birch trees that grow on it are lovely; they too turn gold in the fall. He is trying to avoid getting in Creation's way—just in a different fashion from ours.

"Holy to God" reminds us of another important verse in the Torah, identified as the most important one by Rabbi Akiva: *v'ahavta l'rei-acha kamocha*, "and you shall love your neighbor as yourself" (Leviticus 19:18). Commentaries on the meaning of this verse abound, but two are most relevant here: *V'ahavta l'rei-acha* can be understood to mean "show love to" your neighbor—that is, act lovingly toward your neighbor—because he is "as yourself"—he is just like you. Hillel offers us a second insight, understanding this verse to mean, "What is hateful to you do not do to anyone else" (why should you think that person would not find it hateful as well?).

We need not "love" this person, surely not as we might love a spouse or a close friend, but our actions to our neighbor need to spring from the reservoir of love from which comes our affection for those truly close to us. One of those "truly close to us" is God, whom we are also asked to love: *v'ahavta et Adonai Elohecha*, "and you shall love *Adonai* your God" (Deuteronomy 6:5), the continuation of the first paragraph of the *Sh'ma*. Loving God creates a reservoir of love from which we can do loving acts toward those created in God's image, and so make visible our love for God, as God's love for us becomes visible through the love others show us. Ultimately, even the neighbor who "gets in our way" is not a threat to us. This person too can be a way for us to share the love that God has showered on us—a testimony that we are so filled with God's love that it can overflow into a person whom we might otherwise experience only as thwarting.

As we walk the streets of big cities, where wealth abounds, we often come upon desperately poor people sleeping in doorways, bundled-up old women pushing shopping carts that contain all their earthly belongings, gaunt, wizened men standing at the exit ramps of freeways asking for money for food or shelter. The common wisdom, even of some social service professionals, encourages us not to assist these men and women—"They'll only use your money for drink or drugs." But the wisdom of the Talmud and the Jewish law of compassion argue just the opposite. Though giving to a person who asks is on the lower rungs of Maimonides' ladder of *tzedakah*, it is still a rung. We may not ignore the needs of impoverished individuals even as we ascend the higher reaches of the ladder and give anonymously or so generously that no one in our society is without work and sustenance. Indeed, if we look for the *tzelem Elohim* in these people whom society has failed to take under its wing, how can we do differently? If we give generously to the poor, if our gift is not a handout but the beginning of a dialogue, it becomes a dialogue as well with the One who today may be clothed in the rags of a homeless woman on the off-ramp, as last evening the Holy One was clothed in the gold and lavender strands of a sunset. But today the dialogue is different: "God, how can you have allowed this man to sink to such a state?" "Richard, how could you not have done more to transform a society that permits people to sink to so low a state?"

That is why giving to isolated individuals, as important as it is to reveal more of the image of God in the world, will not alleviate the larger societal ills that cause or contribute to their plight. For while we need to recover the priestly mission in Judaism by letting the band of gold on each person's forehead help to bring him or her closer to God, the Reform Movement has insisted that we also recover the prophetic mission of giving voice to God's complaint against a callous society. Leviticus 19:9 commands us to reserve the *pei-ah*, the corner of the field, for the poor. The corner of the field, the part joining the owner's field with that which does not belong to that owner, is a reminder that the owner shares the field with God. The poor are God's agents, collecting the share that belongs to the Holy One. We learn in the Talmud (*Kiddushin* 41b) that a person's agent is equivalent to the one who engages him or her, further evidence that especially in the poor do we perceive the image of God. *Mishnah Pei-ah* 1:2 tells us that while there is a minimum size of a corner (one-sixtieth of the field), there is no maximum: a corner, like God, is infinitely extendable. In opening the corner to the poor, the farmer enters the space where God dwells. Since the poor are entitled to the sheaves that fall to the ground during the harvest, it is as though God walks beside the farmer, deciding which sheaves shall fall to earth for the poor and which shall stay in the arms of the reaper. This is why the Pittsburgh Principles affirms that we encounter God's presence in acts of justice and compassion. *Tzedakah* is not just a mitzvah, it is a way of realizing God's sovereignty in society.

Two weeks after I was ordained in 1964, I joined a group of seventeen other Reform rabbis in responding to a telegram to the convention of the Central Conference of American Rabbis from Martin Luther King Jr., asking us to participate in a demonstration protesting the segregation of public places in the oldest city in the United States, St. Augustine, Florida. After the seventeen of us were thrown into a segregated jail run by the Ku Klux Klan, steaming in the southern June heat, eating from the baby food jars thrown to us by our jailers, we davened *Shacharit* in our cell, empathizing (more than perhaps we ever had) with the praise of God in the *G'vurot* prayer of the *Amidah* who is *matir asurim*, "the One who releases captives." Marching with farmworkers in Delano, California, sitting in the apartments of refuseniks in the Soviet Union as they taught Hebrew to eager young Russian Jews behind closed blinds, marching for Justice for Janitors, or sharing a seder with workers in sweatshops—no one who shared these involvements in the cause of human justice could escape the feeling that we marched or taught or sang in the presence not only of brave human beings but of the One who was the source of their bravery. For Reform Jews—and for all people devoted to creating a just and compassionate society—work for social justice is ultimately not a political act but a religious one. Work for social justice is an act of *kiddush HaShem*, revealing the holiness of God amid a cruel and often heartless society. Those who trample on the rights of the poor are rebelling against God, and so to fight for their rights is to take up the cause of God. Once again the three themes of the covenant come together in this arena: the Torah reveals to us the will of the God who created all people in God's image, who in redeeming us from Egypt created an empathy with all who are enslaved to cruel taskmasters. The Torah intends that no sooner do we hear the words, "You were slaves [or strangers] in the land of Egypt," that we continue the dialogue by doing all we can to facilitate the redemption of whoever is enslaved at this moment in history. Across the foreheads of each of those oppressed, "Holy to God" is emblazoned for all who wish to see.

Sometimes, though, it is not so easy to see. The night before we were jailed in St. Augustine, we stayed in the homes of members of the black community. The next day we discovered something stunning, and unsettling: when we encountered our black neighbors, we felt safe; when we saw white people approaching, we feared what their intentions toward us might be. On the one hand, we had no trouble seeing the image of God in people who for most of our lives had been strangers to us, were sometimes even feared by us; on the other hand, we found it hard to see that image in the white Floridians, who, we assumed, were among those keeping black citizens in poverty and segregation. In our fear of the faces of the white Floridians, was there fear of what might lurk behind our own faces?

Reflections in a Driver's Mirror

Lurking faces are an increasing phenomenon in urban life. I live in a city where most interactions with strangers take place through the rearview mirrors of our cars. In traditional cities like New York or Chicago, one encounters strangers by walking down the street, but those interactions end as soon as we pass each other by. Driving in heavy traffic, the stranger in the car behind us can be in our mirror for a long time, and so the tailgating driver becomes a metaphor for urban encounters with people whose only purpose in life seems to be getting in our way. When I am driving home after a long day and someone is driving so close behind me that I fear having to stop short, it is hard to look at the face in my rearview mirror and see "Holy to God" on the driver's forehead. But once again, if all I see is an impatient, dangerous tailgater, I am failing to see the *person* behind me, and I certainly fail to see the *tzelem Elohim*. The wickedness of contemporary society is that the anger and cynicism and degradation of so much of the world around us gradually take over the people we think we are and would like to be. Dialogue is impossible, as Buber noted, when we turn a child of God into an "it," a dangerous driver, especially when we respond by reducing ourselves to that "it" as well.

One way to resist this dehumanization (or de-deitization, removing the godly from someone) is to return to Hillel's "What is hateful to you. . . . " Why is this person tailgating me? As the Talmud urges us to do with every unpleasant thing that occurs to us (Babylonian Talmud, *B'rachot* 5a), I need to examine my own deeds. Perhaps I am driving more slowly than necessary. Perhaps I am driving erratically. But let me also look at him. Why should I think he is any different from me? As I want to get home, so does he; as I am irritated by the traffic, so is he. And so rather than glaring at him, let me smile at this newly discovered neighbor and figure out how I can help him reach his goal—by pulling over perhaps and letting him pass. By identifying not with the reduction of this person behind me into an impatient, dangerous driver, but as a person longing to reach home and embrace his family, I am reaching into the reservoir of love from which I feel the presence of the God who created both of us. Out of this consciousness, I elevate us both. For I have transformed this stranger, this other, into my teacher, and I have opened my heart to his wisdom. One of the *Birchot HaNehenin* reads: "Praised are You, *Adonai* our God, who has shared Your wisdom with flesh and blood." Suddenly I am yearning to get home too, suddenly I am overwhelmed by the desire to be with my family, to have that particular encounter with God that, the Pittsburgh Principles reminds us, takes place in the arms of those we love.

To go through all this with an anonymous tailgater is but a fraction of what we need to do with other human beings with whom we share this planet. To confront my fear of the white Floridians in St. Augustine forty years ago, I should have gotten to know whites who opposed integration in my own city, but not only them. To understand each person's holiness we would need to plumb all those qualities that initially make us more aware of our mutual otherness rather than our shared—but very different—divinity. The God who created the lawyer who is descended from a Mississippi slave who is descended from an African tribeswoman is the same God who created the physicist descended from a California railroad worker descended from a Manchu warlord—who is the same God who created a Los Angeles rabbi descended from a Rochester tailor who is descended from Jews of a country whose memory has been lost to our family. This is why we praise the God of Abraham, the God of Isaac, the God of Sarah, the God of Rebekah. Maimonides is right: how can we ever grasp even the hem of such a Being? My tailor grandfather helped to sew a little bit of that hem, and so it is from him and the black lawyer and the Chinese physicist—as well as the flowering bush and the earthquake—that I shall know God. I have more than a lifetime of work to do.

Do Evildoers Reflect God's Image?

Yet neighbors and tailgaters are relatively easy places to find the *tzelem Elohim*. Could we see the image of God in Timothy McVeigh, the man who bombed the Murrah Office Building in Oklahoma City? In Osama bin Laden? In Adolf Hitler? Or closer to home, in the boss who mistreats us day after day? In the man who rapes another neighbor's daughter?

To search for the *tzelem Elohim* is to search for the *n'shamah*, the soul, the essence of a person, before God implanted the *yetzer hatov* and the *yetzer hara*. Even when we are overcome by the presence of someone's *yetzer hara*, we need to continue searching for the *tzelem Elohim*. To deny the possibility of finding it in human beings who have committed awful crimes is to declare that they are more powerful than God, that they have the power to destroy the image that God gave them.

When Adolf Eichmann went on trial in Jerusalem for his crimes during the Holocaust, Martin Buber urged that the Israeli court not give him a death sentence, but commit him to live out the rest of his life working on a kibbutz, facing every day the very people he had wanted to put to death. That brilliant "final solution" to radical evil expressed not only Buber's opposition to capital punishment, but even more his belief that there is something deserving of redemption in every child of the Creation, because each person possesses a *tzelem Elohim*. It reminds us of the absolute command in the Revelation, *uvacharta bachayim* (Deuteronomy 30:19), "Choose life!" Reform Jews read this passage on Yom Kippur morning instead of the traditional portion of the High Priest's rites of sacrificing one goat and sending away the other, laden with our sins, into the wilds of Azazel. Choosing to read this alternative passage is saying that our solution to sin is not to kill sinners (thought the Torah permits it), but to help them find their way to life. Long ago God commanded us to abandon vengeful killing and to subject the accused to a jury trial, and the Rabbis, speaking in the Babylonian Talmud (*Sanhedrin* 37a–b), argued in principle for the abolition of capital punishment. Yes, we should do all we can to hunt down figures like McVeigh and Bin Laden and Hitler, not to kill them (unless they threaten our lives) but to redeem them and thereby show how strong is our belief in God who created every person in the divine image. The Rabbis in the *M'chilta (Bachodesh* 8) asked us to read the Ten Commandments side by side in two columns rather than in a list of ten, so that we would read the sixth commandment, "You shall not murder," as the consequence of the first commandment, "I am *Adonai* your God." If you murder, they suggest, you are destroying the image of God. And if redemption is possible for such criminals as these, how much more so is it possible for those, like a mean boss, who do not seek our lives but only make them miserable.

Of course, not all Reform Jews oppose capital punishment, though in their resolutions over the years, the URJ, the CCAR, and the

Religious Action Center (RAC) have come out strongly against it. There are also a number of scholars who disagree that the *Sanhedrin* text opposes capital punishment. Nonetheless, a weighty segment of the Reform Movement is willing to show how far its belief in "the image of God" extends, that even in the face of the most egregious of crimes it urges preserving life out of a refusal to lose hope in the possible redemption of every human creature of God. Until we are able to look upon such individuals and praise God for "sharing Your wisdom with flesh and blood," we know how much work our society still has to do.

Some readers of the Pittsburgh Principles have asked whether the statement "every human life is sacred" implies opposition to a woman's right to choose abortion. The Reform Movement has long supported the right of women to have control over their own bodies, of which the fetus is a dependent part. While the fetus has the potential to become a human being, in Jewish law it is not considered alive and able to live independently until birth. Jewish law has always affirmed that the perceived needs of the fetus are subject to the expressed needs of the mother's physical and mental health. Of course, because the fetus has the potential to become a life, no decision to abort should be taken lightly, but no one who has faced the crisis of whether or not to bring a baby to term sees the decision as a "light" one. Every mother—and father—knows that to give birth to a child is to give substance to the image of God, but in the mother carrying that child, the image of God already has substance.

To Realize God's Image

How can we stop getting in the way of God's plan and stop seeing others as merely being in the way of our own? The Pittsburgh Principles suggests an ethic of behavior whose mission is to realize the palpable presence of God in our lives through human beings and the natural world. It is a powerful antidote to the perpetual challenge to faith suggested by the charge: "Why can we not see God the way the people in the Bible did, even the way some of the ancient rabbis did?" Moses, who had a dialogue with God through the Burning Bush, is anguished that his people find it so hard to feel the presence of God once the pyrotechnic miracles have given way to ordinary life. After their inability to encounter God leads them to make the Golden Calf, Moses cries out, "Please, show me Your glory!" (Exodus 33:18). To look for God's image in every person—to multiply the moments when we experience the awe of the universe; to act with reverence toward the planet, with justice toward the defenseless and with compassion toward the sinful; to experience the time alone with the ones we love as moments when we see the glory of God—we shall give testimony that God has answered Moses's cry in our own time.

4

How God Commands and How We Respond

We respond to God daily: through public and private prayer, through study and through the performance of other *mitzvot*, sacred obligations—*bein adam la-Makom*, to God, and *bein adam la-chaveiro*, to other human beings.

We strive for a faith that fortifies us through the vicissitudes of our lives—illness and healing, transgression and repentance, bereavement and consolation, despair and hope.

—Statement of Principles, "God," paragraphs 6–7

God's Voice in the Mitzvot

Dialogue with God can begin when we see something startling in nature or when we remember that every person has an invisible "Holy to God" on the forehead. But Jews have long believed that God initiates dialogue in another way as well: through the giving of mitzvot. Later on in this book, we shall discuss how mitzvot come to us through study of Torah, but before the Israelites were given the Torah as a physical object, individuals (Abraham and Sarah, Isaac and Jacob) heard the commanding voice of God. The Israelites heard that voice as they stood at Sinai, where, according to the Talmud (*Makot* 23b–24a), God commanded the 613 mitzvot that make up the Torah. Through encountering each of the mitzvot, we too can encounter the original voice of God.

Mitzvah is a noun derived from the root *tz-v-h,* "command." Why, then, has the Pittsburgh Principles rendered it as "sacred obligation"? And why, when it appears again in the "Torah" section, is it described as "the means by which we make our lives holy"?

"Sacred" of course is a synonym for "holy," and both are words that infuse the people's experience at Sinai. When Moses encounters the Burning Bush, God tells him to remove his shoes because the ground on which he is standing is *admat kodesh,* "holy ground" (Exodus 3:5) — seemingly ground on which one can encounter the Holy One. In Exodus 19, before the giving of the Ten Commandments, there are many directions that the people must follow because they are approaching holy ground. The Rabbis chose as the haftarah to accompany the reading of the Ten Commandments the description in Isaiah of the prophet seeing the angels crying out, *Kadosh Kadosh Kadosh Adonai Tz'vaot,* "Holy, Holy, Holy is *Adonai* of Hosts!" (Isaiah 6:3). For Shavuot, the holiday that celebrates the giving of the Torah, they chose as the haftarah Ezekiel's ecstatic vision of God. These choices make clear that for the Rabbis the meaning of the people's experience of hearing Torah at Sinai was not only the content of the mitzvot but the experience of God's holiness. "Sacred obligation" is a very appropriate way to render *mitzvah.*

Yet "obligation" often means something one has taken on oneself rather than a charge that has been given from without. The English word "commandment" sounds authoritarian, and this is one of the reasons why the Hebrew word *mitzvah* was so slow to enter the Reform lexicon. Its first "official" appearance is in *Gates of Prayer,* published in 1975; the Centenary Perspective omits the Hebrew word and speaks only of "obligations." The 1885 Pittsburgh Platform asserted that "we accept as binding only the moral laws," reflecting the Kantian perspective that all human beings are endowed with reason that mandates the same moral laws for all people, and that other kinds of laws, regulating what they called "ceremonies," were of a lesser order, because they were not universal. As to those, the rabbis gathered in Pittsburgh in 1885 "maintain only such ceremonies as elevate and sanctify our lives, but reject all such as are not adapted to the views and habits of modern civilization." By defining *mitzvot* as "sacred obligations," the rabbis gathered in Pittsburgh in 1999 were willing to endow all the commandments in the Torah with the power "to make our lives holy."

But are they commandments (given from without) or obligations (accepted from within)? Some years ago my wife Carol suggested that mitzvah can be better understood not so much as "I command you!" but "This is something very important to Me that you do." The wisdom of this formulation is that it reflects the covenantal aspect of the relationship between God and the Jewish people, rather than an authoritarian one. "This is something very important to me that you do" is the language marriage partners use with each other. The implication is: "Because of our covenant with each other, I would like you to do this act as a way of showing your love for me. Because you are free not to do it, doing it is a gift you can give me—one you know I will appreciate." The word "commandment" involves a request from a superior power to a lesser power; to see a mitzvah as a gift suggests a mutual relationship—a covenant. Of course, the covenant between God and Israel is a different covenant than that of a marital bond, in that God created Israel. Still, it can be argued that Creation is present in the marriage bond too: both partners to a marriage, or any other permanent relationship, create that relationship and as well create, or at least inspire, new aspects of behavior in each other. The mitzvah is also revelatory, uncovering how God understands the implications of the covenant for both of our actions. And the doing of it is redemptive, transformative: in the Exodus, from slaves to free servants of God; in a marriage, from an existence solely as an individual to a partner in a holy relationship. Mitzvah transforms objects, too: two small columns of wax become vessels for the presence of Shabbat; some leaves and a nubby citrus turn into a *lulav* and *etrog*, vessels for extending the fruitfulness of one harvest into another. The transformative power of mitzvah is an echo of God's own transforming power: the Holy One took some sand and Reed Sea water and transformed them into a miracle, a place where God's holiness was revealed. God took a little mountain and transformed it into the place of Revelation, where God's holiness was also revealed.

Do Moral Laws Take Precedence?

Where the Reformers of the 1885 Pittsburgh Platform chose to divide the "laws" into ethical and ceremonial, Pittsburgh 1999 returns to the more normative Jewish division: *mitzvot bein adam la-Makom*, mitzvot between human beings and God, and *mitzvot bein adam la-chaveiro*, mitzvot between one human being and another. While the "moral laws" were always binding, the 1885 Pittsburghers regarded the "ceremonial" laws as instrumental only if they could "elevate and sanctify our lives." Today, we might argue that the "moral" and "ceremonial" laws are not so clearly distinguishable. We could probably identify Shabbat as a set of "ceremonial" laws, but isn't the prohibition against working one's servant on Shabbat moral? We could probably regard prayer as a ceremonial law, but doesn't the prayer book abound in moral teachings, and is it not a moral requirement to be present for a minyan so that one's neighbor can pray? Surely the dietary laws are ceremonial, but are there not moral implications in the restriction against boiling a kid in its mother's milk? The newer formulation of Pittsburgh 1999 makes no such invidious distinctions between the two categories. Whether they speak of obligations between humans or between humans and God, they are still mitzvot, things important to God that we do.

Yet the distinctions between the two categories of mitzvah are porous as well. What are examples of *mitzvot bein adam la-Makom*? Prayer, study, the dietary laws, wearing a *tallit* and *t'fillin*, observing Shabbat. What are examples of *mitzvot bein adam la-chaveiro*? The prohibitions against murder, adultery, and stealing; the regulations about the goring ox, the corners of the field, restoring lost objects. There are divine and human elements in many of them. Indeed, when I don my *tallit* and grasp the *tzitzit*, the knotted cords, I am instructed to be aware of all the mitzvot of God and to do them—the "ethical" and the "ceremonial," those between God and myself, and between myself and another person. In Leviticus 19:3, behavior to parents is followed by Shabbat injunctions (the order is reversed in the Ten Commandments), and in Leviticus 19:16–19, mitzvot regarding relations with other people are followed by the prohibition against *kilayim* and *shaatneiz*, the mixing of different kinds of seeds and fabrics.

Perhaps the greatest change in using the traditional categories rather than the moral/ceremonial dichotomy is that unlike all the other Reform platforms, the 1999 Pittsburgh Principles does not give either category of mitzvah predominance over the other—neither mitzvot among humans nor with God, neither the ethical nor the ceremonial.

In some ways this is an unsettling statement. Is there really no difference between the injunctions regarding wearing a *tallit* or keeping kosher, and the injunctions against murder or stealing or delaying the payment of wages? The Talmud privileges only three mitzvot: refraining from murder, from adultery (and all other sexual crimes), and from public idolatry are the only mitzvot that may not be violated even if one's life is at stake. All other mitzvot may be violated to save a life, whether one's own or someone else's.

But aren't these three mitzvot all ethical? Not really. Murder, as we saw earlier, has the effect of destroying the image of God in a person; many sexual crimes in the biblical period grew out of the polytheistic practices of the Canaanites and were forbidden because they constituted *avodah zarah*, "foreign worship," as does public idolatry. The Torah rarely gives reasons for mitzvot; the primary reason to do them is because God asked it of us. To assert that the ethical mitzvot are more important than the others is in some ways to replace God's judgment with ours. The Columbus Platform of 1937, while listing the ethical demands first, states later that "Judaism as a way of life requires in addition to the moral and spiritual demands, [Shabbat and other sacred days,] . . . customs, symbols and ceremonies." The Centenary Perspective of 1976 makes the primacy of the ethical explicit: "The past century has taught us that the claims made upon us may begin with our ethical obligations but they extend to many other aspects of Jewish living." These distinctions are absent in the Pittsburgh Principles of 1999.

Placing mitzvot in the context of "respond[ing] to God daily" suggests that the doing of mitzvot is situational—not in the relativistic sense of "what is right depends on the context of the ethical decision," but in the sense that it is the situation that reveals the commanding nature of the mitzvah. Thus, when I set out for the synagogue in the morning, I may be prompted to take my *tallit* and *t'fillin*, but issues of stealing or paying workers on time do not apply. When I sit down to pay my bills and the question of whether I should pay the phone company or my gardener first, decisions of wearing a *tallit* do not apply. The need to choose between ethical and ceremonial mitzvot rarely arises. However, if I am rushing off so as not to be late for morning prayer and my gardener comes to the door, having finished his work and asking for payment, I would have a conflict between a *mitzvah bein adam la-Makom* (prayer) and a *mitzvah bein adam la-chaveiro* (paying the gardener on time). And while prayer is ceremonial and paying the gardener is ethical, there is an ethical element in the morning prayer as well, if, for example, I am needed for a minyan (a quorum of ten required to say important prayers such as Mourner's *Kaddish*). I could resolve the tension by quickly writing out a check to the gardener and making haste to services. Sometimes, though, the conflict cannot be resolved so easily. In such cases we may not be able to do both mitzvot, but may have to postpone one while we do another. The Talmud recognizes that sometimes one may be exempt from one mitzvah if circumstances require the doing of another (Babylonian Talmud, *Sotah* 44b). The implication is that since we do not know the reasons for the mitzvot that God gave us, we should try to do as many as we can, and when despite our best intentions we have to abrogate one or another, we should acknowledge our lapse with a feeling of regret, or by offering a prayer of forgiveness (more about this later).

But is not this area of "reasons for the mitzvot" a place where the covenantal notion of "this is very important to me" breaks down? When our partner uses that language, we can usually understand why the requested action is important. In the Torah, the reasons are not always apparent, particularly with the *mitzvot bein adam la-Makom*. Why should it be so important to God what we eat, what we put on our bodies, the times of day when we pray? We know that the reasons for "what is very important to me" are not always clear to the people we love either: Why must I mow the lawn now? Why should we see this movie that has gotten such bad reviews? Why should we invite the Schwartzes over when they never reciprocate? Often the answer is simply, "Because I would like to." When God gave the Torah, the Israelites responded, *naaseh*—we will do it; and later, *naaseh v'nishma*—we will do it first, and in time we will come to understand why. When the Israelites haggle with Moses, it is never over the mitzvot; it is only over physical things—food and water, fear of physical harm. God gave them mitzvot, and they responded by doing them. For Reform Jews, mitzvah-doing is first of all a way to participate in the dialogue with God.

God's Voice in Prayer and Study

Among the mitzvot of this dialogue with God are prayer and study. How did prayer become a mitzvah? The Torah includes a large number of "sacred obligations" relating to the *korbanot*, the offerings that brought the worshiper nearer (*k-r-v* in Hebrew, the root of *korban*) to God. The offerings were to be brought to the *Mishkan*, the Tabernacle in the wilderness, which later gave way to the Temple in Jerusalem. After the Temple was destroyed in 70 C.E., the Rabbis determined that the offerings henceforth brought to God be offerings of the heart, or prayer. The Reform Movement has always adhered to the traditional schedule of prayers: *Shacharit* in the morning, *Minchah* in the afternoon, *Maariv* in the evening. While we know that these formal prayer services emerged out of the schedule of sacrificial offerings that in Second Temple days were accompanied by prayer services, the Reform Movement has also taught the midrashim that the services during the day originated much earlier—with Abraham, who arose early in the morning; with Isaac, who meditated in the afternoon as he walked out to look for the arrival of his bride; and with Jacob, who had an encounter with God as he lay down on a rock at Bethel in the evening. We have also taught the midrashim that in the prayer of Hannah, mother of Samuel (I Samuel 2:1–10), lies the structure underlying the *Amidah*, the prayer of the eighteen (now nineteen) *b'rachot*, and many other rabbinic tales that desire to trace the authority of public prayer back to the earliest times and the earliest figures of Israel's spiritual history.

Before there were institutions like the Union for Reform Judaism and the Hebrew Union College, the Reform Movement was defined by its synagogues and its prayer book. Isaac Mayer Wise hoped that his prayer book, *Minhag America* (The American Rite), would win the hearts of all American Jews; David Einhorn issued his *Olat Tamid* as a radical alternative to Wise's, and the Central Conference of American Rabbis published the first official Reform prayer book, *The Union Prayer Book,* in 1895. Though the *Union Prayer Book* was superseded by *Gates of Prayer* in 1975, which itself is being replaced by *Mishkan T'filah,* the existence of an "official," authoritative prayer book of the Reform Movement has been one of the instruments that has held us together through tensions and disputes for over a hundred years and has been a visible symbol of the authority of the movement's liturgical practice. In anticipation of the publication of the new siddur, the Union for Reform Judaism began a Worship Initiative intended to stimulate congregations to use music, text, and movement to deepen the experience of prayer for Reform Jews. All these examples constitute evidence that the Reform Movement hears the call to prayer as a mitzvah.

One of the tensions Jewish prayer has always faced is between the ideas contained in two Hebrew words, *keva* and *kavanah. Keva,* meaning "fixed," refers to the set texts of the liturgy, the *matbei-a hat'filah,* the "coin" of prayer. *Kavanah,* meaning "intention," refers to the degree to which the worshiper seeks to stand in the presence of God, to feel near to God, to turn the "fixed" words on the page into offerings to God. Reform Judaism emerged in a world in which the prayer service was very long, prayed entirely in Hebrew at a very fast pace. Much of it was chanted in an undertone, with everyone seeming to progress at a different rate. *Keva* was dominant—all the words of the siddur had to be offered so that one could fulfill the mitzvah of prayer. The Talmud argues that fulfilling a mitzvah rarely depends on *kavanah*—if you do the specified things, you are "*yotzei,*" you have fulfilled your obligation. Determined to make the "decorum" of Protestant services available to Jews, the Reform Movement opted for *kavanah* over *keva.* The number of required prayers was reduced to give time for worshipers to "pray" while they were reading (not chanting) them, giving them silent time to meditate on their own, to the accompaniment of soft organ music that would encourage people to feel themselves in the presence of God.

In the past fifty years, the Reform view of *keva* and *kavanah* has altered some, but in an odd way. As *Gates of Prayer* replaced the *Union Prayer Book, keva* increased. There were more prayers taken from the traditional siddur, in Hebrew and English, and in *Gates of Prayer for*

Shabbat and Weekdays, the gender-sensitive book published in 1994, transliteration was added so that worshipers could offer more of the Hebrew prayers themselves, even if they did not read Hebrew letters. *Kavanah* also increased, with a greater variety of services, appropriate to a greater variety of theologies, more meditations, and a companion volume, *Gates of Understanding*, with notes and commentaries intended to deepen worshipers' knowledge of the prayers they were offering. *Mishkan T'filah* shows an increase of both *keva* and *kavanah*. Some prayers that were excised from the *Union Prayer Book*, like the third paragraph of the *Sh'ma*, have been restored as options. Some texts from the Sephardic (Spanish-Portuguese) liturgy have been introduced. Commentaries will appear on the same page as the texts, along with poems to enhance the worshipers' ability to offer the prayers more intensively to God. All English prayers will be written in poetic form, in part to encourage prayer leaders to chant them, understanding that offering a prayer to music may not only impress its meaning on the mind but enable it to elevate the soul to God as well. Chanting, we have learned, does not hinder *kavanah*; rather, it enhances it. As the organ enhanced *kavanah* in the nineteenth century, Reform has incorporated other instruments in recent years as well: not only the guitar, a gift from the folk music revival of the 1950s and '60s, but flutes, clarinets, cellos, violins—even tambourines, bells, and shakers that relatively unschooled worshipers can learn to play to give vent to the music of prayer inside them. Reform Jews feel more comfortable using their bodies in prayer as well, bending and bowing as a sign of submission to God for *Bar'chu* and for the *Avot V'Imahot* and *Modim* in the *Amidah*; standing on tiptoe to reach the celestial heights as we anticipate the angels' "Holy, Holy, Holy"; stepping closer to the throne of God at the start of the *Amidah* and stepping back when finished. Others break out into the aisles during the Song at the Sea or the Torah procession, shaking their instruments and dancing for joy at their redemption and at the Revelation. Reform diversity means that some Reform Jews will do this and others will stand in one place, all increasingly respectful of the different ways in which their congregation draws near to God. Increasing numbers of male and female Reform Jews cover their heads, place a *tallit* over their shoulders, and sometimes even put on *t'fillin*. My favorite sight at services at the Hebrew Union College is watching *tallit* and *t'fillin*-clad young women, their heads covered, sitting next to bareheaded, bare-shouldered young men whose *kippot* are the roof of the synagogue or the great blue sky. Both are praying with *kavanah*, and they rejoice that the College synagogue is a place where everyone feels free to pray as their own private dialogue with God encourages them.

If to a liberal, a mitzvah means "something important to me that you do," why is prayer important to God? Usually we negate that, saying that prayer is important to human beings. But I believe the former definition still holds. God is called *yosheiv t'hilot Yisrael*, "the One enthroned upon the praises of Israel" (Psalm 22:4). I believe prayer is a mitzvah important to God because God is rendered palpable, present, when the Jewish people (and, for their communities, other religious people) sing God's praises. Our praises make the invisible God as tangible as the words we offer, the music we sing, and the movements our bodies execute. When we turn from praise of God to prayer, our petitions demonstrate our belief that God has the power to answer our prayers—we spread the word of God's power in the world. Our prayers do more than benefit us; they are a *kiddush HaShem*, a celebration of the holiness of God in a godless world.

Not only revitalized prayer but study is a hallmark of the transformation of Reform Judaism in the past two decades. Summer and winter study programs have exploded across the continent, Shabbat morning Torah study programs have increased, and wherever leaders of the Reform Movement gather, intelligent people come together in *chevruta* study (in pairs), eager to tackle the heart of a text and to engage a teacher (lay or clergy) in an increasingly sophisticated manner. Are those engaged in this intense learning "respond[ing] to God," as the 1999 Pittsburgh Principles suggests? And how is study a response to God?

Certainly many Reform Jews, like other liberal Jews, see study as intellectually stimulating, pushing them to sharpen their minds through analysis and understanding of difficult texts because they know that the reward of the inquiry will be wise and beautiful insights. But viewing study as one of the mitzvot given by God, derived from "You shall teach them diligently to your children" (Deuteronomy 6:7), also suggests that the ideal is to see ourselves as learning at the feet of God.

The prayer immediately preceding the morning *Sh'ma*, called *Ahavah Rabbah* (Great Love), asks: "For the sake of our ancestors who trusted in You, whom You taught the laws of life, be gracious to us; teach us. . . . Give light to our eyes through Your Torah, and may our hearts cleave to Your mitzvot." This prayer suggests that the ability to understand a piece of Torah text indicates that God has answered our prayer, that God has enlightened our eyes, and that the teaching we have understood is a gift from God. Increasing numbers of Reform Jews ask to preface a lecture or a study session with this *b'rachah shel mitzvah* (the blessing offered before doing a mitzvah): "Praised are You, *Adonai* our God, Majesty of time and space, who has shared Your holiness with us through Your mitzvot, commanding us to engage with words of Torah." Maimonides was right: in his *Hilchot Talmud Torah* (The Laws of Torah Learning) 5:13, he notes that student and teacher are indispensable to each other, each one sharpening the other, "as a small branch may set fire to a small tree." While teaching, I have often felt that words were tumbling out of me that I did not form, that I was merely a vessel for the Original Teacher of Torah to spread teaching to this roomful of learners.

Illness as a Window on God's Presence

The growing belief that God is with us when we pray and study has made it easier for Reform Jews to see God's presence in the more personal aspects of our lives as well. The Pittsburgh Principles articulates this new awareness as a struggle: "We strive for a faith that fortifies us throughout the vicissitudes of our lives." If prayer is not the mere mouthing of words or singing of songs, but the entering into a personal and communal dialogue with God, surely we can enlarge the text of that dialogue to include concern about a loved one's illness, about the paths our children are taking, about our guilt at actions we wish we could undo, about a bitter loss, about the darkness of our lives. While Reform Jews have always included these private thoughts in their prayers, the Reform Movement of today encourages us to share these prayers with a loving community, to bring these concerns into a study session on texts that speak to them. Most Reform synagogues now offer prayers for healing whenever the Torah is read, asking people to call out the name of someone for whom they would like a blessing of healing, following which the rabbi or other prayer leader offers a *Mi Shebeirach*, asking the One Who Blessed (the meaning of *Mi Shebeirach*) our ancestors to bless these individuals today with healing of body and soul. This has long been a Jewish tradition, though not in Reform circles. In reintroducing it, we acknowledge that when we read the Torah it is as though we all stand together in the presence of God, hearing the voice of God teach us about the Patriarchs and Matriarchs, and we ask the God who permitted Sarah, Rebekah, Rachel, and Leah to bear children, and who answered Moses's prayer to heal his sister Miriam, to grant healing to us as well.

Why was the *Mi Shebeirach* prayer omitted from Reform (and Conservative) prayer books for so long? Perhaps because it was perceived that to ask God to heal the sick was to ask for a miracle, to defy the "rational" view that illness would take its natural course. Asking God to intercede might set up unrealizable expectations. But the omission may also have been borne of the same theology that excised the second paragraph of the *Sh'ma*, the *V'hayah Im Shamoa* (Deuteronomy 11:13–21), and the prayers in the *Amidah* that specifically ask God to send rain during the rainy season in the Land of Israel. But these prayers do not ask God to step outside the natural cycle; they affirm that prayer is a human contribution to that cycle. The liturgy of healing emphasizes the power of human prayer in the universe and encourages us to take the *keva* that is the set prayer and apply to it all the *kavanah*, all the concentration, that we can muster to influence the forces that open up the heavens and send down rain. Prayer is also a part of the natural cycle of healing: we importune the same Creator of healing who empowers physicians and nurses. As they strain to direct all their skill toward the healing process, so do we need to strain to direct all our *kavanah* to the Source of that healing. Reform Jews in the twenty-first century have learned that we too have a role to play in that process.

If our loved one does not pull through, does that mean we did not play our part, that we did not pray fervently enough? Prayer is but one of the factors that affect a person's healing. Sometimes even the most fervent prayers, the most skilled doctors and nurses, the most loving care, are not sufficient to conquer a disease whose power is no match for any earthly force. In the Book of *Kohelet* we read: *Eit laledet v'eit lamut*, "There is a time to be born, and a time to die" (Ecclesiastes 3:2). Jewish tradition believes that each of us has our assigned time to die, which is not revealed to us. Skilled medical care and loving prayer can help make sure that a person lives out that time, and can sometimes even extend it, as King Hezekiah was rewarded with an extra measure of life (Isaiah 38:1–5). Some Jews believe death comes arbitrarily; others, following *Kohelet*, that it is part of the divine plan.

For those who agree with *Kohelet*, *Birchot HaNehenin* offer a prayer to be said when we hear of a death and when a ribbon is torn at a funeral: *Baruch atah Adonai, dayan ha-emet*, "Praised are You, *Adonai*, the true Judge"—the One whose judgment of when it is our time to die is in accord with truth. Whatever we believe about its timing, death can be a moment to reopen the dialogue with God. As it took my family some time after the earthquake struck to offer a prayer to the One whose power fills the world, it usually takes some time after we have lost a loved one to feel able to cry out to God about our loss. Traditionally Jews are exempt from doing mitzvot in the time between a death and the funeral; we work our way back into responding to God's calls gradually over the seven-day (or, for many Reform Jews, three-day) shivah period, the thirty-day *sh'loshim*, and the eleven months of saying *Kaddish*. But those milestones are reminders that though grief may cloud our eyes and ears from sensing God's presence, the Holy One has never left us, and we are never outside the presence of the Holy One, not for three days or seven, not for a month, not for a year. If we let friends offer words of comfort or read psalms or poems in collections like *On the Doorposts of Your House* with us, we can start to unblock our ears and begin to see through the tears the human messengers of *HaRachaman*, the Compassionate One. No wonder the Rabbis emphasized the importance of the communal response to the Mourner's (and every other) *Kaddish*: *Y'hei sh'meih rabba m'varach l'alam ul'almei almaya*, "May God's name be blessed forever, in every time and space." A loving friend and a profound text can remind us of the blessings we have been given even though the personification of many of those blessings is gone. What we became in the presence of that person we remain, and those qualities remain a gift that we now can try to give as a blessing to others.

Transgression as an Opening to God

As healing and comfort are to illness and bereavement, so is repentance, *t'shuvah*, to transgression. As comfortable as most Reform Jews have become with the word and the idea of mitzvah, we are still uncomfortable with its opposite, *aveirah*, "transgression, crossing over the boundary." Jewish ethical action begins with the idea of a path, a way, a *derech* filled with mitzvot. When we fail to do a mitzvah, or when we do it imperfectly, we cross over the lines of that path into the area of *ra*, of chaos, beyond it. But as we have crossed over, so we can return. To confess our misdeed, to ask forgiveness, to repair what we have taken, is called *t'shuvah*, "return," for through these corrections we have returned to the path. The evidence, however, still remains of our *aveirah*, of our crossing over, and only God can repair that. That stain lingers on in our guilt, in the discomfort of the person we have wronged, in the memory of the disruption we have wrought in the harmonious order of life. God repairs all this by blotting out the stain, by erasing the discomfort, burying it, for which the Hebrew word is *kaparah*, usually translated as "atonement." It is what we seek on the Day of Atonement, Yom Kippur (from the same root as *kapara*), but we need to seek it all through the year as well. In the daily *Amidah*, there is a prayer asking for forgiveness, which we are urged to offer every day.

What does it mean to say that we sin, that we commit transgressions? It is a particularly complicated question for Reform Jews in dialogue with God, who may hear the requesting voice of some mitzvot but not of others. Are we committing a transgression when we fail to perform the mitzvot that we have not heard God ask us to do?

At this point it is important to consider the system advocated by the great German Jewish philosopher Franz Rosenzweig, who taught along with Martin Buber in Frankfurt, Germany, in the 1920s. Rosenzweig understood the commandments in two ways, using the language of the Bible itself. He divides the commands in two: *Torah* and *mitzvot*. He translates *Torah* by the German word *Gesetz*, meaning a corpus of laws that is set down for us, the entire body of 613 mitzvot. But *Torah* becomes *mitzvot* only when the laws speak to us, when they become *Gebot*, that is, when we are bidden to do them. When Rosenzweig was once asked whether he had put on *t'fillin*, he replied, "Not yet," implying that for him *t'fillin* were part of *Torah, Gesetz*, set down for the whole people, but were not yet a *mitzvah, Gebot*—he had not yet felt bidden to do it himself. What does this distinction imply? *T'fillin* are included in the written Torah, but if we have not felt individually commanded by God to wear them, we may only be potential violators of this part of Torah, not actual violators, because *t'fillin* has not yet become a mitzvah for us. This is another reason why the 1999 Pittsburgh Principles has made an important step in identifying mitzvot not only as a part of Torah—the second main section of the document—but as a part of our experience of God as well, the first main section.

The question of *aveirah* brings us back to the issue as to whether ethical mitzvot should be privileged above other mitzvot. Surely whether or not we have heard in our dialogue with God the prohibition against murder, we are transgressors if we kill—or steal, or commit sexual crimes, or cheat someone. But of course we *have* heard these commands. Living in societies that have turned these mitzvot into civil and criminal law, we have heard them loud and clear, and even though we may obey them because we wish to remain out of jail, we know that many societies derived them from the Bible, believing that they were part of natural law and the law of God. A midrash (*B'reishit Rabbah* 16:6) claims that in the Garden of Eden and after the Flood, God gave all human beings seven mitzvot regarding the establishment of courts of justice and prohibitions against blasphemy, bloodshed, idolatry, incest, stealing, and eating flesh cut from a living animal. Our families and our schools have instilled these commands in us, even if we have discovered only years after that they were originally laws that came from God.

If we are actual sinners in regard to ethical mitzvot and only potential sinners in regard to the others, does this not also say that the ethical mitzvot are more important? I would argue that for all the above reasons the ethical mitzvot are givens, as they are in any relationship. The importance of the *mitzvot bein adam la-Makom*, particularly the "ritual" mitzvot, is their uniqueness to the *Jew's* covenant with God. God may expect all people to obey the ethical mitzvot, but God asks us to obey the others as part of our unique covenant. Reform Jews striving to hear what God wants us to do know that when we feel called to wear a *tallit*, to say the prayers in the siddur, to keep aspects of Shabbat and kashrut, we are fulfilling a portion of our particular Jewish relationship to God. Having heard this call, when we fail in those mitzvot, it is important that we feel we have done something wrong and try to rectify it. How can we build these mitzvot so thoroughly into our lives that falling short becomes harder and harder to do? Each new commitment that we feel ready to accept deepens our relationship with God. That relationship is also deepened when we confess to a breakdown in that commitment and open ourselves to feel God listening to our regrets and (as God has promised) compassionately forgiving us. If we never respond to the call to do a mitzvah, we shall also never experience the momentary distance when we transgress it and the fullness of God taking us back when we do *t'shuvah*. Is it worthwhile taking the risk to respond to a call to do a mitzvah if it means that if we fail we may commit an *aveirah*? It is similar to the risk we take in any serious relationship; the more commitments we make, the more we strive to be faithful to those commitments, the deeper our mutual love becomes, and the deeper the compassion when one of us stumbles and earnestly tries to regain our footing. We know that prayers for healing that emerge from sickness bring us into God's presence. We need to learn that transgression, as well as doing mitzvot, can also lead us closer to God.

5

A Partnership with Chaos

We continue to have faith that, in spite of the unspeakable evils committed against our people and the sufferings endured by others, the partnership of God and humanity will ultimately prevail.

—Statement of Principles, "God," paragraph 8

Covenant and Tragedy

Which is the greater challenge for a religious Jew: personal tragedy or communal tragedy? Cancer, the death of a child—or the attempted murder of the Jewish people?

What a terrible question—and yet it is one that Jews have had to face as long as we have been a people. For we have suffered as individuals like all people do, and we have cried out to God to heal us, to show us some purpose in our suffering, to answer the question, "Why me?" When healing comes, or when the inevitable human sentence of death is delivered, we can often resume our relationship with God, however altered, battered, or deepened it may be. We know that the question "Why me?" is foolish. We know that sickness and tragedy befall all people, that it is part of being human. The Book of Psalms was written to teach us that.

But when tragedies befall the Jewish people—slavery, exile, expulsion, pogrom, Holocaust, the seemingly endless struggle of the State of

Israel to live securely, justly, and peacefully with her neighbors—"Why us?" is not a foolish question. The Pittsburgh Principles refers to "the unspeakable evils committed against our people." What other people has had to endure them? In ancient times the Assyrians and Babylonians, the Greeks and the Romans, assailed us, then the Persians, the Roman Catholic Church and its minions, Protestant Europe, the Russians and the Poles, the Soviets, the Nazis—one after another after another.

But we forget something. Many of these peoples are no more. While according to the prophets, God enlisted the Assyrians and Babylonians as partners in the divine punishment of Israel when the First Temple stood, once the cruelty of the Assyrians and Babylonians exceeded their mandate, they were destroyed. Ancient Greece and Rome were destroyed, the Nazis were vanquished, and the Soviet Union imploded. Even the Roman Catholic Church has engaged in public statements of contrition for its centuries of persecution, and its power is a shadow of what it was. God has been faithful to the covenant: we are still here, as numerous as the stars in heaven (Deuteronomy 1:10) and our claim on the Land of Israel is stronger than it has been since the end of the Second Temple. "Why us?" It would appear that, like personal tragedy, national tragedy is also part of the human condition. Though God promises Abraham eternal progeny and land, God also warns him that his progeny will be oppressed in a foreign land for several hundred years (Genesis 15:13). Yet, in keeping with that covenantal promise, those who survive are offered the promise of a partnership with God. The same is true for the nations: as God entered into a partnership with Assyria and Babylon to effect the divine will, so other peoples who have survived the ravages of war see themselves as allies of God when it is widely believed that they have a just cause. The 1885 Pittsburgh Platform asserted this quite boldly:

> Christianity and Islam being daughter religions of Judaism, we appreciate their providential mission to aid in the spreading of monotheistic and moral truth. We acknowledge that the spirit of broad humanity of our age is our ally in the fulfillment of our mission, and, therefore, we extend the hand of fellowship to all who cooperate with us in the establishment of the reign of truth and righteousness among men.

What the 1885 Pittsburgh Platform did not envision, however, was that these religions and the peoples who practiced them would emerge from the Great War less than thirty years in the future as wounded partners with God. For the late nineteenth century Reformers, the sufferings of the centuries were past:

> We recognize in the modern era of universal culture of heart and intellect the approaching of the realization of Israel's great Messianic hope for the establishment of the kingdom of truth, justice and peace among all men.

It was not to come so soon. The arrogance of the political and religious powers of the nineteenth century were brought low by the First World War, and the ruins of that conflict gave birth to a virulent regime in Germany, the land that had nurtured the 1885 Pittsburgh rabbis. How could Reform survive such an assault on its founding optimism? Was not nineteenth century Reform rooted in the authority of the "views and habits of modern civilization"? How could the Reform religion of reason so in tune with the "modern era of universal culture of heart and intellect" endure when that era exploded? The rise of Nazism showed terrifyingly that history swerves unpredictably between creativity and destruction, just as nature does, and that no "modern civilization," with all its inner contradictions, can by itself be a reliable guide to conduct.

Yet despite their romantic view of their culture, the 1885 Pittsburghers sowed the seeds for accommodation with a vastly altered society. The last plank of the Pittsburgh Platform recognized not only that the inexorable progress of history needed some human assistance, but that even the "modern era of universal culture of heart and intellect" had its dark side:

> We deem it our duty to participate in the great task of modern times, to solve, on the basis of justice and righteousness, the problems presented by the contrasts and evils of the present organization of society.

That they could say "solve" rather than "address" reveals a confidence that the new century would soon shatter. Still, to condemn "the present [capitalist?] organization of society" is a remarkable bow to realism amid their exuberant romanticism. Because the 1885 Pittsburgh

Platform acknowledged society's weakness, it laid the groundwork for the belief in a necessary partnership between God and human beings. The realist strain swelled with the 1937 Columbus Platform, which more modestly stated that "We regard it as our historic task to cooperate with all men in the establishment of the kingdom of God." In its section on "Social Justice," the Columbus Platform calls on Jewish teachings to be applied to the elimination of a whole catalogue of evils: "of man-made misery and suffering, of poverty and degradation, of tyranny and slavery, of social inequality and prejudice, of ill-will and strife." The 1976 Centenary Perspective, written thirty years after the end of the Second World War, went much further in acknowledging that it was modern society itself that was greatly responsible for the most virulent evil the Jewish people had ever known:

> The Holocaust shattered our easy optimism about humanity and its inevitable progress. . . . The widespread threats to freedom, the problems inherent in the explosion of new knowledge and of ever more powerful technologies, and the spiritual emptiness of much of Western culture, have taught us to be less dependent on the values of our society and to reassert what remains perennially valid in Judaism's teaching.

The authority of "the views and habits of modern civilization" was dead.

The Centenary Perspective also reflects the post-Holocaust struggle between working for the needs of the Jewish people and the prophetic demand for involvement with all humanity: "Judaism calls us simultaneously to universal and particular obligations." But above this struggle hovers the Holocaust as a shadow over the entire document: "We have learned again that the survival of the Jewish people is of highest priority." The Centenary Perspective concludes with a lesson from the ashes:

> We have . . . been compelled to reappropriate our tradition's realism about the human capacity for evil. Yet our people has always refused to despair. The survivors of the Holocaust, on being granted life, seized it, nurtured it, and, rising above catastrophe, showed humankind that the human spirit is indomitable.

Wounded though they may be, the nations and religions of the world were still to be considered potential partners with God.

Every document arises out of a mix of "perennially valid" ideas and the influences of the time in which they were conceived. It is curious that the Pittsburgh Principles does not specifically mention the Holocaust, only "the unspeakable evils committed against our people." On the one hand, one might say that this reflects the period of optimism at the close of Bill Clinton's presidency that pervaded Jewish life in the United States: the Cold War was over; Israel and the Palestinians seemed on their way to establishing a permanent peace; Judaism was flourishing in the former Soviet Union; in a booming economy and the most hospitable environment American Jews had ever known, Jewish life and philanthropy were thriving. Even intermarriage was attracting less attention, in part because we had become used to it, in part because programs of outreach and conversion seemed finally to be bringing a noticeable (if still a minority) group of intermarried families back into Jewish life. The phrase "Jewish survival" occurs nowhere in the 1999 document; Reform rabbis seemed finally willing to believe that, in keeping with the covenantal promise, God was taking care of that. Would the language have been different had the document come into being after the terrorist attacks of September 11, 2001, a resurgence of European anti-Semitism, and the suicide bombs of the Second Intifada? It is impossible to know.

On Ra *and* Yirah

Why does the Pittsburgh Principles differentiate between "the unspeakable evils committed against our people and the sufferings endured by others"? Does this suggest that other people's tragedies are merely suffering, but ours are evil? "Suffering" is a factual word: we can document the nature of people's suffering. When Stalin slaughtered the Kulak peasants in the 1930s, when extremist Hutu tribes massacred the Tutsi in Rwanda in the 1990s, when the Serbian army slaughtered Bosnian Muslims—these acts caused horrible suffering. They made the world shudder and cry, and occasionally, try to stop it.

"Evil," on the other hand, makes a theological statement: it looks not at the facts of a murder but the soul of the murderer. Jewish tradition has tended to identify doers of evil against the Jews as manifestations of

Amalek, the ruler who attacked the rear guard of the Israelites as they were leaving Egypt (Exodus 17:8–16), and who was also the ancestor of the wicked Haman, who, in the words of the popular Purim song, "would have murdered all the Jews." Suffering is suffering; the Pittsburgh Principles only suggests that Jews interpret their suffering as the doing of "unspeakable evil." We do not presume to tell other victims of horror around the world how to interpret the suffering that has been visited upon them.

So what does "unspeakable evils" imply? First, the phrase suggests the unease with which Jews have come to view the popularity of the word "Holocaust" as applied to the destruction of European Jewry. Elie Wiesel popularized the term but increasingly it has come to suggest that there might have been a religious dimension to the Final Solution: that Jews were brought as a burnt offering (the literal meaning of the word), when the Nazis' motives were so horribly opposed to any religious ideas and Judaism has been so unalterably opposed to human sacrifice. The Hebrew word *Shoah* is preferable, meaning "calamity," but the Pittsburgh Principles' use of the term "unspeakable" suggests that any word is limiting and that the horror of the Holocaust exceeds any human attempt to name it. It also suggests an awareness, at the onset of the new century, that the Holocaust might not be the last evil to exceed the reach of human words.

Words came into being with the Creation: "And God said [the words]: 'Light, Be!'" Before there were words, there was chaos, *ra*, as in the foundational verse from Isaiah in which God is praised as *Yotzer or uvorei choshech, oseh shalom uvorei ra*, "Shaper of light and creator of darkness, maker of peace [or wholeness] and creator of chaos" (Isaiah 45:7). Chaos is the state described in Genesis 1:2: "The earth was *tohu* and *bohu*, darkness on the face of the deeps, and a wind of God hovering over the waters." God was present in the chaos, in the presence of a hovering wind, but there were no words. *Ra* is usually rendered "evil," though "chaos" is closer to the original meaning. To describe an event as an "unspeakable evil" thus suggests that it returns us to the state of chaos preceding the words that effect creation.

Where else do we hear of something that cannot be spoken? In the Passover Haggadah's story of the Four Children, the last child is the *she-*

eino yodei-a lishol, "the one who does not know how to ask." A Chasidic interpretation suggests that this child may have the most profound understanding of the four, because this child realizes that the Exodus is so full of *yirah*, of awe, that it renders one speechless. Ordinarily the word *yirah* suggests that we are standing in the presence of God the Creator, watching openmouthed as God's holiness and power explode before us. Every time I visit the Grand Canyon I feel the presence of this inexpressible *yirah*. From the heights of the canyon I marvel at the creative power of the tiny Colorado River cutting a gorge through that massive rock for millions and millions of years. But part of the awe of that place is knowing that one false move, one careless attempt to get in the way of that canyon, could send me hurtling down those miles of rock to my death. *Yirah* is the awareness that where we encounter creation, we can also encounter oblivion. Standing at such a junction brings us into the presence of God.

If events that make us speechless can be encounters with God, can unspeakable events be divine encounters as well? Both adjectives are invoked in the story of Aaron's sons Nadab and Abihu, who are consumed in flames after they offer "strange fire" before God (Leviticus 10:1–3). After their deaths, the Holy One observes: *Bik'rovai ekadeish v'al p'nei chol haam ekaveid*, "Through those who are close to Me My holiness will appear; and upon the face of all the people My glory will be manifest"; the verse continues: *Vayidom Aharon*, "And Aaron was silent" (Leviticus 10:3). Is this verse suggesting that God's *k'dushah*, God's holy presence, is experienced not only in a burning bush that is not consumed, but in burning human beings who are? There are destructive acts whose horror is of such magnitude that it can drag us against our will into an encounter with the dark side of God, the God who hovers over chaos, the God who is the source of chaos, which in Hebrew is *ra*.

What kind of partnership is possible with a God who is the source of *ra*?

Ra by itself is neutral, a kind of raw energy. The Rabbis continually stress that *ra* has the potential of playing a beneficial role in the world—without it there would be no passion, no appetite; no eggs would be laid or humans born. Indeed, one midrash argues that the suffering inherent in *ra* is part of God's pronouncement that the world after the creation of humanity was "very good" because the chastening role of suffering purifies human beings to enter the life of the world-to-come (*B'reishit Rabbah* 9:7–8). But unless *ra* is governed by *tov*, its opposite, *ra* becomes destructive: passion becomes lust and rapine; appetite becomes greed. The opposite of *ra*, *tov*, is also neutral. *Tov* basically means "order"—that which contributes to the creation and the harmony of the universe. When God pronounces light and seas and dry land and vegetation and creatures *tov*, God says: This is leading us away from chaos into order. In many ways it is human beings who decide whether the neutral *ra* will become evil and whether the neutral *tov* will affect goodness. It takes the human partnership with God to hold *ra* at bay and to use its neutral energy in the service of *tov*, of order and harmony. God created mitzvot that humans might partner with God to turn chaos into harmony. The Pittsburgh Principles affirms the faith that this human partnership is unshakable, even though there will always be human beings who will try to unleash *ra* to turn the world back into unspeakable chaos.

Does Reform Recognize Amalek?

We have looked at Martin Buber's suggestion for the sentencing of Adolf Eichmann as an example that we are not to despair of looking for the *tzelem Elohim* even in the most egregious of assailants. Yet the Reform Movement has always been uncomfortable with the traditional notion that the heirs of Amalek are still around, that there are individuals who are the embodiment of evil, ready to wipe us out. A refugee from Hitler's Germany himself, Rabbi W. Gunther Plaut, in his editing of the 1981 Torah commentary of the Reform Movement, chose to omit the traditional haftarah reading for the Shabbat before Purim, Shabbat Zachor ("Remember"), on which we are to recall what Amalek did to us because Amalek's descendant, Agag, was an ancestor of Haman. The haftarah is a bloody tale of Samuel's insistence that King Saul spare no effort to wipe out the men, women, children, and possessions of the Amalekite descendant. As Rabbi Mark Washofsky suggests, "Due to the violent nature of the Samuel passage, Reform practice substitutes a selection from the Book of Esther,"[1] which includes no mention of Haman's descent from Amalek. While Rabbi Plaut included the traditional reading in his 1995 haftarah commentary, the earlier omission reflects a belief that we are to view each evildoer in a separate light. No matter how heinous his or her crimes, we can persist in seeing the person as redeemable, even as a potential partner of God.

Which haftarah reading shall we adopt, that of 1981 or that of 1995? The earlier reluctance of the Reform Movement to recognize real human beings as Amalek is an impressive statement of faith for us at the turn of the twenty-first century. Contrary to the expectations after the end of the Cold War, human suffering seems to be on the increase, and with every new suicide bombing in the Middle East "unspeakable evils" against Jews also seem to be on the rise. To label a person Amalek is to say: There is no reasonable way to deal with this person; his sole desire is to annihilate the Jewish people. This is one explanation for the anguish in the early years of the century as to whether Yasser Arafat was a "partner" for peace with Israel or not. The real question was: Is Arafat Amalek? Few Reform Jews wished to answer in the affirmative, which, in the face of all that he either unleashed or condoned, argued forcefully for faith in even the most unlikely human beings.

By the time of the Nazis' rise to power, Reform Judaism had become primarily an American movement. Some of the leading Reform rabbis and scholars in Europe escaped abroad or were brought to the United States in the 1930s. Reform was not really tested in the ghettos and the camps, but only in its responses in North America. The only liberal rabbi of note to endure the Holocaust in Europe was Leo Baeck, who was interned in Theresienstadt and lived to be liberated and teach in liberal seminaries in Britain and the United States. While in Theresienstadt and after his release, Baeck wrote a remarkably hopeful book, *This People Israel.* Denying that there is "in the world the principle of evil," Baeck argued that whatever befalls a person or a people is a "'messenger' which God sends to him":

> A life fulfills itself when it understands and accepts that which is sent to it. A life goes astray when it does not find the possibilities which are innate in it.[2]

Does this suggest that if Amalek is still at work in the world, he too, like the Babylonians and the Assyrians, could be considered a messenger of God? Leo Baeck himself would probably have demurred. But for those of us who did not live through the Holocaust, should we not be able to ask whether even evil human beings fit into the jigsaw puzzle of God's plan? Using Baeck's language, can we consider even these as messengers—unwilling ones, unconscious ones, yet in their terrible way calling, demanding, obstructing, arguing, wounding, murdering? The dialogue that history forces upon us is often brutal. But Baeck is very clear: "A life goes astray when it does not find the possibilities which are innate in it." A voice screams to us out of the darkness, sword in hand: "Do you dare rise to my challenge?" This is not the kind of dialogue we had imagined God would institute. Is the Holy One still choosing people like Sennacherib and Nebuchadnezzar as partners? Should we view today's tyrants as evil forces operating on their own, or can we believe that opposing them might help us fulfill God's will in the world? The prophets saw the message of these monarchs' advance to be: Submit, and go into exile as punishment for your sins. Knowing that today's Nebuchadnezzars are not likely to be satisfied with merely exiling us, we are more likely to see the "possibilities . . . innate in" their advance to be the questions: What is our higher purpose in the world? If we are as uncountable as the stars, what is the nature of the world we are to shine upon? If it is our destiny not to stand idly by, do we advocate containment of this new tyrant, the seeking of allies to assist us, or, if all else fails, resistance?

The ongoing travail of the Jewish people in Israel reminds us that though the Holocaust is long past, those who wish to rid the world of Jews are very present. What is of course different is that Jews now have a state of their own, a state that will continue to be a factor in the foreign affairs of the West. Even if a secure peace is established between Israel and the Palestinians, the mutual wariness of Israel and her Arab neighbors, not to speak of Israel's putative nuclear capabilities, is likely to keep America vigilant on Israel's behalf for a very long time. In part, but only in part, because of this, what is also different is that the most powerful nation in the world is attentive to the needs and demands of its Jewish community. Both these factors mean that for Jews to be ever on the lookout for another Holocaust will be literally self-destructive. A people with a state needs to turn that state into a partner with God in the fulfillment of the oldest Jewish dreams for both humanity and itself. As a people, we now have the ear of the greatest power in the world, and for the foreseeable future we may also continue to have a share in that power—in politics and culture if in no other spheres. Jews must therefore be vigilant to help steer the United States into the role of a partner with God and make partnerships with all the forces in American society and beyond that also wish to steer this country in that direction. Aside from Jewish "defense" organizations, many Jews have withdrawn from active involvement with churches—and certainly with mosques—to create a national religious force for justice and peace. As Jews connected to Israel or America, we have a message for both countries: *you must prevent unspeakable events from happening to anyone*; you must prevent your nation from causing such events to others. We must not forget the Holocaust and its horrible magnitude, but we should also not forget what America did to Vietnam, and what Israel did in Lebanon.

Should the Second Intifada or, *chas v'shalom*, its successor, continue, our people must move beyond a response to terror of either picking up our shattered limbs and weeping bitterly or imposing more and more oppressive military measures on the Palestinians. The Reform Movement has argued for decades that military might is not by itself the way to security. So long as Israeli settlers occupy significant parcels of land on the West Bank, there can never be a secure peace with the Palestinians. From at least the time of the 1999 Camp David summit, that has been clear. We—Israelis and American Jews—are no longer passive observers of our fate. Until Israel is psychologically strong enough to negotiate not as an occupying power but a neighboring power, the suicide attacks will continue. If they continue after a Palestinian state is established, Israel knows well what to do. But her claim as a seeker of peace is undermined so long as she is an occupier. American Jews must be at least as clearheaded as the American president and the Israeli prime minister were in 1999. As part of God's faithfulness to the covenantal promise, a significant part of the power to prevent an escalation into the unspeakable is now in Jewish hands as well as in Arab and Palestinian hands.

How can we be so certain? demand those who see suicide bombings as the harbinger of a new Holocaust. Why do you think Amalek has gone away? Is not the story of Samuel's demand for the destruction of the Agagites back in the Reform canon?

The question is, should it be back in the canon? The Mishnah, after all, says (*Yadayim* 4:4) that after the exile in Babylonia all the nations of the world got mixed up. From this principle, it has been argued that all the mitzvot relating to destruction of the Canaanites, the other seven nations, and the Amalekites, are put on hold, because until the Messiah comes we will not be able to know who they are. As Reform embraces more and more of Jewish tradition, let us be sure that what we embrace is in keeping with our other commitments. It is one thing to reduce the embodiment of evil to a game—drowning out the name of Haman with noisemakers at a raucous Purim reading of the Book of Esther. To use that book as the haftarah reading on Shabbat Zachor, as *The Torah: A Modern Commentary* does, is fitting to Reform. The way to deal with the mitzvah to remember Amalek is to recognize the strength we have to keep him at bay and to laugh at the threat, because to reduce each distinct threat against us to a common root *is* laughable, and unhelpful. Vengefulness is the fantasy weapon of the weak; magnanimity is the weapon of the strong. Reform discontinued the fasts of commemoration of the various stages in the destruction of the Temple, primarily because of our belief that the Temples fell as part of the divine plan to replace Temple sacrifices in the Land of Israel with prayer, through which Jews all over the world could encounter God and fulfill their mission to turn the world to God. Tishah B'Av serves still as a powerful anchor to the consequences of the loss of sovereign power—a loss that, the prophets and the Rabbis argued, was caused by Israel's own arrogance. But the lesser fasts, from a post-Holocaust perspective, can lead us either to bemoan our fate or fantasize revenge on our enemies, neither of which take into account Leo Baeck's call that we see tragedy as a messenger of our mission in the world. As people with some power, neither self-pity nor vengefulness helps us play our role as partners with God.

The question of whether personal tragedies or our people's tragedies are the greater is, of course, ultimately not a question at all. The people's tragedies are unspeakable because so many individuals suffer, and our appreciation of the horror of a communal tragedy is shaped by our knowledge of how terrible is one single tortured death, let alone a multitude. But with the birth of Israel and the rise of American power, Jews can look upon an approaching avalanche of *ra* in the world not with passive horror but with determination to stop it, alleviate it, or punish it. We cannot wait until the avalanche is upon us or upon anyone, but rather we and the nations we can influence must be watchful and do all we can to turn it aside. If all our efforts prove futile, then, like Leo Baeck, we must look to see the message within it, heeding it with all the wounded power at our disposal. Even unspeakable *ra* has a purpose in the world—and if we have done all we can to prevent it but it descends upon us anyway, then let us, like the rabbi teaching in the concentration camp, strain to hear its message and speak the most powerful words we know until *tov* returns to all the creatures of God.

6

With God after Death

We trust in our tradition's promise that, although God created us as finite beings, the spirit within us is eternal.

—Statement of Principles, "God," paragraph 9

Our Immortal Soul

The accomplishment that inspired God to call the Creation not only *tov* but *tov m'od*, "very good," was us. Indeed, we can almost hear God breathing:

> *Vayipach b'apav nishmat chayim*, "And through the nose God pumped in [Adam's] pores the breath [*n'shamah*] of life."
>
> Genesis 2:7

God, who but five days earlier appeared as a wind hovering over the depths, now channels that wind into the nostrils of the first human being: breathing in, the wind becomes breath; breathing out, the breath returns to wind. Wind into breath into wind into breath—our bodies are but membranes through which God moves through the world.

Each morning we praise God for the gift of our *n'shamah*, and as we do so we reenact God's breathing it into us. *Atah v'rataaah*, "You created it," we chant in the prayer called *Elohai N'shamah*, drawing out the *aaaah* to feel the breath leaving us to join the wind; *atah y'tzartaaah*, "You shaped it," and the wind becomes breath again; *atah n'fachtaaah bi*,

"You pumped it into me," creating me anew continually this very morning. Because of Genesis 2:7, and because it is similar to *n'shimah* (breath), *n'shamah* is also one of the Hebrew words for "soul." We experience our soul through our breath because we first became aware of it when we began to breathe. The soul is our life. When I kissed my father's forehead after he died, I was stunned by how cold he was. "He's not there," I said aloud. His soul had departed. Where did it go? The simplest answer is: back to its source in God.

> The souls of the righteous are in the hand of God,
> And no hurt shall befall them.
> In the eyes of the foolish they seem to have died,
> And their departure is regarded as misfortune,
> And their going from us as destruction.
> But they are at peace,
> And their hope is full of immortality.
> Having been chastened a little, they shall receive great good,
> For God has tested them
> And found them worthy of Himself.
>
> The Wisdom of Solomon 3:1–5

These verses, thought to date from the first century B.C.E., reflect Jewish views in the early rabbinic period. Part of this section appears as a reading in the 1961 edition of the CCAR *Rabbi's Manual* and is much in keeping with the Talmudic views expressed a few hundred years later:

> Rabbi Eliezer said: The souls of the righteous are hidden under the Throne of Glory, as it is said, "Yet the souls of my lord shall be bound up in the bundle of life," but those of the wicked continue to be imprisoned.
>
> Babylonian Talmud, *Shabbat* 152b

In subsequent ages, however, belief in the immortality of the soul waxed and waned. Medieval philosophers differed as to its validity, as did modern thinkers, with some arguing that there was a common soul of the Jewish people that was immortal and others asserting that individual souls were immortal as well. It was perhaps this ongoing argument that led the rabbis of the 1885 Pittsburgh Platform to reemphasize the doctrine of the immortality of the soul, to return to the beliefs so clearly stated in rabbinic literature:

> We reassert the doctrine of Judaism that the soul of man is immortal, grounding this belief on the divine nature of the human spirit, which forever finds bliss in righteousness and misery in wickedness.

If the rabbis of Pittsburgh 1885 wished to make immortality a major element of Reform Judaism, it is not clear that they succeeded. There is no mention of it in the Columbus Platform, and while there is a beautiful statement about immortality in the Centenary Perspective, its inclusion was apparently a struggle. The primary author of the 1976 document, Eugene Borowitz, noted the "intellectual problems" presented by the absence of any scientific or experiential evidence of life after death:

> It came as no surprise, then, that the question was raised in our committee (and by several rabbis who responded to the first draft circulated) as to whether this topic required a statement at all. For many people it is a matter of little or no importance. . . . The committee, though conscious of the intellectual problems it faced and how little it could honestly say in their face . . . felt that such positive faith as could be given utterance deserved a place in the statement.[1]

Given this degree of skepticism, how remarkable is the lyrical sentence in which the Centenary Perspective encapsulated the issue:

> Amid the mystery we call life, we affirm that human beings, created in God's image, share in God's eternality despite the mystery we call death.

Less than twenty-five years later, the turn of the twenty-first century found a very different viewpoint on this question. This time it was rabbis in the field who urged the task force to include a statement on immortality, and in all the arguments about the text this was one issue that was never questioned. The writings of Elisabeth Kübler-Ross, the proliferation of Jewish texts on death and mourning, even lectures and articles by various Reform rabbis on resurrection, have all contributed to a new fascination with the human condition after the body is no more. The spread of Jewish mystical writings has surely affected this new interest. Indeed, in his brief treatment of the subject in the *Encyclopaedia Judaica*, Gershom Scholem argues:

> In contrast with speculations in medieval Jewish philosophy, in Kabbalah immortality of the soul is not a matter requiring justifi-

cation and defense in the face of doubts and arguments. To the kabbalists immortality of the soul was an incontrovertible fact based on
the primary doctrine of the soul common to all, that the soul and all
its parts are a spiritual entity (or spiritual entities) whose origin (or
origins) is in the supernal worlds and from the divine emanation,
and that it evolved downward and entered the body only to fulfill a
specific task or purpose. Its special spiritual essence guarantees its
immortality after death.[2]

How the Soul Learns Torah

One reason for this new emphasis on the soul's immortality may be that
the word "soul" has become popular in the Reform Movement. A collec-
tion of essays by major Reform figures, *Duties of the Soul* (edited by Niles
E. Goldstein and Peter S. Knobel [New York: UAHC Press, 1995]),
deals with the role of mitzvah for liberal Jews. The title suggests that the
doing of mitzvot begins not with the mind, as Maimonides would have
argued, but with the soul, the part of a Jew that originates with God's
creation of us. This notion would have horrified the 1885 Pittsburghers,
who argued that only the moral laws were binding precisely because they
originate in the mind—in the individual intellect and in the reason that
is common to all human beings. By seeming to place the locus of commandedness for Jews in the soul, this group of Reform rabbis suggests
that Jews may have a different authority for action than non-Jews. The
new Reform siddur, *Mishkan T'filah*, uses the word "soul" several times.
The blessing offered at the conclusion of the Torah reading praises God
for *notei-a b'tocheinu chayei olam*, "implanting within us eternal life" and is
immediately followed by a praise of God for giving us the Torah. This
prayer suggests that what makes a soul "Jewish" is its infusion with
Torah while the person is on earth.

But if the soul of the Jew is informed by Torah, what do we make of the
following passage from *Mishkan T'filah*?

> Where does the soul go at night? Perhaps it reunites with the
> Eternal Soul, the Breath of All Life. Fully restored, the individual
> soul returns. Thus, each day, we are renewed.
>
> Commentary to *Modeh Ani, Mishkan T'filah*, 2003 draft, p. 100

If the soul enjoys a nightly reunion with God, why does it need Torah study? Isn't it being nurtured from the very source of Torah? Perhaps this passage suggests that upon rejoining its source in the God of all souls, each soul shares with its Creator the insights it has learned from human Torah study during the day. In this way, just as God inspires the Oral Torah that Jews teach when they are awake, God is in turn inspired by the further development of the Oral Torah when day is done. Perhaps one of the reasons the kabbalists were so drawn to studying Torah at midnight was the desire to participate in this nocturnal interchange between human teaching and divine, when God's inspiration and human insight become one.

This new consciousness of the ways in which Torah study nurtures the soul may well be leading a growing number of Reform Jews to affirm the ancient belief that their study not only puts them in closer touch with God in life, but also contributes to the eternality of the soul and its return to God, the source of Torah, after death. This idea suggests that immortality not only is based on the soul's divine origins, but is a consequence of the effort to deepen Torah learning. Doing mitzvot has traditionally been accompanied by the hope for a reward in the world-to-come, the place in which the soul resides after death. This new emphasis on the role of Torah study in the soul's development, though, seems to be based less on a concern about ultimate reward and punishment than on a desire to improve the soul's journey in this world: to help train the *yetzer hatov* to dominate and channel the *yetzer hara,* and so in death to return the soul to its Source more imbued with Torah than when it was implanted.

This interplay of the soul learning Torah during the day and sharing it with God at night suggests another dimension to the dialogue between the Jew and God—an "inner dialogue," perhaps, between the soul, God's representative in the body, and God the Source of all souls. For if my soul was alone with God before it was implanted within me, my soul knows much more Torah than I have ever added to it. There is a legend that before a child is born, the angel Gabriel teaches the soul the entire Torah. Just before the soul is implanted in the baby aborning, the angel slaps the baby on the mouth, producing the baby's first cry, and all the active knowledge flies away. The point of the story seems to be that the foundation for future study was laid by the angel, and the reason the child, and then the adult, can learn is because of a prenatal predisposition to do so. I have mentioned that sometimes in teaching a class I have found words coming from my mouth that seemed to come from beyond myself. Perhaps what I experienced was my soul "taking over" from my conscious mind, that is, speaking through my mouth and my hands and my eyes truths the soul learned not from me but from its sojourn with God.

Will the Soul Rejoin the Body?

In arguing that there has been a renewed respect in Reform Judaism for the work of the soul in each of us, I am cognizant that there has not been a parallel affirmation of the return of the soul to the body, that is, the idea of resurrection. One might have expected that the Pittsburgh Principles' reflection of renewed interest in the immortality of the soul would also have extended to resurrection.

Some Jews still think that resurrection is only a Christian idea, unaware that certain statements in the Hebrew Bible formed the basis for Christian belief. The creation of humanity out of the dust of the earth reflects a view that, in the messianic time, earth-dust will once again produce a new human race. In Isaiah 26:19 we read:

> Let Your dead revive, Your corpses arise!
> Awake and sing joyously, dwellers in the dust!

The same image appears in Daniel 12:2:

> And many of those who sleep in the earth-dust shall awake;
> Some to eternal life and some to shame and eternal contempt.

The next verse is more specific in describing those who will merit eternal life:

> And those who are wise [maskilim] will shine like the shining of the
> firmament,
> And those who turn many to justice [matzdikim] will shine like the
> stars forever and ever.
>
> Daniel 12:3

Resurrection is a belief that Reform has rejected for most of its history. The Pittsburgh Platform of 1885 traces the Reformers' opposition to its supposed non-Jewish origins:

We reject, as ideas not rooted in Judaism, the beliefs both in bodily resurrection and in Gehenna and Eden (Hell and Paradise) as abodes for everlasting punishment and reward.

Writing thirty-three years after he authored this sentence, Kaufmann Kohler, though still opposed to the idea, treats resurrection more empathetically as a dichotomy of belief:

Certainly it is both comforting and convenient to imagine the dead who are laid to rest in the earth as being asleep and to await their reawakening. As the fructifying rain awakens to a new life the seeds within the soil, so that they rise from the depths arrayed in new raiment, when touched by the heavenly dew of life, will those who linger in the grave arise to a new existence, clad in new bodies. . . . Whoever, therefore, still sees God's greatness . . . revealed through miracles, that is, through interruptions of the natural order of life, may cling to the traditional belief in resurrection, so comforting in ancient times. On the other hand, he who recognizes the unchangeable will of an all-wise, all-ruling God in the immutable laws of nature must find it impossible to praise God according to the traditional formula of "Reviver of the dead," but will avail himself instead of the expression used in the *Union Prayer Book* after the pattern of [David] Einhorn, "He who has implanted within us immortal life."[3]

Einhorn's substitution appeared in the closing sentence of the *G'vurot*, the second prayer in the *Amidah*, the central prayer of the evening and morning service. This language altered the text from a praise of God who rejoins souls to bodies, to a praise of God who implants an eternal soul within us. Thus the belief in resurrection was officially replaced with the belief in the immortality of a soul steeped in Torah. In keeping with this significant thematic change, the *Union Prayer Book* also changed the phrase *m'chayeih hameitim*, "Reviver of the dead," in the body of the prayer to *m'chayeih hakol*, "Reviver of all things." The changes had profound implications, beautifully portraying God as a power who imbues all things with life, but completely obliterating the idea of resurrection. *Gates of Prayer*, published in 1975, additionally changed Einhorn's conclusion of the prayer to *m'chayeih hakol*, bringing it closer to the form of the traditional version, but maintaining the elimination of resurrection. An attempt by some Reform rabbis to restore the original *m'chayeih hameitim* was defeated soundly by a formal vote of the Executive Board of the Central Conference of American Rabbis in the early 1970s. The only place in *Gates of Prayer* where the traditional language appears is in a version of the *G'vurot* in Shabbat evening service VIII, and it was accepted there only "because of its interpretive use."[4]

This continued rejection of the idea of resurrection was based in part on what Kohler called its opposition to "the immutable laws of nature." But are the laws of nature really opposed to resurrection?

One of the lessons we learn from science is that matter is not destroyed, but merely changes its form. When the body is buried in the earth, it gradually decays and mingles with the dust, leaving only the skeleton. Ezekiel (chapter 37) foresees the miracle through which flesh and sinew grow onto the dead bones. We may understand this as analogous to the process whereby solid ice becomes water, is then transformed eventually into a vapor, which under the proper temperatures congeals again into ice. God's reversal of the natural process of the disintegration of flesh into dust is surely a miraculous act, but it can be understood as an extension of the natural process whereby gases become liquids and solids and back again.

The analogy of resurrection to the transformation of matter has a religious parallel in the transformation of the dust of burial as God described the covenant to Abraham. In Genesis 13:16, God compares the multitude of Israel's progeny to the dust of the earth. It is an apt comparison, since it recalls the climax of the curse of Adam and Eve: "For dust you are and to dust you shall return" (Genesis 3:19). But in the promises to Abraham we see the curse transformed: the dust is eternal, and we the people Israel shall be eternal; the dust that we become after death shall be transformed into the uncountable people we were promised to be.

In the passage from Daniel, there is a hint of the role that we as individuals will have in bringing this transformation about. God's promise to Abraham, it suggests, will be fulfilled not when Jews have multiplied in this world to an uncountable number, but when people have become so wise (*maskilim*) that they have been able to turn each other into doers of justice (*matzdikim*). Here we see the connection between the immortality of souls nurtured in Torah and the resurrection: as each soul learns Torah, it enables the person to become a *maskil*, turning other people into doers of justice. It is they who will "awake" to eternal life.

How sad that the early Reformers did not see how appropriate this idea is to a Reform perspective! The nineteenth-century Reformers rejected the belief that the world would come to an end with the advent of a Messiah who was an heir of King David, sitting in judgment on the righteousness or injustice of humanity. Rather, they believed in the arrival of a messianic age, based on the positivist view that humans will develop into ever more righteous beings, until the earth becomes populated with people who will bring about an eternal reign of justice and peace. That is exactly what the Daniel verse suggests: that if human beings can turn others into wise doers of justice, we can enable the souls and bodies to awake together from the earth and—in Isaiah's words—to sing.

Our conviction of this inevitable progression was shaken by contemporary events early in the twentieth century; while we can no longer accept this kind of positivism as inevitable, we can still—indeed, as Reform Jews, we *should*—see it as possible if we are devoted to our religious task.

There are other reasons to reconsider resurrection as well. While some argue that belief in resurrection impedes a mourner's ability to accept the finality of a loved one's death, others suggest that it supports a ritual that emphasizes that finality. More and more Reform Jews are adopting the practice—once rejected as brutal—of filling in the grave with earth before the mourners depart. They see themselves as "planting" the one they love in the earth, rather than turning away and leaving the task of filling in the grave to strangers. They appreciate being able to accompany their dead to the very last moment, and indeed filling in the grave does help mourners accept the finality of a person's death. If the body is "planted," will it sprout, as the traditional *G'vurot* prayer suggests? If we believe the soul is immortal, why should we deny ourselves the possibility that that soul may one day reanimate the body of our beloved?

If the conservation of matter gives us some hope that we might again encounter those we have lost, some will ask whether we really want to. Aside from questions as to whether the reunion will be too frightening to endure, many argue that mourners should concentrate their attention on adjusting to their new life, learning to survive in the absence of their beloved.

But living "in the absence of one's beloved" still suggests a relationship to the other person. The physical departure of the dead does not cut off the emotions we nurtured as a result of their presence. None of us is *ever* alone—we are all connected with hundreds of individuals, part of the infinite connections with God. Of course the mourner lives *in the absence* of a beloved, but *t'chiyat hameitim*, resurrection of the dead, suggests that there is a shape to the absence; that as it had a beginning, so will it have an end. It promises that we shall meet our beloved ones again in the flesh. While waiting for the ultimate reunion, they shall have been purified by their souls' long association with God, as shall we; what we found lacking in our living parents (and what our children found lacking in us) we shall find was there all along. Indeed, the more we look forward to that reunion, the more we may be inspired to teach our souls wisdom and turn ourselves and others into the *matzdikim*, which for Daniel was a description of the awakening of bodies to their long-absent souls. I will be able to kiss my father again, and this time he will smile.

Given the absence of resurrection in the Pittsburgh Principles, is it appropriate to devote so much attention to it? Users of *Mishkan T'filah*, the new Reform siddur, will see that *t'chiyat hameitim* has at last been embraced as a viable option for contemporary Reform Jews. While the basic version of the *G'vurot* prayer uses *m'chayeih hakol*, it does restore the praise of God who sends down rain in winter and dew in summer—the language that led to Kohler's evocation of the rain awakening new life in the soil. *M'chayeih hameitim* appears in parentheses. The new siddur also offers a wonderfully ambiguous translation of the troubling phrase: not "You revive the dead," but "You revive what was dead," combining some of the beauty of "Reviver of all" with the possibility for the resurrection of whatever is dead in the world. This felicitous rendering is intended to appeal both to those Reform Jews who are attracted to the mystical idea of resurrection and to those who prefer the belief in the renewing presence of God in all nature. In this reminder that "resurrection" can be understood as God's metaphorical promise to bring new life to the desiccated aspects of our existence, Kohler's dichotomy between miracles and the order of nature may have been resolved.

The final paragraph in the Pittsburgh Principles' section on God opens for Reform Jews the opportunity to see the few years we spend on earth in the context of an eternity spent in the presence of God. Our souls were one with God before they were breathed into us at birth, and the dialogue we carry on with God in the flesh can be seen as but a segment of a conversation that will continue for eternity. If, as the kabbalists believe, life on earth is but a parenthesis in the soul's experience, how important it is for us to nurture the animating force inside us with all the awareness we can muster of God's presence in the world, in others, and in ourselves.

> In all these ways and more, God gives meaning and purpose to our lives.

THE
REFORM JEW
IN DIALOGUE
WITH TORAH

7

Revelation and Relationship

We affirm that Torah is the foundation of Jewish life.

We cherish the truths revealed in Torah, God's ongoing revelation to our people and the record of our people's ongoing relationship with God.

We affirm that Torah is a manifestation of *ahavat olam*, God's eternal love for the Jewish people and for all humanity.

—Statement of Principles, "Torah," paragraphs 1–3

Does Torah Come from Sinai?

The authors of the original Pittsburgh Platform would be surprised at the inclusion of the word *Torah* in the 1999 Pittsburgh Principles, since the Hebrew appears nowhere in their document. But Kaufmann Kohler uses the word often in his *Jewish Theology,* thirty-three years later. It features prominently in both the Columbus Platform and the Centenary Perspective, and today it has become an important part of the vocabulary and the life of active Reform Jews.

But what does it mean? According to the Columbus Platform, "The Torah, both written and oral, enshrines Israel's ever-growing consciousness of God and the moral law." In the Centenary Perspective, "Torah results from the relationship between God and the Jewish people." One of the interesting differences between the two statements is that Columbus speaks of "the Torah" as a single work—either the Five Books of Moses, or the Written and Oral Torah—while the Centenary Perspective speaks of "Torah," a wider usage, encompassing the entire tradition of text, commentary, interpretation, narrative, and philosophy sprung from God's initial words at Sinai.

If "Torah" was omitted from the Pittsburgh Platform of 1885—the authors preferring to use the English word "law"—the word "Sinai" is omitted from the 1999 Pittsburgh Principles, and indeed from all four Reform statements of belief. For Y'hudah HaLevi, the fourteenth-century philosopher and poet, the Torah's authority rested on what he considered the fact that more than 600,000 Israelites at Sinai saw the Torah being given and heard the Ten Commandments. The Rabbis argued that what Moses heard encompassed the entirety of Torah—that is, all truth—but his physical limitations required that he could write only so much down. Aware of this limitation, God dictated those parts of the Torah that Moses was able to commit to writing in such a way that they would contain hints of the rest of the Torah, which were to emerge through centuries of study, questioning, and arguing. That which was to be filled in was called the Oral Torah, and while some of it was eventually written down into books of midrash, Mishnah, Gemara, and other collections, some of it is still being brought into being today. For the Jewish people, "Sinai" became, if not a historical fact, certainly a metaphor for the experience of the Revelation of Torah. The third draft of the Statement of Principles attempted to incorporate that metaphor:

> Reform Judaism embraces the story of the Jewish people which tells of three great encounters with God: Creation, our redemption from Egypt, and our standing together at Sinai. . . . Standing at Sinai, the Jewish people heard God reveal the Torah.

The context tried to make clear that "standing at Sinai" is part of our "story." Despite HaLevi's opinion, the Revelation at Sinai does not need to be understood as historical fact. Indeed, the Reform Movement tried to replace bar mitzvah with the rite of confirmation, held on Shavuot, the holiday on which we mark the giving of the Torah, so that the confirmands might be seen to be standing at Sinai themselves. Kaufman Kohler and a Rochester, New York, rabbi named Max Landsberg, a radical Reformer, wrote the following in the 1902 edition of the *Jewish Encyclopedia*, in an article on "Confirmation":

> As [Shavuot] celebrated the occasion when the Israelites at Sinai, of their own free will, declared their intention to accept the obligation of God's Law, so those of every new generation should follow their example and declare their willingness to be faithful to the religion transmitted by the Fathers. . . . [Confirmation] becomes for all a renewal of the Sinai covenant.[1]

Remarkably, almost one hundred years later, the mention of Sinai in the third draft of the Statement of Principles met with an uproar, a reminder that the liberal movements in Judaism—Reform, Conservative, and Reconstructionist—had moved away from Kohler's broad understanding of the word, seeing "Sinai" instead as an affirmation of a questionably historical event.

J, E, D, and P: Where Is God's Word?

Beginning with the Jewish philosopher Baruch Spinoza in the seventeenth century, and taken up a century later by Protestant scholars, the argument developed that the Torah was not delivered all at once by God to Moses at Mount Sinai, but arose in stages as an amalgam of texts compiled over different periods in different parts of the Land of Israel, using different names of God and reflecting differing views of original stories, laws, and traditions learned from other peoples in the ancient Near East. Many of these scholars sought to trace the documents back to an urtext, an original human document from which others were derived. They could never find it and so called their theories the "Documentary Hypothesis," which in essence held that the Torah comprised four main strands: J (thought to be completed in 1000 B.C.E.) for the sections in which God is called *YHVH*—in German JHVH, or "Lord"; E (from the same period) for the sections in which God is called *Elohim* or "God"; D, primarily the Book of Deuteronomy (from around 620 B.C.E.); and P, the Priestly redactor, who organized the earlier documents around 400 B.C.E. Despite the name this theory was given, its adherents believed it was not merely a hypothesis but the truth. While Isaac Mayer Wise rejected the notion that the Torah was a series of human documents, his faculty at the Hebrew Union College accepted it, and once he died, it was taught to future Reform rabbis, and to future Conservative rabbis at the Jewish Theological Seminary as well.

Whatever amount of truth there may be in this hypothesis, it is not conducive to the desire to see in Torah an avenue to the will of God. The Documentary Hypothesis has raised many questions for modern Jews as to why the Torah should be accepted as an authority if it is but a pastiche of human writings. More recent generations of biblical scholars, having decided to work with the text that exists rather than try to discover a single urtext, have concentrated not on the question of who wrote the Torah but why its contents were handed down in their particular order and style. Contemporary biblical scholarship is thus more congenial than older scholarship to looking at "the Torah" as a whole, rather than seeing it as various documentary fragments. Considered as a whole, it is easier to speak of the Torah as a document inspired by God, even as a document reflecting what God desired the Jewish people to know, or, as many Reform Jews hold, a document revered by the Jewish people as the guide to Jewish behavior, whatever God's direct contribution may have been.

I hope that we can move further than that. The preamble to the 1999 Pittsburgh Principles cites as one of the great contributions of Reform Judaism its ability "to bring faith to sacred texts without sacrificing critical scholarship." One of the aspects of faith in the Pittsburgh Principles is the clear affirmation that Torah includes God's ongoing Revelation to our people. In other words, through studying Torah we may actually uncover something of what God spoke to us long ago. It is my hope that in years to come we will be able to reconnect the storied experience of Israel at Sinai that we celebrate on Shavuot and at confirmation to the document we ritually celebrate as stemming from that place, even if most Reform Jews continue to believe that the Torah we possess is from human hands and not the hand of God.

This is not the only time we wrestle with the relationship between fact and observance. On Shabbat we celebrate the culmination of Creation, even though most of us believe the Creation took place over billions of years and not in six days. At the Pesach seder, we try to be faithful to the Haggadah's admonition to see ourselves as though we too came forth from Egypt, even though we now know that many archaeologists and other biblical scholars have doubted the historicity of the event. The factual nature of something is different from the celebration of it, though the celebration may encourage us in further study, and the study deepens the power of the celebration. We cannot celebrate the act of receiving a document written in different locations over several hundred years; we *can* celebrate a text given amid great drama on a mountain one day in late spring. The celebration says: "We, sitting here, received the Torah at the same time the Jewish people has believed it was received; we, sitting here, received the gift of the culmination of Creation at the same time the Jewish people believe it was received; we, sitting here, received the experience of rescue from Egypt at the same time the Jewish people did." How we analyze the background of those ritual events falls not in the realm of observance but in the realm of study.

Yet study and observance need not be doomed to permanent estrangement. Part of our joy in celebrating the gift of Torah needs also to stem from a belief that embedded in Torah is something of what God spoke to us on that storied mount. Can we find God's words in a Torah that most Reform Jews believe was a human creation?

The answer lies in how we understand one of the most radical and creative elements in Reform views of Torah. All four statements of principles of the Reform Movement assert that God's Revelation was not static, fixed, and immutable through all the millennia, but is ongoing and continuous, its correct interpretations changing with the times. The Pittsburgh Platform of 1885 proclaimed:

> We hold that Judaism presents the highest conception of the God-idea as taught in our Holy Scriptures and developed and spiritualized by the Jewish teachers, in accordance with the moral and philosophical progress of their respective ages. . . . We hold that the modern discoveries of scientific researches in the domain of nature and history are not antagonistic to the doctrines of Judaism, the Bible reflecting the primitive ideas of its own age. . . .

The Pittsburgh Platform, implying that everything in the "Holy Scriptures" is of human authorship, does not use the word "revelation."

The Columbus Platform of 1937, also an advocate of human authorship, does use it:

> Revelation is a continuous process, confined to no one group and to no one age. Yet the people of Israel, through its prophets and sages, achieved unique insight in the realm of religious truth. The Torah, both written and oral, enshrines Israel's ever-growing consciousness of God and the moral law. . . . As a depository of permanent spiritual ideals, the Torah remains the dynamic source of the life of Israel.

The Centenary Perspective of 1976 makes a similar point:

> Torah results from the relationship between God and the Jewish people. The records of our earliest confrontations are uniquely important to us. Lawgivers and prophets, historians and poets gave us a heritage whose study is a religious imperative and whose practice is our chief means to holiness. Rabbis and teachers, philosophers and mystics, gifted Jews in every age amplified the Torah tradition. For millennia, the creation of Torah has not ceased and Jewish creativity in our time is adding to the chain of tradition.

On one level, the Pittsburgh Principles of 1999 is of a piece with these in its balance of "God's ongoing revelation . . . and . . . our people's ongoing relationship with God." The idea that the Revelation of Torah is ongoing is a great improvement over the assertion in the 1885 document that Revelation is progressive, that each age has a greater insight into God's will than the age before. The Talmud actually argues the opposite, that each age offers a dimmer mirror of Revelation than the age before. The twentieth century taught us to be wary of both these extremes—a century that created Nazism can hardly be seen as more enlightened than any century before it, but some of the insights of philosophy, science, and culture in this century have certainly revealed aspects of God's nature and power that were hidden from earlier ages. The countless radical changes from the Talmudic age down to our own have necessitated the growth of new insights to apply the Torah—or move beyond it—to help us cope with those changes. And change, Reform has always believed, has been part of God's design for the universe. How else can we understand a God who *m'chadeish b'chol yom tamid maaseih v'reishit,* "continually renews the work of Creation every day" (siddur, *Yotzer*)?

New Windows on Old Revelations

But we can embrace ongoing Revelation and still believe that God's word can be found within it. The problem with the earlier platforms' discussion of Torah emerging from Israel's experience with God is their subjectivity. The Pittsburgh 1885 and Columbus Platforms ("the Torah . . . enshrines Israel's ever-growing consciousness of God and the moral law") see Torah as a wholly human endeavor. The Centenary Perspective traces these endeavors to a "relationship between God and the Jewish people," indicating that God plays a part, even though it is the people that records the relationship. To that statement the Reform rabbinate of 1999 added the belief that God has also *objectively* revealed something to the Jewish people. The Pittsburgh Principles sees Torah as the product of a dialogue in which God and Israel each make a contribution. The Pittsburgh Principles does not spell out which parts of Torah it believes are "God's revelation" and which are but the record of our relationship with God. How could we know that? The separations between them are, at present, unrecoverable. But if we believe that imbedded in the Torah we possess is not only our people's memory but God's own words, that is a powerful argument to consider Torah as authoritative for Reform and all other Jews. What happens then when cultural changes awaken us to what we perceive as unjust or wrongful statements in the Torah? The law requiring stoning of the stubborn and rebellious son (Deuteronomy 21:18–21) has since Mishnaic times appeared to be at odds with the mainstream of Torah law, or perhaps with the collective Jewish experience, and was long ago rendered impossible to carry out.[2] Laws dealing with homosexual practice have in this generation collided with the collective experience of a growing number of Jews and Jewish institutions (including the Reform Movement) and remain at odds with the mitzvah of belief in God who created all human beings *b'tzelem Elohim*. Differing ages reveal that laws appropriate for one period may not be appropriate for another (e.g., new insights into the nature of children or of sexual orientation). Can these new insights also reflect the will of God? Did God reveal these new insights, or were they part of "our people's ongoing relationship with God"? We may believe they are both.

Passages that we once tended to dismiss as primitive or irrelevant have taken on new meaning as new ages have looked at them with different lenses. Mary Douglas's book *Purity and Danger* (Routledge, 1966) has helped us look beneath the surface of the so-called "leprosy" passages in Leviticus, as the *JPS Torah Commentary* to Exodus (1991) and Moshe Levin's book *Melechet Ha-Mishkan* (1968) have invited us to examine the symbolism of the minutiae of the descriptions of the *Mishkan*, the Tabernacle. That word has even made its way into the title of the new Reform siddur! A law that used to evoke our derision is the prohibition against *shaatneiz*, mixtures of linen and wool (Leviticus 19:19, Deuteronomy 22:11). Why should God prohibit such an innocent combination? But Rabbi Charles Arian has reminded me that the mitzvah prohibiting *shaatneiz* requires that one look closely at the ingredients of a garment one is considering buying. Doing so allows us to consider other things we might look for: Who manufactured this garment? Was sweatshop labor employed? Were the employees paid a decent wage? Not only is much attention given to the garments of the High Priest, but the very first garments humans wore were crafted by God. There is therefore an inherent holiness to something as mundane as clothes. *Oshek*, oppression, does not mix well with holiness. Our ongoing relationship with God has helped us find new (or old!) revelation in these arcane passages.

Of course, for those who say that Torah is the product of the Jewish people but not the word of God, it is easier to attribute outmoded mitzvot to the fallibilities of human intellect and imagination; I for one would argue that this is too easy. The Jewish people has wrestled with some of these issues for many generations, all the while keeping the Torah intact, out of an *angst* at seeming to overrule the will of God. We Reform Jews too are committed to keeping the Torah intact. The Reform Movement has never presumed to edit out objectionable passages from our Torah scrolls, nor have we ever officially departed from the tradition of reading from every Torah portion during the year, though some individual rabbis may omit one or two. This faithfulness to the unabridged Torah scrolls in our arks is testimony to a belief that somewhere deep down, we too believe that the Torah is something more than a mere human document.

By defining Torah as the dialogue between God's ongoing Revelation to our people and our people's ongoing relationship with God, we may not merely say: What the Torah says is nonsense. Instead we need to say: What the Torah says may have been the will of God in the past; our experience leads us to believe that God's will has enlarged, or that our growing experience is enabling us to understand a new dimension of God's will. We may also argue that such harsh sections as the stubborn and rebellious son or the penalties for homosexual behavior demonstrate a tension between God's *midat hadin* and *midat harachamim* (qualities of judgment and compassion), leaving it up to "our people's ongoing relationship with God" to soften "God's ongoing revelation." We might even wonder whether the God who saw all things from the beginning placed these harsh statements in the text to challenge us to reach beyond them. We were ready to challenge the stubborn and rebellious son in the second century; sadly, it has taken us eighteen more to challenge the statements on homosexuality. God, for better or worse, is patient.

How shall we deal with this ongoing dialogue between us and the texts of the Written Torah and an ever-developing Oral Torah? We need to act on our changing insights, stand back and listen for God's response and that of the Jewish people, and perhaps in time we shall come to know whether we were correct. I would argue that the gifts of insight and creativity that gay and lesbian Jews are bringing into Jewish life are evidence that we were correct in our changed understanding of God's will, just as the gifts that women rabbis and cantors have brought to Jewish life are a sign that the Reform Movement's decision to ordain and invest them was correct as well.

The realization that our understanding changes of how God's Revelation applies to "our time" underlies the statement that "we cherish the truths revealed in Torah." One of Maimonides' thirteen Principles of Faith states that *Torat emet natan l'amo El*, "God gave a true Torah [or a Torah of truth] to God's people," suggesting that the entire Torah is true. Believing that Torah is a continuing dialogue between God's Revelation and our relationship with God, we know that some statements in Torah do not ring true in all ages. (In addition to dealing with the stubborn and rebellious son and homosexual practice, we should include passages related to slave-holding, the trial of the suspected adulteress, and wiping out the Canaanite nations.) We understand *Torat emet* as a Torah in which truth can be found, and we know that study, experience, and listening are the ways to find those truths. Saying, "I don't like this mitzvah" or "This mitzvah is too difficult for me" is not the way of dialogue with Torah. To ask, "How can I do this mitzvah when I am also commanded to do what appears to be a contradictory mitzvah" is the way of dialogue with Torah.

Torah as a Gift of Love

One of the aids to this dialogue is the following statement in the 1999 Pittsburgh Principles: "We affirm that Torah is a manifestation of *ahavat olam*, God's eternal love for the Jewish people and for all humanity." A number of rabbinical colleagues felt that earlier drafts of the Statement of Principles lacked the reminder that God gave us Torah out of love. As *Gates of Prayer* translates the prayer immediately preceding the *Sh'ma* in the evening:

> Unending is Your love for Your people, the House of Israel: Torah and Mitzvot, laws and precepts have You taught us.
>
> *Gates of Prayer*, 1975, p. 130

This prayer makes it clear that God gave us the Torah out of love and that the mitzvot are a sign of God's love. In the Talmud, a number of prayers were written around this theme, which many scholars believe was originally intended to counter Paul's teaching that the Torah was a punishment for Israel's sins.[3] No, the Rabbis insisted emphatically, Torah was a sign of God's love, not of God's rejection. Indeed, they believed the Torah was the *ketubah*, the marriage contract, as it were, in which the terms of God's covenant with the Jewish people was set down *l'olam*, for all time. Each time we do a mitzvah—be it lighting Shabbat candles, paying bills on time, or studying Torah—we are experiencing the outpouring of God's love, as we experience the love of our human beloved when we walk down the street hand in hand, when we help each other through a difficult situation, when we sit down by candlelight over a private dinner for two.

While this idea suggests that Revelation emerges from our relationship with God, the opposite is also true—the relationship emerges from the Revelation. Some people marry because they have fallen in love (revelation leads to relationship); others fall in love because they have married (relationship leads to revelation). If in our days, after much deliberation, a mitzvah appears to be devoid of God's love, we are entitled to believe that it is no longer the will of God.

The 1999 Pittsburgh Principles, however, reflects another meaning of *olam*, which is "universe." The correct meaning of *olam* is "the totality of time and space." It is appropriate, therefore, to use the phrase *ahavat olam* to mean "love for the world"—and indeed, the Rabbis believed that God gave the Torah to Israel in part so that she could deliver it to the rest of humanity. This is how the early Reformers understood the promise in the chapter describing the giving of Torah (Exodus 19:6), that the Jewish people was to be a "realm of priests and a holy people." As priests help individuals serve God, so a priestly people would help the nations serve God. The Rabbis even suggested that God offered the Torah to the nations first (*Sifrei D'varim* 343), but each one found another verse in it that would destroy their identity. Another midrash states that the Torah was delivered in all the seventy languages spoken by humanity (Babylonian Talmud, *Shabbat* 88b), so that when they were ready for it, Torah would be accessible to them. To properly carry out this mission, the Reformers believed, God intended that the First and Second Temples be destroyed, enabling Israel to go out into the world carrying the Torah of truth with them. Outreach initiatives to intermarried couples and to "unchurched" Christians have been based on these classic Reform positions.

Is Torah the Foundation of Our Life?

It is against this background of a life lived in dialogue with a Torah that includes God's direct Revelation and Israel's ongoing experience of God that the Pittsburgh Principles affirms that "Torah is the foundation of Jewish life." It is an assertive statement; it is not "Torah *should* be the foundation of Jewish life," but "Torah *is* the foundation of Jewish life." To those who would say that Zionism is the foundation, we would argue that the foundation of Zionism is the Torah's view of the Land of Israel as the place that God destined for Jews; to those who say that family traditions are the foundation, we would argue that those traditions, where they are significant, are based on mitzvot in the Torah. And even to those who would say that God is the foundation (as the Pittsburgh Principles indicates by placing first the section on God, the basis of the universe), we would say that as Jews we are guided in our view of God's nature and God's will by Torah. In some ways, of course, it is a foolish argument. The entire structure of the Pittsburgh Principles, as it is for the Centenary Perspective, is God, Torah, and Israel, meaning the Jewish people. Jewish faith depends on all three together, but Torah is the foundation of them all.

"But I'm not observant," we can hear people say. "How can you say Torah is the foundation of *my* life?"

And here would be my response: God, the giver of Torah, plays a role in your life, as we have argued in earlier chapters, because you believe in the interconnections in the universe, and the sum of those connections is one definition of God. You feel obligations to other people, and while you may have learned them from parents or school or society, most of them are echoed, or originate, in the Torah. You are probably philanthropic, and the roots of the impulse to give *tzedakah* are also from the Torah. Whatever the level of your Jewish knowledge and observance, you are most likely aware of the High Holy Days and Chanukah, and probably of Passover as well, and you probably know that Friday night through Saturday is the Sabbath. You probably remember the basic stories in the Torah about Abraham and Sarah, Moses and Miriam, and you have probably wrestled with the issues around a *bris*, around bar or bat mitzvah when a boy or girl is called to the Torah, around marriage, divorce, and death. All of these originate in laws or stories in the Torah.

The question of our mythical interlocutor, "How is Torah the foundation of *my* life?" is a significant question for Reform Jews to ask. The Pittsburgh Platform of 1885 suggested that "the views and habits of modern civilization" were the governing features of the Reform Jew's life, and the Columbus Platform and Centenary Perspective do not deal with the question. In the third draft of the Statement of Principles, the following statement was made, which aroused the ire of some readers:

> In the worldview of Reform Judaism's founders, modernity was the center, the scale on which we measured what was valuable and enduring in Jewish practice and belief. Looking back at a century which has witnessed some of the greatest gifts and the most awful

consequences of modernity, we proclaim that the mitzvot of the Torah are our center, and Judaism is the scale by which we shall judge the modern world.

Is that true? Some people commented that at most, Torah and modernity share the center of our lives, but not Torah alone. While the final version of the 1999 Pittsburgh Principles skirted the issue by speaking of Torah as the foundation only of Jewish life, the debate is an important one. Most American Jews—even synagogue goers, Shabbat observers, and students of Torah—would agree that they spend much more time reading the newspaper, watching the evening news, going to films, listening to favorite music, and driving to work and school, than they do considering issues of Judaism. And yet, the more involved that Jews become in Jewish life, the more we read the newspaper and watch the evening news *as Jews*, the more the land God promised us in the Torah hovers at the back of our minds, the more we become interested in whether artists are Jewish or utilize Jewish themes, the more we are interested in learning the *b'rachot* that can turn an everyday commute into a series of encounters with God. Is that Torah? you may ask. Isn't much of that simply "enhanced Jewish identity"? But as we have argued, Torah is the root of our Jewish identities.

Beyond these activities, we would probably also affirm the centrality of such American values as freedom and equality. But while freedom and equality may be central to us, are they "the center"? Jews have always understood freedom to be a predicate. We don't subscribe to the idea of freedom as a noun, freedom as an abstract. Rather, we believe in the freedom to do, the freedom to act. When Moses spoke God's words to Pharaoh, "Let My people go" (Exodus 7:26), that was only part of the sentence. The rest was, "that they may serve Me." The Rabbis note the similarity between the Hebrew word for freedom, *cheirut*, and the Hebrew word *charut*, "inscribed" (Exodus 32:16, *Pirkei Avot* 6:2), as the Ten Commandments were on the two tablets. Freedom is both freedom *from* oppression, and freedom *to* observe Torah. As for equality, this too is a complicated word for Reform Jews. We have struggled for equal rights for women, gays and lesbians, and others often denied the right to fulfill themselves in American or Jewish society. But here too we have struggled for equality *to do* something, such as to learn and practice

Torah. Abstract concepts in American values become concrete in Judaism, and so to say that Torah and her mitzvot are the center of our lives means that we see American values like freedom and equality as instrumental in helping us achieve our central commitment to Torah. Of course, where Torah seems to preach inequality or oppression, we might say that the American values argue against them, but I would prefer to say that the mitzvot of freedom to learn and practice and the mitzvah of belief in a God who created all people equally in God's image argue against the mitzvot that would limit freedom.

Perhaps in a decade or two we will be ready finally to assert that the mitzvot of the Torah are the center for American Jews as well.

8

Hebrew: The Language
of Revelation and Relationship

We affirm the importance of studying Hebrew, the language of
Torah and Jewish liturgy, that we may draw closer to our people's
sacred texts.

— Statement of Principles, "Torah," paragraph 4

From Bitter to Sweet

There is an old custom, associated with the start of a child's formal
Jewish education, in which parents pour honey on a page of Hebrew text
for the child to lick. The meaning of this ritual is not subtle: children
are encouraged to associate sweetness with the Hebrew language and to
believe that the more Hebrew they learn, the sweeter life will be. One
of the *b'rachot* that precedes the study of a Torah text begins:

> *V'haarev na Adonai Eloheinu et divrei Toratcha b'finu*: Make the words
> of Your Torah pass sweetly into our mouths, *Adonai* our God. . . .
> May we and our offspring and the offspring of Your people the
> House of Israel become familiar with Your name and selfless learn-
> ers of Your Torah. . . .

So important has Hebrew study been in our tradition that embark-
ing upon it becomes a ritual of the life cycle, much like circumcision,
baby naming, or bar/bat mitzvah.

The ritual associated with the beginning of Hebrew learning raises an important question about the role of Hebrew in the Reform Movement. While that role has changed dramatically since the movement's inception, we have not been clear as to whether it is instrumental (Hebrew is important because it leads to an understanding of text) or intrinsic (Hebrew is important *as a language* independent of the thoughts expressed in it). The rationale given in the Pittsburgh Principles—"that we may draw closer to our people's sacred texts"—suggests an instrumental purpose. I would argue that the way this sentence entered the Pittsburgh Principles affirms that Reform Jews are encouraged to develop a regard for the Hebrew language because of the value of the language itself.

Hebrew abounds in the new Pittsburgh Principles. No fewer than twenty Hebrew words or phrases appear in the document, in vocalized Hebrew letters, in transliteration, and in translation. The only Hebrew word besides *Torah* to appear in any other platform is *aliyah*, in the Centenary Perspective. The task force that proposed the 1999 document firmly desired to demonstrate to the Reform Movement that on the eve of the twenty-first century, Hebrew—the ability to both read and understand it—was important to Reform Jews.

Things were not always so. When Reform was beginning in Germany, a debate about the importance of Hebrew was one of the factors that led to the splitting off of rabbis like Zecharias Frankel, who felt that his more radical colleagues were insufficiently devoted to the language. Those who followed him would eventually go on to found the Conservative Movement. Even a relative traditionalist like Abraham Geiger had a great deal of ambivalence about the language as a vehicle of prayer. A Hebrew stylist himself, he conducted his own services almost entirely in Hebrew and valued its retention because, as historian Michael Meyer explains, "it still possessed deep historical associations." At the Frankfurt (Germany) Rabbinical Conference in 1845, however, Geiger joined the vast majority in voting that "there was no *objective legal necessity* for retaining Hebrew in the service." This was in keeping with the passages in the Mishnah (*Sotah* 7:1) that clearly state that one may offer the major prayers in any language one understands. However, the conference was nearly unanimous in holding that "retention of

Hebrew was *subjectively* necessary." When voting on the question of whether there might be other "objective" reasons for retaining Hebrew besides the legal ones, only a bare majority of 15 to 13 concurred. Geiger and a number of others opined that "they and most other German Jews were more affected by German prayers than by Hebrew ones."[1]

Within the next decade, the same issue would arise on American shores. Isaac Mayer Wise published a prayer book called *Minhag America* (The American Rite), which included much of the traditional prayer book in Hebrew with complete translation, while David Einhorn published one called *Olat Tamid* (An Eternal Offering), of which only a portion was in Hebrew. The radical Reform rabbis on the East Coast preferred Einhorn's book, but congregations preferred Wise's, which was intended not only for Reform Jews but for the entire American Jewish community. As the radical Reformers won out in Pittsburgh in 1885, so did their prayer books, and Einhorn's spare use of Hebrew became the model for the early editions of the *Union Prayer Book*. While there were whole sections of Hebrew in Einhorn's book, like the *Union Prayer Book* it spawned, many of the Hebrew prayers appeared only on the right-hand side and could easily be ignored, leaving the worshiper and the leader to conduct as much of the service in English as they wished. Indeed, as a little boy attending High Holy Day services with my parents for the first time, I asked what the strange writing was on the opposite page in the prayer book, to which my father replied, "Oh, that's for people who don't know English."

The preliminary edition of the *Union Prayer Book*, published in 1892, included transliterations of *Bar'chu*, the first sentence of the *Sh'ma*, and the refrain of *Mi Chamochah* immediately following the Hebrew text. For reasons now unknown, this edition was hurriedly withdrawn, and in 1895, in what commonly became known as the first edition, the transliteration was removed. Like Einhorn's book, it opened right to left like an English book, reinforcing the understanding that English was the language in which the book was intended to be prayed. A survey taken in 1906 showed that "while most Reform synagogues had retained at least some passages in the ancient tongue," over 100 had eliminated all Hebrew text.[2]

What explained this widespread antipathy to Hebrew? The most obvious answer has to do with the viewpoint expressed in the 1885 Pittsburgh Platform that the mores of the surrounding civilization were to govern the religious life of American Jews.

"The views and habits of modern civilization," so lauded by the Pittsburgh Platform, included the conviction that only one language was appropriate for Americans to know. Most Jewish immigrants did not know Hebrew, since it was the language of the shul, where the younger generation usually felt uncomfortable, or of a very small circle of intellectual Hebraists. The "real" Jewish language was Yiddish, but it too was assaulted on every side—by German Jews who called it "jargon" because it sounded like a corruption of their mother tongue, and by non-Jews because it wasn't English. These reactions to Yiddish caused many second-generation American Jews to be embarrassed by the language.

This embarrassment not only contributed to the demise of American Yiddish, but had a powerful effect on Hebrew as well. Yiddish is written in Hebrew letters, like all Jewish languages that were created out of the tongues spoken by the different peoples among whom we lived. But Yiddish ceased, for the most part, to be anything but a spoken language, as young people were too embarrassed to be seen reading a Yiddish newspaper or book. This self-consciousness ultimately resulted in the tragic phenomenon that the alphabet that Jews had used for thousands of years to communicate with each other and with God had almost died out in early twentieth-century America. It looked as though "the offspring of Your people the House of Israel" were destined not to become learners of Torah, at least not in Hebrew.

To compound this phenomenon, early generations of immigrant children who were forced to learn Hebrew to become bar mitzvah usually found it a barbaric experience. For my father, the most memorable ritual associated with Hebrew School was not licking honey off a page but being rapped on the knuckles by the hapless *melamed* who taught him. To him, the meaning of this ritual was also not subtle: a language communicated in that oppressive environment was itself oppressive. While rulers on the knuckles had no place in the enlightened Jewish schools the Reform Movement set up as the century progressed, the pedagogy was often dull and continued the impression that Hebrew was the language of oppression, while English was the language of freedom and acceptance.

As native-born Americans began to enter the rabbinate and Jewish education, however, the view of Hebrew as a language of beauty and insight began to spread in the Reform Movement. More creative ways to teach Hebrew were developed, as was the realization that Hebrew mattered not only because of its actual content, but also because of the feelings or memories it evoked. Hebrew is nostalgic, filled with memories and history, and it tied the speaker to an ancient past even without being understood. This is precisely why Geiger favored the resolution at the Frankfurt conference. By 1937, the Columbus Platform endorsed "the cultivation . . . of Hebrew" as one of the "customs, symbols and ceremonies as possess inspirational values."

The Role of Israel

After World War II, Hebrew came to occupy an ever greater place in the affections of Reform Jews. With the destruction of European Jewry, Yiddish no longer provided a living tie to the Jewish past. Rather, with the Jewish state a reality, Hebrew became the tie to peoplehood, providing a tangible connection to the State of Israel. As more rabbis, cantors, and laypeople began to travel and study in Israel, Hebrew became more familiar, resulting in an increased desire to utilize it in worship and study. In 1971 the Hebrew Union College began to require first year rabbinic students (and eventually education and cantorial students as well) to study at the College's Jerusalem campus for a year, taking an ulpan (intensive Hebrew conversation course) and then text courses, some of which were taught in Hebrew. The purpose was not so much to make these future leaders of American Reform fluent in Israeli Hebrew but to make the learning of Bible and Rabbinic Hebrew less tortuous through immersion in the Hebrew-speaking culture of Israel. After the Six-Day War, many Reform synagogues switched from the Ashkenazic pronunciation of Hebrew to the Sephardic, as is used in the Jewish State. Whereas some Orthodox groups who had also made the switch would later revert to Ashkenazic pronunciation in order to distinguish between the ordinary Hebrew of the Israeli street and the holy tongue of the siddur and sacred texts, Reform Judaism took the opposite approach: teaching students sacred texts in the context of learning Israeli Hebrew so that the language of siddur, Bible, and midrash would be as familiar as the language they spoke every day. Returning from Israel, rabbinic, education, and cantorial students wished to use their newfound Hebrew skills and so began to introduce more Hebrew into the services they led.[3] Meanwhile, the new Reform prayer books, trying to assist Reform Jews in coping with the increasing amounts of Hebrew in the service, began offering transliterations, but in the back of the book. Reform Jews of all ages began to take serious classes in Hebrew, despite the struggle it represented for some.

What led to the fundamental changes in our understanding of the languages Jews should know? Was it merely that Reform Jews were more secure in America and no longer felt they needed to prove their citizenship through ignorance of Jewish languages? This is, after all, the same generation that began giving their children biblical or Israeli names and, later on, American Jewish immigrant names like Max and Sophie. As our feeling of security grew, we became more clearheaded about what American cultural pressures had done to Jewish languages, as they had to all immigrant languages. The ethnic awakening of young American Jews in the late 1960s and early 1970s, influenced by similar developments among Blacks and Latinos, made them aware that America had given them many things but had also taken away their historic languages—or, more accurately, had created the conditions that made it easy to obliterate those languages. Though a few young Jews tried to learn Yiddish, most of them saw that as a lost cause. However, their regret about losing a knowledge of Yiddish made many determined to implant Hebrew firmly in the American Jewish consciousness. Their determination did not stem, by and large, from Zionist commitments; the majority wanted not so much to learn Israeli Hebrew but the Hebrew of the prayer book, the Bible, and rabbinic literature.

Nonetheless, as more and more young Jews and their parents went to Israel, one of the ways to retain their ties to the Land upon their return was to continue their Hebrew study. Since there were more opportunities to use Hebrew in prayer than in conversation in North

American Jewish life, that was the route they took. In the world of Jewish education, educators have struggled with the approach that Hebrew education should take: should the emphasis be on texts, connecting to the Jewish past, or on conversation and reading and writing the Hebrew of the Jewish present? That's an unfair dichotomy, the proponents of textual Hebrew argue—prayer and study are an increasingly vibrant part of the Jewish present! It is clear that when we teach Hebrew for use in Israel, we teach out of a commitment to the language as a vital, integral part of Israeli society and culture. But what is our motivation for encouraging Hebrew as a language for liturgy and text study? The reply in the Pittsburgh Principles, "that we may draw closer to our people's sacred texts," suggest that Hebrew is primarily useful as a means to acquire understanding of the prayer book, the Bible, or the Talmud, but other purposes are present as well.

Hebrew and Holiness

Hebrew has long been known as *l'shon hakodesh*, usually translated as "the holy language," but also meaning "the language of holiness," the language that conveys *k'dushah*. The use of the definite article is significant, as Jews have traditionally not believed that other languages are holy tongues. The Babylonian Talmud (*Shabbat* 88b) states that the Torah was given in all the seventy languages that humans speak, suggesting that since God gave the Torah, one can find holiness in other human languages. But when we study Hebrew we are working with the very syllables that God used not only to give the Torah but to create the world (*Vayomer Elohim,* "Y'hi or," *va-y'hi or*, "And God said, 'Be, light!' and light was."). It is one thing to read and analyze the language of Shakespeare or Faulkner; it is another to read and analyze the language that God both *created* and used in order to create the entire world. The third draft of the original Ten Principles used the phrase "holy tongue" as a title of the ninth principle, which affirmed "our people's belief that God endowed the Hebrew language with a particular measure of *kedushah*." Some colleagues expressed discomfort with this usage, primarily out of a sense that it sounded chauvinistic. But any Reform Jew who has wrestled with texts in Hebrew, any Reform Jew who has studied the liturgy sufficiently to know what the Hebrew original means and how much the language is connected to God's creative acts—those Reform Jews will affirm that the feeling washing over them is very different from that which they receive when they pray or study in English.

Just as the language of a letter written long ago by someone we love can carry us back to the early times we spent together, the Torah is like a love letter to us from God. Shakespeare and Faulkner were never our beloved, but God is. When we read the Torah, we are transported back to the moments we spent at Sinai. Hebrew for us is not only the means to understand God's truth and the truth of God's interpreters, Hebrew is part of that truth, as the love letter itself is part of our relationship. God spoke in that letter, revealed a bit of God's nature, and God spoke it to each of us.

What do we need to do to learn that language, to pray in it, to read the ultimate love letters, and to write our own? Clearly, for Bible and other text study we need to be able to read the Hebrew and to know the alphabet. We need to know its remarkable grammar that takes two or three letters and sculpts a word, then adds some other letters to the front or the end and smoothes them down, and shapes a more subtle word, and another and another, until we have sculpted a whole building all from letters. Its door is open, and we walk inside the text, sniff out the crannies, look out the windows, sit luxuriantly in the chairs, and stretch out on the ancient floors. You have to know a lot of Hebrew to comprehend an entire village of buildings made out of words. This metaphor emerges from the Hebrew language itself. The word for the structure of verbs, *binyan*, means "building," and the sheer majesty of its construction is one of the sources of the holiness of the language.

But when we pray, we want to do more than just enter into the nooks and crannies of the words. We want also to open the windows and reach out to the God who built the house for us; we want to run out of the doors and breathe the sweet air and take in the mountains and the seas—as well as the smoke and fire and rain. Seeing Hebrew as a language conveying intrinsic holiness enables us to do that. For prayer is not so much reading and studying as speaking—singing even, shouting, whispering, weeping, exulting. And to speak and sing and shout and whisper in Hebrew we do not need to be able to read it. We can reach out to God in Hebrew whether we know the alphabet or not.

To Pray in Transliteration Is to Pray in Hebrew

The way to pray to God in Hebrew if you don't know the alphabet is to pray in transliteration—Hebrew words written with English characters. At the end of the twentieth century, transliteration had become the vehicle to liberate Jews who could not read Hebrew from the margins of Jewish prayer. Resistant to the idea that Hebrew sounds could convey holiness whether or not people understood their meaning, past leaders of the Reform Movement came to believe that people had to learn to read Hebrew before they could pray in it. For this reason, Reform prayer books rarely included transliteration until the publication of *Gates of Prayer* in 1975. But even in this siddur transliterations were relegated to the back of the book, difficult to find. Other Jewish groups accepted the value of transliteration more easily. Hillel services often transliterated every prayer, Conservative prayer books transliterated some of them, and in 1998 ArtScroll, the publisher of prayer books for newly Orthodox and others who wish to observe the strictest interpretations of halachah, published a completely transliterated weekday and Shabbat siddur. As with so many other issues, the Reform Movement's views on transliteration have begun to change.

The siddur is not primarily a text of liturgy—it is a book to pray from. In the new Reform siddur, *Mishkan T'filah*, every major Hebrew prayer will be transliterated so that everyone may pray to God in the Hebrew tongue, tasting some of the *k'dushah* that resides in it, and with that taste take wing from the windows of the house of holy words and speak to God.[4]

Hebrew has thus not only an instrumental value for prayer, it is an integral part of prayer itself, so much so that we are now willing to encourage people who cannot yet read Hebrew with their eyes to offer it with their mouths. Still, we are committed to training their eyes as well. Along with other liberal movements in Judaism, in addition to teaching Hebrew to children in a creative way, we have developed programs to teach adults to read Hebrew. But it has become clear over the past two decades that merely having a class is insufficient. Adults want to celebrate what they have learned, and so we have realized that just as praying is a ritual, learning Hebrew needs to partake of a ritual as well, just as it does for the child licking honey off the Hebrew page on the first day of school. There is *k'dushah* in learning as well as in prayer. Most Reform synagogues now offer an adult b'nei mitzvah class whose members celebrate the culmination of two or more years of Hebrew and Torah study with a public celebration in the synagogue in which they demonstrate their knowledge by reading from the Torah, just as thirteen-year-olds do. This new ritual suggests that as a bar or bat mitzvah ("child of the mitzvah"), these adults understand that learning Hebrew is essential to fulfilling many other mitzvot. As *Gates of Prayer* reminds us, quoting from the Mishnah but adding an interpretation, *Talmud Torah k'neged kulam,* "The study of Torah [in Hebrew!] is equivalent to them all, because it leads to them all." In celebrating their adult bar or bat mitzvah, they can feel themselves surrounded by the sweet holiness of the mitzvah to study Torah.

The threat that Hebrew learning would die out from "the offspring of Your people the House of Israel" has been eased.[5] We know that only a minority of Jewish children who learn Hebrew will use it in their adult lives, yet by affirming that the expression of Hebrew has an intrinsic value whether we understand its meaning or not, we have taken important steps to help that minority grow. First, we have increased the amount of Hebrew in the Reform siddur, and second, we are encouraging people to pray in Hebrew even before they can read it. To help them move on from there and use Hebrew instrumentally, we have encouraged college students to take some of the growing number of Hebrew language courses on campus, and we are offering synagogue adult study programs in Hebrew language, Hebrew Bible, and other Jewish texts. Beekeepers will tell you that gathering honey is hard work; they will also confirm what the rest of us know as well: eating a little honey makes you want more, and its sweet taste can linger in your mouth for a very long time.

9

Called by Torah

We are called by Torah to lifelong study in the home, in the synagogue, and in every place where Jews gather to learn and teach. Through Torah study we are called to *mitzvot*, the means by which we make our lives holy.

We are committed to the ongoing study of the whole array of *mitzvot* and to the fulfillment of those that address us as individuals and as a community. Some of these *mitzvot*, sacred obligations, have long been observed by Reform Jews; others, both ancient and modern, demand renewed attention as the result of the unique context of our own times.

—Statement of Principles, "Torah," paragraphs 5–6

How Reform Jews Won Their Freedom

"We . . . Reject All Such"

Reform Jews have always been free to direct the shape of their religious lives.

But is that really true? The 1885 Pittsburgh Platform makes it clear that some practices are off-limits for Reform Jews:

Today we accept as binding only the moral laws, and maintain only such ceremonies as elevate and sanctify our lives, but reject all such as are not adapted to the views and habits of modern civilization. . . . We hold that all such Mosaic and rabbinical laws as regulate diet, priestly purity and dress originated in ages and under the influence of ideas altogether foreign to our present mental and spiritual state. . . . Their observance in our days is apt rather to obstruct than to further modern spiritual elevation.

The rabbinic authors of this document, expressing not only their own beliefs but also views popular with Reform congregants, laid down a dictum that held fast for over a hundred years. From 1885 on, to be a Reform Jew meant in part to refrain from adopting specifically Jewish modes of dress, diet, and purification.

To "reject" something is to make a powerful statement. How, in what is widely perceived as the most permissive Jewish movement, did such a restrictive view take hold? When Reform Judaism was developing in the United States, "the views and habits of modern civilization" were themselves quite prescriptive as to what was and was not proper behavior. American society frowned on covering one's head indoors, looked upon wearing a *tallit* or *t'fillin* as foreign and, increasingly, "Orthodox." For Reform Jews who had grown up in Orthodox homes, tales proliferated of what they saw as the corruption of kosher supervision ("My grandmother told me to give the rabbi a dollar and he would declare the chicken kosher"). "Purity," meanwhile, raised the specter of dirty, humiliating mikvehs (ritual baths), and the enforced sexual separation of husbands and wives (*nidah*) that seemed much less protective of "family purity" (*tohorat hamishpachah*) than degrading to the menstruating woman. For many Reform Jews, "diet, . . . purity and dress" were artifacts of a confining Old World culture they could not wait to leave behind.

But as the twentieth century advanced, many Reform Jews, happy in their strict nonobservance of these once troubling practices, often failed to notice that the rest of the Jewish world was beginning to take a new look at what their parents had rejected. Past midcentury, the old rules about covering one's head indoors had started to loosen, and in Israel new kinds of head coverings had begun to emerge. Even the name changed. Instead of the (to Western ears) ugly-sounding *yarmulke* or "skullcap," Israelis coined the much crisper word *kippah* (head covering) and created a cottage industry of hand-crocheted headpieces. Here, as elsewhere, language was also helpful: a modern Hebrew word helped an old practice sound attractive.

The Jewish World Begins to Change

As the 1960s progressed, the thin blue and white silk bar mitzvah *tallis* and the austere, even forbidding, black and white *tallis* began to be joined by *talleisim* (or in Hebrew, *tallitot*) crafted in a variety of materials in a variety of colors. In a minyan in which my wife and I were much involved in the early 1970s, one young man wore a batik *tallit*; another wore one made of denim. This was a time of experimentation in Jewish modes of expression, as it was in other areas of life. Many African Americans had begun to wear dashikis and grow their hair out rather than trying to straighten it, expressing pride in their African ancestry rather than shame. Part of the new attraction of the *kippah* and the *tallit* was their value in demonstrating a rejection of their parents' embarrassment with Jewish culture.

Unknowingly practicing a remarkable form of *hidur mitzvah* (doing a mitzvah in the most aesthetic way one can), young Jews in hip *tallitot* reflected a growing comfort at participating in two cultures, not so much Jewish and American as Jewish and countercultural. In the dark days of racial violence and the horrors of Vietnam, many of these young Jews embraced Judaism as itself a countercultural expression. During the nationwide campus strikes called in the wake of the Kent State shootings in May 1970, many Jewish students across the country boycotted all but their Jewish studies classes on the grounds that in those courses they were learning values that could correct the misguided values of 1970s America. Young Jewish seekers in this period wanted a faith that was the antithesis of "the views and habits of modern civilization"; indeed, they sought a faith that would transform those habits.

The publication of the *Jewish Catalog* (Jewish Publication Society) in 1973 celebrated this countercultural explosion of Jewish styles. Young Jews explored them through campus Hillels or other Jewish student groups, older Jews through alternative minyanim or *chavurot* within or outside synagogues in larger cities. Some of these Jews were members of the Reform Movement, and they brought their new practices back into the movement.

Skeptical observers of this period might argue that the explosion of Jewish enthusiasm was not so much an attack on the "views and habits of modern civilization" as an embrace of a changed civilization. The rebellion against the conformist 1950s included a realization that what a previous generation saw as expressions of independence from their Old World past was, at its root, an endorsement of the widespread American belief that this country was to be a melting pot, in which cultural differences imported from Europe should be abolished in favor of what "most Americans" (meaning white Anglo-Saxon Protestants) did, wore, and ate. Most Jewish organizations supported this belief, and those that didn't—like the stereotypic *cheder*—reinforced it by the repressive Old World environments they perpetuated. To uncover one's head, to cast off a worn silk *tallis*, to eat *treif*, all felt like assertions of one's independence, though it was really a surrender to the majority culture that defined "American" as "uniform." When the legitimacy of American values came under scrutiny with the revelation of pervasive racial discrimination, a war increasingly defined as imperialist, and an economic system that created a wide gap between the wealthy and the poor, a growing number of Americans of all ethnic backgrounds started to declare their independence from the conformity that had been the hallmark of their parents' culture. In a number of ways, Jews who had grown up Reform were declaring their independence from that culture just as their parents and grandparents had separated themselves from Old World civilization. The Centenary Perspective itself noted that one of the things "we have learned" since the late nineteenth century was "to be less dependent on the values of our society and to reassert what remains perennially valid in Judaism's teaching."

Another fervent tenet of Reform also came under attack in this period. The Pittsburgh Platform of 1885 declared that "we consider ourselves no longer a nation, but a religious community." Over time, this sentence was popularly misquoted as "we are no longer a nation, but a religion." Countercultural Jews were not so sure. Even Mordecai Kaplan's early attempt to declare us members of a religious civilization—two civilizations actually, Jewish and American—no longer seemed so attractive to Jews who felt uncomfortable at how American civilization had crushed so many aspects of the Jewish one. Wearing religious symbols, Reform and other Jews enlisted religion in the battle against cultural conformity.

Reform Jewish homes began to wear religious symbols, too. As beautiful mezuzot began to appear on the market, Reform Jews began to buy them, practicing the mitzvah of affixing God's Word to the dooposts of their homes. Fear that they or their homes would be labeled as "Jewish" had given way to the increased desire to be so identified. Was this a religious adherence to the mitzvah, or an ethnic celebration of the growing definition of "American" as a person free to display signs of one's particular identity? Books of Reform Jewish practice were now listing mezuzah as a mitzvah; synagogues were affixing them to their doors, as was the Hebrew Union College. The early Reformers retained the instructions about mezuzot in the first paragraph of the *Sh'ma*, though perhaps only with a symbolic intent, conveying the message that as you enter your house, remember that it should be a home dedicated to Jewish belief and practice. The more literal observance of this mitzvah beginning in the 1970s and '80s can be seen as a fulfillment of the liturgical commitments of the early Reformers.

But was wearing a batik *tallit* a religious act as opposed to merely an act of ethnic identity? Surely not all Reform Jews who bought or crocheted their own *kippot* believed that the *tzitzit* they wore on Shabbat prodded them to keep the mitzvot. Yet when they opened *Gates of Prayer* (published in 1975) the word *mitzvah* leapt out at them countless times. While the paragraph regarding *tzitzit* was absent from the *Sh'ma* in that prayer book, as it was in the *Union Prayer Book*, the reason for the *tzitzit* at the end of the third paragraph was retained: "that you may remember all My mitzvot and do them." Many Reform Jews, however, felt that a *tallit* increased the *kavanah*, the intentionality of the prayers, viewing it as a fulfillment more of the mitzvah of prayer than of *tzitzit* per se. If they saw affixing a mezuzah as a religious act at all, they most likely saw it as an affirmation of a mitzvah being practiced by a wide range of American Jews, which they wished to share. The older image of Reform as almost a separate religion was losing ground in this period, as "*Jewish Catalog* Judaism" offered up a welter of new ways to paint one's home in Jewish colors. One saw this phenomenon on campus particularly: "Are you Reform or Conservative?" one student would ask another. "I'm Jewish!" would be the enthusiastic reply. On the activity cards they distributed, Hillel Foundations began adding to

"Conservative, Reconstructionist, Reform, Orthodox" the option "Just Jewish."

Rejectionism Confronts Autonomy

But this growing transdenominationalism had a downside. Jews who learned to wear *tallitot* and *kippot* in a minyan or a weekend retreat entered their Reform synagogues and would sometimes find themselves stared at or given hostile glares. The most classical of synagogues would dispatch an usher to request that people remove their head coverings. The rejectionist stance of the Pittsburgh Platform of 1885 extended its long arm into the synagogue a hundred years later and made the growing ranks of Jews who wore these garments feel increasingly uncomfortable. Some Reform Jewish laypeople (and rabbis) suggested that wearing such garb was out of place in Reform synagogues and that their wearers should seek out Conservative synagogues instead. Later, during the debates on what would become the Pittsburgh Principles, Rabbi Robert Seltzer labeled the suggestions of incorporating more observance into Reform as "Conservative Judaism Lite" ("This Is Not the Way," *Reform Judaism* 27, no. 2 [1998]: 23).

The resurfacing of the rejectionist argument raised many questions about the sincerity of the famed case for "autonomy" that was such an important part of the Centenary Perspective of 1976. Interestingly, it appears in that section of "our obligations" entitled "Religious Practice":

> Within each area of Jewish observance, Reform Jews are called upon to confront the claims of Jewish tradition, however differently perceived, and to exercise their individual autonomy, choosing and creating on the basis of commitment and knowledge.

If that was what those who wore a *kippah* and *tallit* were doing, they received scant support for acting as true Centenary Perspective Jews. Instead, they were often branded as traitors to Reform by people who suggested that, in the spirit of the Pittsburgh Platform of 1885, the only proper Reform choice was a choice *against* diet, dress, and purity. It was a reminder that despite the affirmation of inspirational "customs, symbols and ceremonies" in the 1937 Columbus Platform, and the

1976 affirmation of knowledgeable choice among different kinds of Jewish observance, the original Pittsburgh Platform had not been superceded, but remained in force. Most Reform Jews maintained that only the moral laws were binding, and what could possibly be moral in covering one's head or wearing a fringed garment?[1]

Even if the *tallit*-wearers of the 1970s and '80s had been welcomed, there was a basic flaw in the autonomy argument. "Choice" is a problematic idea in religion. If early Reform thinking circumscribed the freedom of Reform Jews to choose certain kinds of observance patterns, what did it mean by saying that Reform Jews could choose? Choice is a rational process: I determine my goals for Jewish life, consider the pros and cons, benefits and costs, to particular observances, and how they do or don't fulfill goals, and then decide which to accept. While this may be the way in which we make business decisions or decide which courses to take in college, there are few other major decisions we make in this fashion. Aesthetics play a role, relationships and other aspects of our personal history play a role, instinct plays a role, and in religious decisions, God plays a role. The idea of autonomy began as a Kantian construct, related to his belief that humans made decisions based on moral principles inherent in each individual's rational processes. In the twentieth century, "choice" became associated with "freedom," the ability or the right to make decisions without compulsion. Yet the rejectionist aspect of the Pittsburgh Platform of 1885 raises doubts about whether for much of its history the Reform Movement has truly wanted its members to be autonomous, free to make choices at odds with what the leaders of the movement believed was authentically Reform. It is possible to suggest that the insertion of autonomy into the Centenary Perspective might have been meant as a corrective to the prohibitive aspects of the old "diet, purity and dress" clause. However, it is more likely that it was meant as a concession to those opposed to the growing traditionalism in the movement and a reassurance that each Reform Jew should make decisions on one's own, unimpeded by the influence of halachah or the "norms" of other segments of the Jewish people. Conflicting with this sentiment was the publication by the CCAR of authoritative volumes like *Gates of Mitzvah, Gates of the Seasons,* and *Gates of Shabbat* (based on the earlier *Shabbat Manual*), all of which use the language "It is a *mitzvah* to . . . ," itself borrowed from the *Guide to Reform Jewish Practice*, published as early as 1957 by Rabbis Frederic Doppelt and David Polish. This language suggests that the movement itself desired to set standards for practice that "autonomous" individuals would, of course, be free to accept or reject, but which would provide an incentive to follow.[2]

The authors of the Centenary Perspective, most of whom favored the move toward increased observance, would probably argue that the guides to Reform practice did not contradict autonomy, but encouraged it. After all, autonomy was to be exercised "on the basis of commitment and knowledge," and the existence of guides indicating what the Reform rabbinical body believed was appropriate practice would provide the knowledge that could help individuals make appropriate choices. But a generation of Reform Jews wrestling with the question of autonomy left a growing number of Reform rabbis and laypeople convinced that more was involved in their religious decisions than an isolated "autonomous" decision based on reading guides and trying out various mitzvot. David Ellenson, Kaufmann Kohler's most recent successor as president of the Hebrew Union College, rejects the "Kantian notion that defines autonomy as the act of an internalized conscience directed by will and guided by duty. Dialogue and response must supplement, if not replace, an abstract commitment to duty and principle."[3] With the proliferation of guides to practice, collections of *t'shuvot*, and the modeling of observance at camps, Reform campus groups, and adult *kallot*, more and more Reform Jews came to see "autonomy" as an unremarkable given in a free, democratic society and looked for religious guidance, even direction, from their movement. In the 2003 Supreme Court decision declaring that private homosexual behavior was no longer to be considered criminal, Justice Anthony Kennedy wrote: "Liberty presumes an autonomy of self that includes freedom of thought, belief, expression, and certain intimate conduct." If being a free American "presumes" autonomy, an American religious movement must stand for much more than that; it can certainly offer direction that free individuals may accept, reject, or modify.

Committed Reform Jews growing up in a movement that has been offering direction for decades knew that mitzvah did not mean only a practice that was *called* a mitzvah. A mitzvah also meant something that was commanded, even if the command was understood as "this is something very important to Me that you do."

From Autonomy to Mitzvah

A command is a call—it involves a voice different from one's own. Autonomy suggests that the individual adopts or rejects a practice or belief based on a solely internal process of ratiocination. Mitzvah suggests that the individual is in conversation with another: a text, or the God who issued the mitzvah in the first place, or members of the people Israel who have been listening since Sinai. This is why the 1999 Pittsburgh Principles removed the language of autonomy and choice and substituted the idea of dialogue. There is no system, moral or otherwise, that can cause any body of Reform Jews to "reject" a mitzvah for another Reform Jew. The Pittsburgh Principles asserts that each Reform Jew has the right, indeed, the obligation, to enter into dialogue with the mitzvot, because as Jews we have been involved in that dialogue since Sinai. It is the right of every Reform Jew to emerge from that dialogue affirming a mitzvah, declaring one is not yet ready to accept it, or even rejecting it. But the dialogue must precede the decision, or it is not really a decision.

Dialogue takes place through study. Sometimes study is *lishmah*, "for its own sake," to understand a text from the inside out, to understand its history, its grammatical formations, its place in the Jewish canon, or to seek the answer to a particular question. Study is a lifelong commitment for Jews. We are enjoined to teach our children, or to provide study opportunities for them (Deuteronomy 6:7).[4] We are obligated to hear the Torah read in public and to study it ourselves, to hear it call to us, and then to read the text of the call, pore over it, involve ourselves in it, and figure out the answer to three questions: "What did this call mean when it was first uttered?" "What does this call mean to us, in this generation or in this place?" and "What is this call saying to me?"

The traditional understanding of the manner in which the Torah was given to Moses reinforces this dialogic sense of its authorship. Rabbi Akiba and Rabbi Ishmael debated whether God intended every word to be interpreted on its own, including the generally untranslated grammatical particles, or whether God used the human idiom to deliver the Torah so that human beings would see it as a part of their own language. Underlying their two positions was a common agreement: God intended for human beings to find their own meanings within the Torah. As noted earlier, the Torah could not be dictated in forty days and nights unless God gave Moses a summary—the "chapter headings" (*rashei p'rakim*)—of what God wanted to communicate. What Moses wrote down was the *Torah Shebichtav*, "the Written Torah," within which God planted the seeds of the *Torah Sheb'al Peh*, "the Oral Torah," the fulfillment, the completion of the written text. Inherent in the written text we possess is the voice of God calling us to look, to notice the grammatical oddities, the seeming contradictions, the unusual words. God calls us to search for the answers, not only in our lexicons, but in other texts, rabbinic texts, the texts of our own time and our own experiences. Preceding the Torah *b'rachah* that learning be sweet for us is a blessing praising God for commanding us *laasok b'divrei Torah,* to immerse ourselves—to soak ourselves—in the words of Torah. Torah study is a response to the questions, the demands, and the calls that God has written into the text and that its human transmitters preserved for us.

Pirkei Avot, "The Ethics of Our Ancestors," (1:6), advises: *Asei l'cha rav uk'nei l'cha chaver,* "Make a teacher for yourself and acquire a study companion for yourself." The *rav,* the teacher, is the one who helps us discover what Torah meant in its own time and in ours. While the study companion is helpful in those questions too, the *chaver* is essential in the third: "What is the call of this Torah passage saying to me?" For if study is to be a dialogue, it is important that it not be a theoretical dialogue between a book and me, or a dialogue in my head between God and me. The dialogue needs to be personified, by a teacher who inspires us to reach deeply into and beyond the text, or by a *chaver* who helps us let the call of Torah reach deeply inside ourselves. Torah study calls us to mitzvot, the Pittsburgh Principles tells us, which it here describes as "the means by which we make our lives holy."

The previous section of this book explored *mitzvot* as a way to bring us into the presence of God. In this section, mitzvot are the means of bringing Torah into our presence, of infusing our lives with holiness and transforming the ordinary parts of our lives into holiness. We have examined the word "holiness"—*kodesh* and *k'dushah* in Hebrew—before. We have seen that like the ground on which Moses encountered the Burning Bush, holiness is an experience of God's presence. To see Torah study as a dialogue means that we are studying the text God delivered at Sinai not only for its immediate hearers to soak up ("What did this call mean when it was first uttered?"), or only for our people today to soak up ("What does it mean in our generation?"), but also for me to soak up: "What is it saying to me?" No matter how many mitzvot we bring into our lives, no matter how many "traditional" prayers and practices we incorporate, what characterizes a Reform approach to Torah is this insistence that Torah calls to each individual and that the individual responds out of the uniqueness of each one of our lives. It is not an autonomous choice, but a call from outside and a response from inside. Yet it is also a call from inside each of us: "What should I do in this situation? How can I make Shabbat a more profound part of my life? How can this verse of Torah that seems to be calling to me help inform my life this week, today?" The call is not mediated through the Reform Movement, nor from the halachah as interpreted by an authoritative committee, but directly from the Torah itself as we study it alone or, preferably, with a *chaver* or a Shabbat morning study group. The published guides of the Reform Movement certainly rank among our teachers and even our *chaverim*; they are among the sources of the Oral Torah through which we listen to the voice from Sinai, but they are not a "Reform halachah," a set of rules that all Reform Jews must follow. The call for an individual response is unique to Reform Judaism; it refutes the notion that Reform is "Conservative lite" or even heavy, as the Conservative Movement understands its relationship to Torah in a much more authoritarian manner. It has little in common with the language and symbolism of the Reconstructionist Movement, which is opposed to the notion of a God who calls through Torah or any other means. We need not fear, if we feel called to do mitzvot similar to those observed by Jews in other movements, that we are betraying Reform. It is the individual nature of the call, not that to which we are called, that marks our response a Reform Jewish one.

A Call to Individuals and Communities

The Pittsburgh Principles goes further. Mitzvot, the document continues, "address us as individuals and as a community." If the unique Reform aspect of heeding mitzvot is individual, how can the mitzvot address us as a community?

The question is an important one, for even though we have altered the language of the individual response from "autonomy" to "dialogue," we have retained the locus of response in the individual. Yet even the 1885 Pittsburgh Platform spoke of Judaism as a "religious community." Furthermore, we are of course a community—we are found in synagogues, in summer camps, in Reform groups on campus, in a common College-Institute, in meetings and gatherings of the Union for Reform Judaism. We have developed common prayer books, rituals, and music, with which most of us feel comfortable. Whether the rabbi and cantor determine the nature of the prayer service or whether they work with a ritual committee, most Reform synagogues can speak of "our service" as something they feel part of, whatever their critique of it might be. Moreover, most synagogues operate in a democratic fashion, with majority votes, and if most decisions are made by the synagogue board, the most significant decisions often involve a meeting of the congregation as a whole.

However, I think the Pittsburgh Principles implies more than a democratic vote. By suggesting that mitzvot can address Reform Jews as a community, the Pittsburgh Principles suggests that among the souls who stood at Sinai were some who thousands of years later would become embodied as Reform Jews, and the communities into which they would form themselves were present at the mount as well. The Reform communities existing today are the fulfillment of what existed potentially at Sinai, and so a synagogue may properly listen for the call from Sinai just as an individual may. "What mitzvot call to us as a synagogue, no matter whether they call to individuals or not?" a community may ask. "The Shabbat practice of our members varies widely, but what does the mitzvah of Shabbat practice say to us as a whole?" Synagogues recognize that they are obligated to create a community in which members may observe Shabbat through worship, Torah study, Shabbat meals, and *Havdalah*, and learn how to observe it in their own individual homes. Many synagogues now observe Mitzvah Day, offering many opportunities for individuals to go out into the community to assist the poor and homeless. In general, the calls of Shabbat or Mitzvah Day are easy to recognize. But the calls of some mitzvot are less clear: Should a synagogue heed the call of kashrut, since most of its members do not keep kosher? Like heeding the call of Shabbat, a synagogue may decide it wants to *kasher* its kitchen as a learning experience for its members, so they can discover what keeping kosher means. As more members do observe kashrut, the synagogue's meal service would then be hospitable for them. The question of a community hearing a call to mitzvot that its members may not (yet) observe illumines one of the differences between the Reform and the Conservative Movements. While Conservative Jews do not all observe Shabbat or kashrut, they join a Conservative synagogue because they want to belong to an institution that values such practices, holding them up as an ideal. A Conservative Jew might say, "In supporting a synagogue that observes—and whose rabbi observes—kashrut, I feel I am helping to sustain this mitzvah even if I myself do not observe it." In the heated debate in the Reform Movement surrounding the Statement of Principles, one of the charges made by some dissenting congregants was that "the rabbis were getting too far out in front of the laypeople." These comments revealed a crucial idea of the Reform Movement: that rabbis and laypeople are partners in the legitimation of mitzvot in the synagogue. It thus may be irrelevant whether a rabbi observes kashrut as an individual; the challenge is for the rabbi and lay leaders to move the synagogue to observe kashrut— and other mitzvot—if this mitzvah calls them.

What are these "new" mitzvot? Let us examine some of the mitzvot to which a Reform individual or community might feel called at the beginning of the twenty-first century.

When Diet, Dress, and Purity Call Us

A Movement of Mitzvot

In describing these "new" mitzvot, the Pittsburgh Principles offers a broad definition:

Some of these *mitzvot*, sacred obligations, have long been observed by Reform Jews; others, both ancient and modern, demand renewed attention as the result of the unique context of our own times.

Reform Jews from the outset have observed a great many mitzvot. We have been faithful to the mitzvot of the Jewish calendar, to a greater or lesser degree to the preservation of Hebrew, to the study of Torah and the preservation of the cycle of Torah readings, to the ancient structure of prayers, and to the basic celebrations of the major and minor holidays. We have been committed to a large number of the mitzvot governing relations between human beings, going so far as to reinterpret mitzvot originally connected to a very different society. The Reform Movement has provided a significant body of responses to the question, "What does this call mean to our generation?"

Some observers of the new openness of Reform Jews to traditional practice have tended to measure the "success" of this development by the number of mitzvot we observe and the degree to which our practice conforms to Orthodox or Conservative understandings of halachah. But this misses the point of the direction in which Reform Judaism is heading. As much as we have remained faithful to the mitzvot that undergird basic Jewish practice, so have we creatively expanded some of those mitzvot, refusing to believe that the seventeenth-century *Shulchan Aruch* marked the endpoint of Jewish responses to God's call. We have written new prayers that have brought us closer to God, we have summoned our teenagers to Sinai on Shavuot and our children to consecration on Sukkot, we have called women to receive rabbinic ordination and cantorial investiture, and we have opened our congregations and our leadership to serious Jews whatever their sexual orientation or the presence of non-Jews in their families. For us, the issue is not how we can be faithful to halachah, but rather, how we can expand halachah to be faithful to the call of God to build a sense of holiness into the widest swath of our life.

But before we can creatively expand areas of longstanding Jewish practice, we need to confront our fears of it, indeed our rejection of aspects of it, a rejection that "the unique context of our own times" may well have rendered obsolete. We began this chapter with a discussion of the manner in which Jews in the last third of the twentieth century responded to "other" mitzvot, particularly those in the long taboo realms of dress, purity, and diet. Despite the growing interest in these three areas during the heady days of the 1960s and '70s in North America, the greatest controversy in the original drafts of the Pittsburgh Principles arose over dress, purity, and diet. The most significant changes were made in these three areas to allow the document to be passed by the Reform rabbinate and win the general approval of Reform laity.

The text that proved the flash point in the discussion of the third draft of the "Ten Principles for Reform Judaism" (appearing in *Reform Judaism* in November 1998) was the following:

> In the presence of God we each may feel called to respond in different ways: some by offering traditional or spontaneous blessings, others by covering our heads, still others by wearing the *tallit* or *tefillin* for prayer. Some will look for ways to reveal holiness in our encounters with the world around us, others to transform our homes into a *mikdash me-at,* a holy place in miniature. Some of us may observe practices of *kashrut,* to extend the sense of *kedushah* into the acts surrounding food and into a concern for the way food is raised and brought to our tables. Others may wish to utilize the *mikveh* or other kinds of spiritual immersion not only for conversion but for periodic experiences of purification. Some of us may discover rituals now unknown which in the spirit of Jewish tradition and Reform creativity will bring us closer to God, to Torah, and to our people.

The three most controversial sets of mitzvot mentioned here are, of course, *t'fillin,* kashrut, and *mikveh.* Why should that be?

How T'fillin *Can Bind Reform Jews*

T'fillin are surely the variety of "dress" that is most unsettling to Reform Jews. They are not any more intrinsically exotic than a *tallit* or a *kippah* (though they are much more difficult to put on), but they are perhaps the least familiar. *T'fillin* are worn only on weekday mornings; few North American Reform synagogues offer regular weekday services.[5] While Jews can don them while praying at home on their own, personal daily prayer from the siddur at home has not generally been normative Reform practice. There are some who can be seen at URJ national and regional conventions putting on *t'fillin,* and the number is growing at some of the campuses of the Hebrew Union College, but for most Reform laypeople this practice continues to appear very foreign, the epitome of the bearded patriarchal figures in genre paintings scowling down in judgment on the life choices of Reform Jews. At the same time, though, the *b'rachot* to be said before putting them on have appeared in Reform liturgy since the 1975 edition of *Gates of Prayer.*

Why does *t'fillin* call to some Reform Jews?

I first encountered *t'fillin* in the traditional minyan of a Conservative synagogue in Cincinnati, which we were assigned to attend as liturgy students in my first year as an HUC rabbinic student (over a decade before the first year in Israel was instituted). An older man in the minyan taught me how to put them on, and I felt very drawn to the ritual of binding a fragrant little box containing the *Sh'ma* and other passages to my arm, which would bump against my heart and bind my head. As a *kippah* makes me aware of the presence of God hovering over me and my thoughts, directing the fruits of my mind upward, the verses of the *Sh'ma* around my head remind me of the blessing of God who *oteir Yisrael b'tifarah,* has crowned Israel with glory—not our own glory, but God's. If our heads move through morning prayers surrounded by the glory of God, how noble might our actions be if we could continue to be conscious that we were swathed in that same glory throughout the day! And how filled with the strength of God's holiness might be our hands if they could feel in all our waking hours the press of God's unique sovereignty! In each box of the *t'fillin* are verses from the Torah (Exodus 13:1–10 and 13:11–16; Deuteronomy 6:4–9, the first paragraph of the *Sh'ma*; and 11:13–21, the second paragraph of the *Sh'ma*). All these passages speak of wearing an *ot*, a sign, on one's hand and arm, and the Exodus passages relate the sign to the strong arm of God in rescuing Israel from Egypt. It is as though the press of leather into our skin was God's redeeming arm, strengthening our own[6] and acting through us. Each box of the *t'fillin* is inscribed with the Hebrew letter *shin* for *Shaddai*, one of the names of God signifying Almighty, but also *shadayim*, "breasts," suggesting the nurturing power of the God who bore us in the divine womb, *rechem*, the root of *rachamim*, "compassion."[7]

A discussion of *t'fillin* must also address the problems that the reclaiming of some traditional garb by Reform Jews has raised for Jewish women. Having grown up in homes where *yarmulke, tallit,* and *t'fillin* were options only for men, Jewish women entering college or facing the do-it-yourself Jewish revolution in the 1970s often felt uncomfortable putting them on. As Jewish women increasingly wished to celebrate their gender as well as their religion, to don traditional Jewish garb seemed to affirm one at the expense of the other. The proliferation of new styles of *tallit* made that garb easier, as women could choose garments that resembled shawls they might ordinarily wear. But how to cover their heads? The *yarmulke* was clearly a male symbol; the newer, crocheted *kippah* was more hip, but still felt male; and the snood (a variety of a French beret) or *tichel* (a head scarf), head coverings often worn by married Orthodox women, did not feel right to women outside that community. Gradually some women began to add more feminine elements to the *kippah*, like braided borders or faux pearls. One such *kippah* is even on display in the Israel Museum. But of course there remains great variety in the styles of women's ritual garb. Some women wear the same *kippot* men do; others may choose to wear a *tallit* without a head covering. Whether consciously or not, the mitzvah prohibiting the wearing of clothes of the opposite gender (Deuteronomy 22:5) has exerted a powerful effect on women who have felt called to the mitzvot of ritual garb. Today some women are also beginning to wear *t'fillin*, though so far there has been little innovation in this area. I know of only one woman who has created a unique set of *t'fillin*. Rabbi Judith Abrams of Houston, a creative, spiritual teacher of Talmud, wears *t'fillin* made of linen, in part out of observance of the ban against *tzaar baalei chayim*, causing pain to animals. As of this writing, her example has not been followed, in part, surely, because of the artistry required to make them.

Nonetheless, Rabbi Abrams's *t'fillin* are an example of a new dimension to Reform Jewish observance suggested by the Pittsburgh Principles' endorsement of heeding the call to "ancient and modern" mitzvot. Many Reform Jews hear the call of more than one mitzvah at a time: Rabbi Abrams hears both the mitzvah of *t'fillin* and the mitzvah of *tzaar baalei chayim*. Her solution to answering the call of both is to choose linen straps rather than leather ones. Because Reform Jews are called as individuals, it is crucial for a Reform approach to observance that we express our freedom to expand the traditional understanding of certain mitzvot to embrace complementary, or even, as we shall see, contradictory, mitzvot. I have heard the call not only to put God's words upon the doorpost, but to be conscious of the mitzvot that apply to each particular room. On the doorpost of my office at the Hebrew Union College is a mezuzah in which I have inserted not the traditional passages of the *Sh'ma* but the passage about the values of Torah from Psalm 19:8–12, as a reminder that I am to study and teach in my office as well as doing "work" there. A Reform Jewish home might well have a mezuzah at the entrance to the living room with texts from Genesis 18:1–5 or 24:31–33, discussing *hachnasat orchim*, welcoming visitors; texts at the entrance to the dining room from Genesis 1:29–31 or 9:3–4, or Deuteronomy 14:2–21, enjoining appropriate foods, and from Deuteronomy 8:7-10, enjoining blessings after a satisfying meal; at the entrance to the bedroom, portions from Genesis 2:21–22 or 28:10–17, which deal with Adam and Eve's lovemaking and Jacob's dream, or the love poetry of Song of Songs 3:1–5 or 4:16. Here too we see a difference between Reform and Conservative Judaism: the halachah may not only be *corrected* to meet changing needs, but *expanded* to enlarge the awareness of the holiness potentially present in our lives.

Dietary Practice: An Example of Halachic Expansion

Opportunities for a Reform expansion of the halachah appear also in kashrut, the second controversial word in the earlier draft of the Pittsburgh Principles. Kashrut in the Torah stems from many sources: Leviticus 11:1–23 bans specific creatures that according to Maimonides, were part of the idolatrous practice of the surrounding nations, thus creating a separation between Jews and non-Jews in that most critical area of human behavior, eating.[8] Kashrut has also been interpreted as an extension of the role played in the Temple by the *shulchan*, usually translated as "table" but also meaning "altar." With the Temple destroyed, the dining table became the Jew's new altar, on which foods prohibited in the service of God in the Temple were prohibited as part of a meal. In this way the mitzvot related to eating became another way to serve God. We celebrate the *k'dushah* of the food God brings to our table by saying *b'rachot* (*HaMotzi* and *Birkat HaMazon*) and are urged to engage in table conversation appropriate to a holy place. Observing the multiple laws of traditional kashrut extends that *k'dushah* not only to the eating of food, but to the buying and preparation of it as well as cleaning up when the meal is done.

To these already far-reaching actions, some Reform Jews are suggesting additions. The mitzvah of avoiding *tzaar baalei chayim*, one of the seven Noachide laws the Rabbis believed were enjoined on all people, has motivated a growing number of Jews to ban veal from their tables, as well as *pâté de foie gras* (goose liver paste). Calves and geese raised for these foods are penned and fed under horrific conditions, and refraining from eating them helps lessen the incentive for farmers to treat these creatures in this fashion. This is another example of how communities as well as individuals may feel called by a mitzvah. The larger the community called to ban creatures victimized by such practices, the greater the chance that the practices may be curtailed in the wider society. Should this expanded practice of kashrut spread in the Reform Movement, a committee might be set up that would explore which slaughtering houses use the most humane means of *sh'chitah* (kosher slaughter) and urge that Reform Jews buy only from them.

Another mitzvah affecting diet in our days is *lo taashok et rei-acha* ("Do not oppress your neighbor" [Leviticus 19:13]). Our neighbors include the men and women who plant, harvest, and produce our food in fields and factories and who, for the most part, work under painful physical conditions for shamefully low pay. Periodically their chief champion, the United Farm Workers Union, will urge boycotts of foods produced under these cruel conditions, and for decades the Reform Movement has supported these calls. Reform Jews moved by this issue refrained for years from eating grapes when they were under the farmworkers' ban. At this writing, grapes are no longer banned, but certain other foods are. Just as Orthodox kashrut supervisors will issue periodic advisories informing consumers that this or that product is now on or off the approved list, so the Reform Movement might issue similar alerts indicating what foods should be avoided by those who feel called to support the farmworkers' cause. Expanding the realm of kashrut to include mitzvot not traditionally included is further evidence that when the Reform Movement adopts mitzvot, it does not imitate other movements, but hears them in a manner consistent with "mitzvot long observed by Reform Jews." This development constitutes not only an expansion of the halachic process but an attempt to integrate mitzvot that used to be considered in the realm of "customs and ceremonies" with those that used to be considered in the realm of "social justice." The Pittsburgh Principles implies, as we have noted earlier, a break with these artificial distinctions, which are in any case antithetical to a system of mitzvot all of which belong to but one realm: the will of *HaKadosh Baruch Hu*, of the Blessed Holy One.

Kashrut is controversial, of course, because it touches one of the most basic elements of life. Our relationship to food begins minutes after we are born, when a baby begins to cry for its mother's breast. The food habits with which we grow up tend to remain with us for life, which is one of the reasons to raise children in a kosher home. A Reform kosher home must be filled with love and humor and the absence of the stringent obsessiveness that led so many Jews to reject kashrut. Still, the idea of changing one's food habits can feel very threatening. Despite the permissive language of "some" and "may" in the third draft of the Ten Principles, many people read the description of what "some Reform Jews may" do as a statement that "all Reform Jews should" do them and that they are bad Jews if they do not. It is curious, though, that in a time that has seen the single "American" omnivorous diet dissolve into a welter of vegetarian, vegan, low-carb, low-sodium, macrobiotic, lactose-free, sugar-free regimens, with which most hosts desirous of fulfilling the mitzvah of *hachnasat orchim* are happy to comply, only kashrut seems to arouse hostility. However, many Reform Jews today refrain from pork, others from shellfish, and a somewhat lesser number from eating milk and meat together. If someone were to count those Reform Jews who observe one or more of the mitzvot relating to kashrut the results would show that many Reform Jews have built one or more dietary mitzvot into their lives.[9]

Deepening the Mikveh

If food is a controversial arena, so surely is sex. While the Talmud contains many passages discussing how sexual relations between married couples can increase awareness of the *k'dushah* between them, this has been an area in which the Victorian sensibilities of Reform's birth led its decorous nineteenth-century rabbis to remain silent. We are overdue for a sensitive discussion from a Reform perspective on how lovemaking can bring a loving couple closer to God even as they come closer to each other. The only topic touching on sexual practice on which the early Reformers spoke regarded the institution of *mikveh*. It was recommended at the Frankfurt Conference in Germany in 1841 but denounced by the Cincinnati Reform rabbi David Philipson, who expressed horror at its practice in 1888.[10] Traditionally, women are to remain separate from their husbands during the period of their menstruation (*nidah*), at the conclusion of which they are required to immerse in a *mikveh* of collected rainwater (*mayim chayim*, "living water"). This practice of ritual purification dates back to Torah rituals surrounding the Tabernacle. Classically, one of the first structures a Jewish community would build would be the *mikveh*, so that husbands and wives might enjoy normal sexual relations.

There is a spiritual dimension to the *mikveh* that early Reform failed to appreciate, in part because of the dreadful condition of so many *mikvaot* when the movement was in infancy and even long after. In her earliest writing on the subject, Rachel Adler wrote that the condition of the menstruating woman, *tum'ah* (from the adjective *tameh*, usually translated "impurity"), was really a confrontation with the intersection between death and life, as the eggs representing potential new life flowed out of the woman's body without having been fertilized. This confrontation is not peculiar to the menstruant: men experiencing a seminal emission also feel the outflow of semen that did not produce new life, and men and women who enter a graveyard suffer the *tum'ah* of contact with the literal end of life.

> In all creation is the seed of destruction. All that is born dies, and all that begets. Begetting and birth are the nexus points at which life and death are coupled. They are the beginnings which point to an end. Menstruation, too, is a nexus point. It is an end which points to a beginning. At the nexus points, the begetter becomes *tameh*. The fluid on which new life depends—the semen, the rich uteral lining which sustains embryonic life—the departure of these from the body leaves the giver *tameh*. The menstrual blood, which inside

the womb was a potential nutrient, is a token of dying when it is shed.[11]

For a woman or a man in a state of *tum'ah*, immersion in the waters of life can be an experience of rebirth: the renewed hope for fertility and potency, the promise of life renewed following the death of a loved one. As the fetus is cradled in the waters of its mother's womb, as the Israelites were born when they entered and emerged from the waters of the Reed Sea, *mikveh* offers a symbolic experience of birth and rebirth in the waters over which at Creation hovered the presence of God, who is *HaRachaman*, the Merciful One, the Womb (*rechem*) of the world. In an era of immaculate and beautiful *mikvaot*, a small but growing number of Reform men and women are exploring *mikveh* as an experience of cleansing, healing, and renewal after such destructive, sullying experiences as rape, a messy divorce, invasive surgery, and chemotherapy, as well as at the outset of a new stage in life, such as a marriage or a significant birthday. As the CCAR's new Guidelines for Conversion call on Reform rabbis to inform prospective converts about the mitzvah of *t'vilah* (immersion in a *mikveh*), an increasing number of Reform Jews have asked why this beautiful, often transformative experience should be available only to converts, and then only at the time of their conversion. Indeed, the official publication of the URJ, *Reform Judaism* magazine, featured a moving piece on one Reform woman's experience with *mikveh* as long ago as 1975. As of this writing at least a half dozen Reform synagogues (and the Centre for Reform Judaism in Toronto) have built *mikvaot* on their premises.

It is not clear whether, if the Statement of Principles had been written in 2005 rather than 1999, *mikveh* could have been mentioned by name. A group of fifty Reform rabbis met at the CCAR Convention in June 1998, a year before the Pittsburgh Principles were adopted, and discussed an earlier draft that did include a specific mention of *mikveh*. I asked my colleagues in the room whether they thought that its inclusion might be incendiary, and they all shouted, "No! Keep it in!" They believed that the mention of this mitzvah would clearly demonstrate the truth of the language that survived into the final 1999 statement: "We are committed to the ongoing study of the whole array of *mitzvot*." We

Reform Jews are free to consider any and all of the mitzvot; we are not afraid of confronting any of them. To my enthusiastic colleagues that night, *mikveh* was a symbol of the rebirth of a robust Reform Movement ready to take its place at Sinai, open to hear the call of whatever mitzvot it was ready to receive. Though in the end, *mikveh* was not included in the 1999 Pittsburgh Principles, I believe my colleagues have been proved correct.

While the dialogic language of call and response finds its origin in the philosophy of Franz Rosenzweig, it can also be found in the personal religious experiences of Reform Jews. I conclude this chapter with an account of some of my own in the hope that they will strike a chord with other Reform Jews. I had been wrestling with issues of kashrut through all my years at the Hebrew Union College. In the year of my ordination as a rabbi, I attended a meeting at a classmate's apartment, and his wife served a lunch of salami and cheese sandwiches. As she approached me with the tray, I felt a sense of revulsion sweep through me. I could not accept the sandwich. As I smiled and said, "No thanks," I realized that the time had come for me to stop eating meat and milk together. From deep inside, I knew I had been called to follow this mitzvah. I had a similar experience many years later regarding wearing a *kippah*. Six months in Israel had led me to put on a *kippah* when I prayed or studied, but then to remove it. I felt increasingly uncomfortable with removing it, because it seemed to suggest that God was present when I prayed or studied but not at other times, and I knew that was not true. One evening, chairing a meeting at the Los Angeles Jewish Federation dealing with spiritual concerns, I donned my *kippah* as a rabbinic colleague began a beautiful study session on a Chasidic text. When he finished, and I was to begin the meeting itself, I instinctively reached for my *kippah* to remove it, and could not. Why should a meeting prefaced by such an uplifting teaching partake of less *k'dushah* than the study session? Once again, I felt called, this time to the mitzvah of covering my head throughout the day. I believe, in the midst of our studying and wrestling with the mitzvot, that God does call to us when the Holy One believes we are ready to receive the call.

Through Torah, God calls each of us every day. Blessed be each day that we are able to respond.

10

Torah in the World:
Revealing Holiness in Time and Space

We bring Torah into the world when we seek to sanctify the times and places of our lives through regular home and congregational observance. Shabbat calls us to bring the highest moral values to our daily labor and to culminate the workweek with *kedushah*, holiness, *menuchah*, rest, and *oneg*, joy. The High Holy Days call us to account for our deeds. The Festivals enable us to celebrate with joy our people's religious journey in the context of the changing seasons. The days of remembrance remind us of the tragedies and the triumphs that have shaped our people's historical experience both in ancient and modern times. And we mark the milestones of our personal journeys with traditional and creative rites that reveal the holiness in each stage of life.

—Statement of Principles, "Torah," paragraph 7

A Reform Shabbat

Why does a book like this need a special chapter on Reform observances? Does Reform approach Shabbat, the High Holy Days, Festivals, and life-cycle events differently from other Jews? Or rather, does Torah call us to these events differently from other Jews?

One Shabbat afternoon some years ago, after davening at the minyan near our house, my family joined our *chavurah* for a Shabbat afternoon by the ocean. All afternoon, as we studied Torah and enjoyed a *S'udah Sh'lishit*, the third Shabbat meal, we watched the surf, still high from recent rains, roll majestically over the sands, arraying them in a gown of foam that turned from blue to purple to pinkish gray as the sun reclined lower and lower in the sky, retiring at last in orange splendor behind the blue-mist mountains of the Coastal Range. Protecting the tall *Havdalah* candle from the wind, we huddled around it, nurturing each fragile wick until each one's flame kept the others lit. Through a blend of cloves and salt-sea breath, we bade farewell to the *n'shamah y'teirah*, the special Shabbat soul that had animated us all, ending our Shabbat together with a spirited call to the prophet Elijah to come soon across the waves bringing a world that would be altogether Shabbat, where everyone could join together arm in arm as we had.

It was not clear, though, whether everyone in the Jewish world would want to. For as beautiful as it was, there was something quintessentially Reform about that afternoon. To explain why, we need to look at the way in which Shabbat is understood in both the Written and the Oral Torah.

When the fourth commandment, on Shabbat observance, was given, it appeared in two forms: in Exodus 20:8–11, it begins with the Hebrew word *zachor*, "remember": "Remember the Day of Shabbat to bring forth its *k'dushah*." The text proceeds to derive Shabbat practice from the belief that the first Shabbat was the day on which God rested from the Creation. In Deuteronomy 5:12–15, however, the fourth commandment begins with the word *shamor*, "guard": "Guard the Day of Shabbat to bring forth its *k'dushah*." Here Shabbat practice, specifically abstinence from work for ourselves and our servants, is derived from the fact that we were once servants and slaves in Egypt until God freed us to serve only the Eternal.

The Rabbis believed that *zachor* represents those aspects of Shabbat practice that illuminate Shabbat and the culmination of Creation for all humanity, seen in the feminine aspect of the arrival of the Shabbat Queen on Friday evening. They viewed *shamor* as a signpost for those Shabbat practices, particularly the prohibitions of work, spelled out in the particular revelation given to the Jewish people through Moses, a masculine figure, celebrated in the Torah reading on Shabbat morning.[1] Traditional Jewish practice blends the *mitzvot aseih*, the "Thou shalt" mitzvot of *zachor,* with the *mitzvot lo-taaseh,* the "Thou shalt not" mitzvot of *shamor.* The Reform Movement has generally favored the "Thou shalt" *zachor* mitzvot—lighting candles, making *Kiddush* and *Havdalah,* engaging in study and rest—over the "Thou shalt not" *shamor* mitzvot, such as not kindling fire or driving a car, and refraining from carrying, writing, tearing, or repairing. These *shamor* mitzvot are actually a total of thirty-nine activities derived from the kind of work specified for the creation of the *Mishkan,* the Tabernacle or holy place in the wilderness, which the Torah often juxtaposes to Shabbat, the essence of holy time. The Reform preference for *zachor* is clear: it emphasizes the day as a manifestation of holiness rather than a time of restriction, and it is related to the universal aspect of Shabbat—Creation—rather than the particular ones.

For most of the twentieth century, Reform emphasized Friday night observance over Shabbat morning, particularly since the Shabbat morning service, especially if there was no bar or bat mitzvah, has been a relatively recent innovation in Reform. In this sense our *chavurah's* Shabbat afternoon was the epitome of *zachor.* The colors of the sea and the sky gorgeously proclaimed the majesty of God's creation, as its finale, the Seventh Day, drew to its stunning close on the eve of a new week. We learned Torah together, we relaxed on the sand, and we observed the main nonsynagogue event of Shabbat afternoon, the third meal, with its symbolic allusions to the redemptive meal that all will enjoy in the messianic time. We climaxed the day with the *Havdalah* service, committing ourselves, now that the day filled with Shabbat *k'dushah* was ending, to look for the *k'dushah* that lies hidden beneath the ordinary days of the week.

What made our *chavurah's* Shabbat specifically Reform? As filled as it was with *zachor,* so did it ignore many aspects of *shamor.* We had to drive to the ocean, we carried the jackets and blankets and coolers, and because the increasing cold of early twilight was making the children's teeth chatter, we made *Havdalah* a little early. This style of practice is in keeping with the two modes of *shamor* that Mark Washofsky describes from a Reform perspective:

> We might abstain from driving, the use of money, the telephone, the computer and the like. . . . Alternatively . . . one may decide to engage in any number of activities which, though traditionally forbidden on the Sabbath, are done *likhevod Shabbat,* in *honor* of the

Sabbath. One might not drive to the mall to shop, for example, but might drive to a museum and pay the price of admission, because one considers a visit to the museum an act that refreshes the soul.[2]

The *zachor* qualities of our *chavurah's* Shabbat would have been much less restful if we did not believe we could drive to the beach house, bring our own food, and make *Havdalah* before dark. Still, while Reform has bypassed many of the particulars of *shamor*, it has always endorsed its principle of abstinence from work on Shabbat. From the earliest days of the Reform Movement, the rabbis inveighed against those who voluntarily kept their offices and factories open on the seventh day. The fact that many Jews who would have liked to rest on Shabbat were prohibited from doing so by the harsh labor laws of the nineteenth and early twentieth century became a further argument for the Reformers' condemnation of those laws. But in terms of the specific prohibitions, the Reform Movement has generally encouraged its members to define "work" for themselves.

Reform Shabbat observance has generally tended to seek holiness in space, seeking out locations (like the ocean) where one's physical surroundings manifest *hadrat kodesh*, the "beauty of holiness" of the day. Open chapels in our camps are set in aesthetic locations, synagogues (used most often on Shabbat) are as soaring as the means of the congregation can make them or, if possible, feature windows open to beautiful natural settings. Note by contract the little *shtieblach* of traditional Orthodoxy, where the message is clearly that the humble spaces are meant to be transcended by soaring prayer and the observance of Shabbat. A traditional concept that relates to Reform's emphasis on the holiness present in physical space is *hidur mitzvah*, the beautification of the mitzvah. We are enjoined to use the most beautiful *lulav* and *etrog* we can afford, to build the loveliest sukkah we can imagine, to grace our Shabbat and festival table with the loveliest settings and wine vessels we can afford.

Redefining Holiness in Time

While Reform has increasingly sought holiness in space, we have resisted being concerned about the boundaries of holy time. Reform Jews generally light candles not at the halachic eighteen minutes before sunset, but when the family has gathered for the Shabbat evening meal. *Havdalah* often takes place not punctiliously when three stars come out, but when the family is together before individuals break off for Saturday night activities. As a friend once put it to me, "Which is better—to make *Havdalah* when we are all together even if it is before dark, or not make it at all and deprive our child and us of the mitzvah?"

Another way in which the movement "reformed" the traditional understanding of time was in its stance on the second day of holidays. The Reformers argued that since the Jewish calendar had long been fixed, there was no need for Jews in the Diaspora to observe a second day as a way to make sure that at least one of the two days of observance was the correct one.[3] This was a sensible, rational decision, which not only echoes the doubts of the Talmudic sages themselves (see Babylonian Talmud, *Beitzah* 4b), but avoids placing overly burdensome obstacles in the way of moderns called to the first steps of observance. Nonetheless, it ignores the benefits that can accrue to a two-day observance. In the Diaspora, we often need one day just to separate us from the deeply ingrained, ordinary habits of everyday life so that we can really appreciate the change that has occurred once Pesach or Sukkot or Shavuot has arrived. To extend the first day to two could give us the length of time we need to fully appreciate the transformation of time from an ordinary March or October to the holy time of Pesach or Sukkot. In *Eretz Yisrael* we are surrounded by the *k'dushah* of space; lacking that in the Diaspora, we need a second day to more fully absorb the *k'dushah* of time.

A popular theme in business courses is "managing time." Jews have an interesting take on this topic: there are roughly 136 days in the traditional Jewish year that have an aspect of *k'dushah* attached to them, including the month of Elul preparing us for the High Holy Days, the ten days of *t'shuvah* between Rosh HaShanah and Yom Kippur, and the 49 days of counting the Omer (*S'firat HaOmer*) between Pesach and Shavuot that prepare us to receive the Torah. If we make ourselves conscious of the special *k'dushah* inherent in all those days, how rich and reflective might our time become! If we engage in fifteen minutes of reflection on how we might correct our wrongdoings each day of Elul, how much more profound would be our observance of the High Holy Days! If we spend time reflecting on one of the kabbalistic themes of each of the seven weeks of the Omer period, how much we would recover of the almost vanished *k'dushah* of the day we stood at Sinai! For example, the first week we could concentrate on strengthening our capacity for love (*Chesed*), the second on exercising the power (*G'vurah*) of restraint, the third on creating a splendid (*Tiferet*) balance of compassion and truth, the fourth on winning victory (*Netzach*) over our hesitation to relate, the fifth in acknowledging (*Hod*) others empathetically, the sixth in seeking a foundation (*Y'sod*) of sexual purity, and finally, the seventh week, in experiencing the sovereignty (*Malchut*) of God experienced as the *Shechinah*, the indwelling Divine Presence, sometimes perceived as the feminine side of God.[4]

There is one aspect of time that the Reform Movement has unequivocally endorsed. As the Pittsburgh Principles says, "Shabbat calls us to bring the highest moral values to our daily labor." One of the traditional understandings for categorizing the days of the week by number rather than by name is to see each one as a step toward Shabbat. Sunday is thus *Yom Rishon*, the first day toward Shabbat, Monday *Yom Sheini*, the second day, and so on. It is a custom to look each day for an object, a reading, or a thought to bring to Shabbat, that we might see the Seventh Day as a culmination of the week. Just as we welcome Shabbat with a psalm representing each day of the preceding week, we can dedicate each day to the observance of Shabbat as the week progresses. Similarly, if we are aware that each day is a piece of Shabbat, it can lead us each morning to be conscious of the quality of our actions that day, that they might be a fitting gift of that day to Shabbat. When we are tempted to gossip, to lose our temper, to take something that is not ours, we are encouraged to ask, "Is this an action that will let me make this day a gift to Shabbat?"

Reflections on Holy Days

Though we ask forgiveness for those actions in the *Amidah* prayer every weekday, one period in the year, the High Holy Days, is particularly dedicated, in the words of the Pittsburgh Principles, to "call[ing] us to account for our deeds." We have noted earlier that Reform Jews committed to do mitzvot should by definition also be committed to recognizing when we commit *aveirot*, violations of mitzvot. Reform *machzorim* have always included the three parts of the Shofar Service, affirming the importance to Reform Jews of *malchuyot*, the recognition of God's sovereignty over our lives; *zichronot*, remembrances of the covenant with humanity (through Noah) and Israel (through Abraham and Sarah); and *shofarot*, the echoes of our standing at Sinai (more evidence that the Reform Movement affirmed this event) and the promise that we shall hear the call of the future redemption in the messianic age. No sooner have we emerged from the High Holy Days than we are invited to build and enter the sukkah, and then follows the entire cycle of the seasonal Festivals and other special days. Does Reform Judaism suggest a particular approach to the Festivals? The Columbus Platform and the Centenary Perspective merely mention the various seasonal observances, while the Pittsburgh Principles reminds us that Shabbat and the Jewish seasonal occasions are not merely celebrations but are dedicated to specific actions. These are *religious* events, not merely times for enjoyment. Like Shabbat, these times are dedicated to a purpose, offering us ritual opportunities to deepen the moral quality of our lives. Once again, significantly for a contemporary Reform Jewish approach, we see how the ethical and the ritual are intertwined.

The description of the three Festivals—Pesach, Shavuot, and Sukkot—reflects another aspect of this integration:

> The Festivals enable us to celebrate with joy our people's religious journey in the context of the changing seasons.

As the *Birchot HaNehenin* enable us to transform an event of nature into an acknowledgment of the presence of God, so, in keeping with our growing desire to connect with the environment, through the Festivals we can commemorate the change of seasons as an event in our people's and our personal histories. Spring, the emergence of the land from winter, does not only occur for all creatures; it is an outward sign of our Pesach emergence from Egyptian slavery. The first fruits of summer are a time to receive the first fruits of that emergence, which is the giving of Torah. Autumn not only marks the harvest that will shelter us from approaching winter; it is a time when we experience God's *sukkah*—shelter from the fragilities of life—and renew our movement's commitment to spread that shelter over as many of God's creatures as we can. Shabbat came into being as the culmination of the Creation of all that lives, but its observance was a gift only to the Jewish people. While the seasons are common to all people, we have been given particular holidays as a special gift to experience a part of those natural occurrences revealed only to us.[5]

The greater attention that Reform Jews have been paying to the inner life encourages us to be attentive to the instruction to be joyful in the festival (*v'samachta b'chagecha* [Deuteronomy 16:14]). *Simchah* is a different kind of joy from *oneg,* the joy prescribed for Shabbat. In the siddur we are told that those who keep Shabbat call it *oneg.* "Call" is the same word as "name," and we know that to name something is to summon its inner being. *Oneg* is an innate part of Shabbat, as is *k'dushah.* On Shabbat we are to plumb the joyousness that God implanted in the holiness of Shabbat when God took the restful breath that brought it into being. But since the Festivals came about through the dialogue of God and Israel's experience, *simchah* seems to partake not of God's nature but of our own as part of the historical Jewish people. *Simchah* is what *we* bring to the Festivals; we are to plumb its depth in our memories of Israel's history and bring it into the day—even if we are feeling sad or mournful. By doing so, whatever else we may be experiencing when a festival comes around is to be accompanied by joy. The seven-day shivah mourning period is to be canceled by a festival as a reminder that we need to understand our personal loss in the larger light of the season and our people's history. It is not easy to do.

Expanding the Festivals

Simchah is the festival equivalent of the *zachor* element of Shabbat: building a beautiful sukkah, waving a majestic *lulav,* making an elaborate ritual out of the nighttime search for *chameitz,* setting an elegant seder table, festooning the house with greens and flowers for Shavuot. As Reform Jews we should explore creative ways to expand these external stimulations of *simchah:* filling the sukkah with samples of our own harvest in school, work, and the community; gathering a harvest of food baskets in conjunction with local food pantries; creating a yearly calendar of poor people's needs for different months and committing our synagogues to providing them; on the night before Pesach, hiding notes of certain behaviors of ours that, like *chameitz*, we would like to clear out of our lives; encouraging our synagogues to contact appropriate agencies to provide names of guests appropriate for us to invite for the seder; festooning our houses with texts that over the year have acquired particular meaning for us. With the explosion of creative synagogue music and the entrance of dance and movement into worship, we can use the publication of *Mishkan T'filah* as an opportunity to reinvigorate our synagogue festival celebrations as well.

The Festivals have their *shamor* equivalent too—details of time, of traditionally prohibited work, the specifications of a proper ("kosher") sukkah, or the kind of foods (*chameitz*, "leavening") that are to be removed for Pesach. Reform Jews have recently come to be much more concerned about these "halachic" matters. While Reform Jews do not always build sukkot according to halachic specifications, more and more are aware of what a "kosher" sukkah is and will explain why theirs does not meet the halachic requirements but does meet their interpretation of the requirements. Reform Jews who remove leavening on Pesach do so in a variety of ways, often diverging from the halachah sometimes from lack of knowledge or time, but sometimes on principle (e.g., "I don't like the invidious distinctions inherent in selling my *chameitz* to a non-Jew").[6]

Some of the most important changes in Reform observance of the Festivals stem from a desire to incorporate women's particular insights and experiences of *k'dushah*. When Reform attempted to reinvigorate Shavuot a century ago by instituting confirmation, part of its rationale was to create a ritual that, in an era before bat mitzvah developed, would be open to girls as well as boys, since both genders stood at Sinai. Girls and boys were also to be consecrated together on Sukkot as they entered religious school. The rediscovery of the Talmudic custom of women abstaining from work on Rosh Chodesh (Jerusalem Talmud, *Taanit* 1:6) as a reward for refusing to give their jewelry to the Golden Calf (*Pirkei D'Rabbi Eliezer* 44) led in the 1970s to the rise of Rosh Chodesh as a women's festival. Women's groups in many Reform synagogues now hold Rosh Chodesh observances monthly, sometimes writing their own liturgies or sharing others', celebrating the waxing and waning of the moon as an external symbol of the monthly flow within their own bodies. What is still seen as a "curse" by women with painful menstrual cycles has been sanctified by Rosh Chodesh rituals into a celebration of a body in tune with the ever-changing night sky of the universe.

While Reform did not invent these monthly commemorations, Reform women have embraced them. In similar fashion, Reform has over the years adopted some of the customs that arose out of the Renewal Movement, bringing them into the "mainstream" of non-Orthodox Judaism. For example, in the new CCAR Haggadah, *The Open Door*, the seder table now features a *kos Miryam*, a cup filled with water in memory of Miriam, in whose honor, a midrash states, a well followed the Israelites throughout the wilderness to save them from thirst. This Haggadah also includes an orange on the seder plate, reflecting "the full inclusion of gay men and lesbian women and their families around the seder table and in Jewish life" or "the presence of women as full participants in the Passover seder."[7] This Haggadah, borrowing from the work of the poet and liturgist Marcia Falk (*The Book of Blessings*), includes blessings to God written in the feminine. The rituals for Sukkot in the CCAR's *Gates of the House* (1976) and *On the Doorposts of Your House* (1994) include a nightly welcome not only for the traditional seven male *ushpizin* (spiritual guests, from Abraham to David), but for seven appropriate female guests as well (the four Matriarchs, as well as Miriam, Hannah, and Deborah).

Changes in Remembrance

Another set of Jewish holidays that the Pittsburgh Principles addresses are the "days of remembrance." What are these? They encompass the ancient ones, Chanukah and Purim, and the modern ones, Yom HaShoah (Holocaust remembrance) and Yom HaAtzma-ut (Israel Independence Day). They also include the fast day of Tishah B'Av. Unlike Shabbat and the Festivals, which Reform has observed enthusiastically and tried to reinvigorate, in the early decades of Reform these "days of remembrance" were also days of ambivalence. The *Union Prayer*

Book insertion for Chanukah was a new creation, recalling the victory of the Maccabees and the rededication of the Temple, but with no mention of the Talmudic account of the miracle of the oil lasting for eight days. The *Union Prayer Book* Purim insertion is a dour piece, dwelling on the threats of Haman but with little allusion to the antic nature of the holiday—defeating the power of the adversary by turning him into a clown. For many years the tradition of a raucous reading of the *M'gillah* was at odds with the Reform sense of decorum in the dignified spaces of the sanctuary. That Reform *M'gillah* readings are now as raucous as those of the rest of Jewry can be seen either as a defeat for decorum or an acknowledgment that *k'dushah* can also be manifest through laughter.[8]

While Israel Independence Day has a service of its own in *Gates of Prayer*, there is a curious omission of any reference to the State of Israel, as opposed to the land and the people and the city of Jerusalem. It is as though, despite the enthusiastic embrace of Zionism by the entire movement since 1967 and in much of it long before, there was still a hesitation as to whether religious expressions could encompass the political entity of the State of Israel. (This omission has been remedied in the pilot editions of *Mishkan T'filah*.) *Gates of Prayer* has a service for Yom HaShoah and Tishah B'Av, the only fast day associated with the destruction of the Temple observed in the Reform Movement. In an era when some zealots in Israel wish to rebuild the Temple on its historic site, now the site of the Dome of the Rock and the Al-Aksa Mosque, the Reform Movement is to be applauded for restricting its commemoration of the destruction of the Temple to Tisha B'Av alone, which, of course, evokes other tragedies as well. Reform classically saw the destruction of the Second Temple as a calamity that in the end had a beneficent effect in dispersing the Jews around the world to serve as lights to the nations among whom we lived. With time, the Reform Movement has broadened its definition of *k'dushah* to include the extremes of laughter and tears, not only for personal sadness (as in a *Yizkor* service) but for national sadness as well. And with the gradual embrace of more and more of the insights of mysticism, we have become more open to the miraculous as well. Does this help to explain why, like other Jews, Reform Jews have begun to invest in longer-burning Chanukah candles? Watching their light slowly grow from night to night and slowly burn down can open the eyes to perceive many visions that reason alone might censor.

Yet the mystic elements of Chanukah often pale amid the real-world conflict with Christmas, as Reform synagogues open their doors to more and more families of intermarriages. Rabbis may inveigh all they wish against observing both holidays, but the tension between the mitzvot of the Jewish holiday and the mitzvah of honoring parents leads many of these families to syncretistic compromises, blurring the distinctions between the faiths. Observing Chanukah in one's home and Christmas in the home of the non-Jewish partner's family works for some, but sometimes the non-Jewish partner insists for this one time in the year on having his or her holiday acknowledged. One of the arguments in favor of conversion in a household that reflects the Jewish calendar and where the children are being educated as Jews is that conversion is a process that helps the once non-Jewish partner move totally away from Christian observances and assists that person's family of origin to adjust to the absence of such observances in their children and grandchildren's home. Another aspect of Christmas in some Reform (and other) Jewish homes is its transformation into a day to do mitzvot of social justice in the non-Jewish community, serving Christmas meals at Salvation Army installations, filling in for Christian co-workers to enable them to celebrate their holiday, and so forth. Amid our continuing ambivalence regarding Christmas, it is appropriate that Chanukah, whose theme is opposition to syncretistic religious practice, should continue to proclaim its uncomfortable message to the contemporary world.

Fasting

At the opposite pole of Chanukah's merriment is the most uncomfortable kind of observance, the fast. What is the Reform Movement's stance on fasting? In an era when "fasting" has become a part of some people's dieting regimens, it is easy to forget that fasting can be a profound religious act. When we abjure both food and water for twenty-five hours (on Yom Kippur and Tishah B'Av) or from dawn to sunset (for the lesser fasts), we begin to burn up our own fat, making a *korban* of part of our own bodies. Fasting is as close as we are permitted to come to human sacrifice. Its intent is to weaken our physical resistance to the soul's yearning to come close to God; indeed, by shrinking ever so slightly our physical being, we melt away some of the barriers between our soul and the God who gave it breath. In addition to the traditional fast days, there have been times of great distress when rabbis would declare a community fast, in the hope that the combined anguish of a self-denying community would move the Holy One to come to their aid. Does fasting (outside of Yom Kippur and Tishah B'Av) have a place in today's Reform Movement?

Because of the political use that right-wing religious groups in Israel have made of rebuilding the Temple, I for one hope we do not resuscitate the Fast of Gedalia (on the third of Tishrei) and the fasts of the Tenth of Tevet and the Seventeenth of Tammuz. With the Temples destroyed, to fast as an act of self-sacrifice suggests that the holiness of the Temple in our days has been transferred to each human person. But the Fast of Esther is not a fast for the Temple. It is an affirmation of the power of fasting to deepen prayer and a reminder of the courage of Queen Esther who, according to the arbitrary rules of her husband the king, might have lost her life when she approached him to plead for the lives of her people. While the other fast days are traditionally meant to acknowledge our complicity in the Temple's fall (as the prophets make abundantly clear), nowadays they tend to become opportunities to wallow in our victimization at the hands of oppressors. This stance can blind us to the fact that whatever the acknowledged cruelties of our enemies, it is also important to look clearly at our own actions and assess whether there is not more we can do. And that is the unambiguous message of the Fast of Esther: Mordecai awakens her to the power she possesses, and she enlists the support of all the people in helping her make the most of it. Especially since the Shabbat before Purim is dedicated to a reminder of the persistent strain of generic evil in those who wish to destroy us, the Fast of Esther is a refusal to see ourselves only as victims of each generation's Amalek, but rather as individuals empowered to take affirmative stands in our own right, after which we have a right to laugh and sing boisterously because such affirmations are the surest way to weaken our fear of the evil that lurks among us.

Celebrations of the Life Cycle: Ancient and Creative

We will return to the struggle between good and evil as we consider the ways in which we commemorate not only the seasonal holidays but also the milestones of the life cycle. These rituals, like the holidays, are ways of bringing Torah into everyday life. While Shabbat is built into the Creation and the Festivals and commemorative days are events in the life of the Jewish people, the celebrations of rites of passage recall events in the personal lives of our biblical ancestors. Abraham is given the mitzvah of *milah*, circumcision (Genesis 17:10–15), in the same utterance as God commands that he and Sarah be given new names, the biblical source not only for circumcision rites but for naming rituals for girls as well as boys. Rebekah is the heroine of the first ritual marriage (Genesis 24:58–67); Moses and Aaron set the pattern of mourning customs (Numbers 20:22–29, Deuteronomy 34:5–8). Yet, just as Shabbat was only given as a mitzvah to the Jewish people a thousand years after it was built into the cosmos for all Creation, the rituals initiated by our "Jewish" biblical ancestors find their origins in the creation of Adam and Eve. *P'ru ur'vu*, procreation, is commanded to them (Genesis 1:28), as is the process whereby adults are to leave their families and "become one flesh" in marriage (Genesis 2:24), and in their act of eating the forbidden fruit, immortality is forbidden them and death comes into the world (Genesis 3:17–19). The stories of Abraham, Sarah, Rebekah, Moses, and Aaron illustrate how God has adapted universal rites into rituals appropriate to the Jewish people. That Ishmael, traditional father of the Arabs, is circumcised at thirteen is itself a hint that God has shaped the universal rites into rituals for other peoples as well.

Despite the periodic debates over the appropriateness of *milah* (Does it inflict unnecessary pain on the child? Does it offer boys a more powerful ritual than is available to girls?), the Reform Movement has embraced *milah* with enthusiasm. Stung by Orthodox *mohalim* who refused to circumcise sons of intermarriages (or parents converted by Reform rabbis), the Reform Movement under the guidance of Rabbi Lewis Barth created the Berit Mila Board of Reform Judaism and began to train physicians skilled in the surgical practice of circumcision to be *mohalim* and *mohalot* (male and female circumcisers), who would do *milah* in the context of a religious ceremony.[9] These *mohalim* and *mohalot* are also trained to lead services that bring baby girls into the covenant as well. While some parents still prefer to name their baby daughters in the synagogue as part of an *aliyah* to the Torah (though both parents and the baby are usually involved, rather than just the father), more and more families are creating their own services to be held at home to make sure that as she grows up the child is aware of how important her birth was to her family and friends. These services began in the 1970s with Hillel rabbis, alternative minyanim, and independent *chavurot*, but the Reform Movement enthusiastically joined in. *Gates of the House*, a home prayer book published by the CCAR in 1976, includes such a rite. One of the most popular rituals for these services has been the lighting of candles, with different people important to the family invited to offer a blessing for the child while lighting a candle, a reminder of the woman's mitzvah of bringing light into the home for Shabbat. Another rite has been the washing of the baby's feet, a sign of welcome, a reminder of Sarah and Abraham's washing of the feet of the messengers who arrive at their tent. Sometimes each guest is given a glass of water to pour into the bowl as they utter a blessing, so that the water with which the baby is washed is filled with the prayers of all who are present. This rite also suggests immersion in the purifying waters of the *mikveh*, the waters of the womb that nurtured the baby, and the role of water at many significant times in Miriam's life.

This jubilant expansion of life-cycle rituals has made itself felt in marriage services as well. Beginning with the heady days of the 1970s, Reform has by and large replaced its once austere marriage ceremonies with exuberant celebrations incorporating old as well as innovative rites. As the Pittsburgh Principles says, "Some of these mitzvot . . . have long been observed by Reform Jews; others, both ancient and modern, demand renewed attention. . . . " In increasing numbers of Reform weddings, a *chuppah* is used (ancient) that is sometimes created for the couple by friends or family (modern), and a cup of betrothal (*eirusin*) is drunk (ancient) and is sometimes passed around to those standing beneath the canopy (modern). The full seven blessings are usually offered over a second cup of wine (ancient), sometimes accompanied by an egalitarian translation read by guests (modern). A *ketubah* is read, though it is seldom the ancient one that stresses only the groom's obligations; rather it is usually a modern, egalitarian text, sometimes written by the couple, and often so beautifully calligraphed and illustrated that it becomes, in the tradition of *hidur mitzvah*, a significant work of art. Rachel Adler, a faculty member at HUC-JIR in Los Angeles, has composed a *b'rit ahuvim*, a covenant of the beloved, in which both partners pledge equal responsibilities in the marriage.[10] In recent years couples have also begun to encircle each other, originally a Chasidic custom incorporating the symbolism of drawing the seven lower *s'firot* around the groom (late ancient). But today's Reform Jews split up the circuits, with one partner walking three and the other partner walking three, and often the two of them making a seventh circuit around a space that their stroll fills with the holiness of the space they will now share together (modern). The song that Rebekah's family sang to her as she departed to wed Isaac is offered today during the increasingly performed *bedeken*, the veiling of the bride, but these days the bride will sometimes give the groom an ornate *kippah* so that the heads of both partners are bedecked with garments that remind them of their obligations to each other, to the past, and to God. Increasingly, Reform couples are following the Chasidic custom of retiring to a private room after the ceremony, though not always with the Chasidic *kavanah* of uniting the feminine with the masculine *s'firot*. Some of them have gone to the *mikveh* and fasted prior to the service, in an attempt to align themselves to the purity of spirit that similar rites inspire on Yom Kippur. A groom may also don a *kittel*, a white knee-length garment tied with a cloth separating the spiritual from the sexual parts of the body, which is worn not only on the Day of Atonement but when leading a seder and in death. The *kittel* is removed and the fast broken in *yichud*, as the bride and groom turn from the focus on the holiness of the marriage rites to the joyousness of the celebration afterward, which is intended to be so exuberant that it will make a permanent imprint on their consciousness, inspiring them to combine holiness and joy in their life together after the wedding. Will they be able to find holiness and joy once the festivities melt away into ordinary life? By dancing and eating and singing and blessing, guests at the wedding have tried their best to assist them.

The outpouring of joy that for many years has marked Reform weddings represents a realization that expressing emotion is a crucial element of religious rites, meant to underscore the meaning of the event being commemorated. Similarly, at funerals the old Reform belief has almost disappeared that mourners needed to be "protected" from the strong outpourings of feeling evoked by lowering the casket in their presence or filling the grave with earth. Modern mourners do not want to repress their feelings and know that they need to fight the natural desire to deny that their loved one has died. These rituals ease the way. They know that filling in the grave is not barbaric, but a way of paying final honor to the dead beloved, escorting this *adam*, this human being, back into the *adamah*, the earth from which God sculpted us (Genesis 2:7, 3:19). Other customs once discarded are also finding their way back into Reform practice. A few Reform congregations have been exploring creating a *chevrah kadisha*, a "holy fellowship" trained in washing and preparing the body for burial, rather than trusting these rites to the anonymous staff at a funeral home. Engaging in these rituals as a community also represents a commitment to replace the fear and revulsion often associated with the dead in Western societies by a more typically Jewish respect for the *k'dushah* of the vessel that once housed a soul sent from God. Rather than concluding the religious rites with the burial, more and more Reform families not only are inviting friends back to the house after the funeral for a *s'udat havraah*, a meal of reconstitution, but are holding "shivah minyans," evening worship for at least three nights, if not the whole traditional seven (*shivah*) days. As these observances increase, it has not been possible for synagogue clergy to conduct them all, which has led to the healthy creation of lay committees trained to conduct these services themselves. Upon arriving at a Reform house of mourning following the funeral, guests are no longer surprised to find a pitcher of water and a towel, enabling them to wash away the environment of death pervading the cemetery with waters symbolizing the life and nurture they wish to impart to the mourners themselves. These gestures of support continue to be reinforced by the ongoing Reform custom that everyone at a cemetery or a shivah minyan joins the mourners in Mourner's *Kaddish*, symbolically praising God for the life that now is gone and reminding the family that friends' voices will continue to shore up the mourners when they falter. Involvement of the community in these new-old rites renews Reform's commitment to inclusiveness, in this case of laypeople as well as clergy. Commemorations of all these "milestones of our personal journeys" bring the words of Torah to life.

Women rabbis and other knowledgeable Jewish women have also created new rites to celebrate specific periods in women's lives. Rabbi Laura Geller may have been the first woman to create a ritual to accompany the weaning of her first child, drawing her inspiration from the biblical mention of such a rite for Isaac (Genesis 21:8). In Reform and Jewish Renewal circles, rites have been created for menarche, menopause, miscarriage, and other life events; *On the Doorposts of Your House* includes blessings and readings for a couple concerned about infertility, confirmation of pregnancy, giving birth, adopting a child, beginning breastfeeding, beginning a child's education, entering college, and celebrating anniversaries. While many of these new rites are for both males and females, it was Jewish women who educated the rest of us on the need to create opportunities to thank God in a Jewish manner for the approach of seasons of life that had heretofore lacked a religious context.

The Reform desire to blend the ritual and the ethical has led us to greater comfort with the struggle of good against evil that shadows many celebrations of the life cycle. Acknowledgment that there was a demonic underside to these milestones was slow in coming to Reform practice. Steeped in German rationalism and an uncompromising commitment to monotheism, the Reformers rejected as the basest superstition the Eastern European custom to sit up all night studying before a *b'rit milah* to ward off the predations of the dangerous succubus Lilith. They may not even have known of the custom to hang a Sephardic *chamsa* (an object borrowed from Islam) around the bedstead of the woman in labor or, another anti-Lilith device, to tie a red ribbon around the infant's cradle. They were certainly uncomfortable with the standard ritual of breaking a glass at a wedding, rejecting its implication that the world without a Temple was a shattered world, and the "superstition" that the noise of the breaking glass would scatter the demons. In post-1960s America, whatever rituals would deepen the meaning of a holy occasion were welcomed, so thoroughly did Reform and other Jews wish to rid themselves of the notion that only Western middle-class customs were appropriate. Furthermore, the explosion of irrationalism that was the Second World War and the Holocaust led a number of Jews—however unconsciously—to desire whatever weapons they could amass to ward off the incursions of evil into the world. Many a groom (or, in fully egalitarian weddings, bride and groom) will now stomp determinedly upon a glass in the knowledge that with unfaithfulness and adultery on the rise and divorce rates rampant, new husbands and wives need all the help they can get. Few if any Reform Jews who practice these rites believe that they reflect anything other than the Pittsburgh Principles' statement that "we affirm the reality and oneness of God." Just as a battle against a visible human enemy does not lessen God's sovereignty over that person but is intended to reinforce it, a battle against an invisible enemy may be seen to strengthen God's hand as well.

Why does the Pittsburgh Principles consider Shabbat, Festivals, and life-cycle commemorations as opportunities to "bring Torah into the world" rather than as encounters with God, which would place them in the first section? We noted earlier that the idea of mitzvah appears both in the section on God and the section on Torah because, as Franz Rosenzweig taught us, as Jews we need to see all the mitzvot in the Torah as calling to us as members of the Jewish people who heard them at Sinai, while we may feel that God addresses us as individuals with only one mitzvah at a time. It is only by studying Torah that we discover the existence of Shabbat and the Festivals and the rites of the life cycle. When we experience some of those observances with family, with friends, at Hillel, or at synagogue, the words on the page are transformed into an individual address: "The time has come for you to consider taking this on."

In a world that seems to isolate human beings more and more from the Creation, when more and more people are crying out for Redemption, the Revelation of Torah seems to call Reform Jews even more forcefully to uncover the *k'dushah* in the changing times and seasons of each of our years. As the setting sun brings moonrise to the waves and hills and flatlands of our lives, Torah calls us to witness not only a beautiful sight but the reenactment of a moment as ancient as our people, or as time itself. The mitzvot of sad and festive days are the means by which we make our lives holy.

II

Torah in the World:
The Prophets and *Tikkun Olam*

We bring Torah into the world when we strive to fulfill the highest ethical mandates in our relationship with others and with all of God's creation. Partners with God in *tikkun olam*, repairing the world, we are called to help bring nearer the messianic age. We seek dialogue and joint action with people of other faiths in the hope that together we can bring peace, freedom and justice to our world. We are obliged to pursue *tzedek*, justice and righteousness, and to narrow the gap between the affluent and the poor, to act against discrimination and oppression, to pursue peace, to welcome the stranger, to protect the earth's biodiversity and natural resources, and to redeem those in physical, economic and spiritual bondage. In so doing, we reaffirm social action and social justice as a central prophetic focus of traditional Reform Jewish belief and practice. We affirm the *mitzvah* of *tzedakah*, setting aside portions of our earnings and our time to provide for those in need. These acts bring us closer to fulfilling the prophetic call to translate the words of Torah into the works of our hands.

—Statement of Principles, "Torah," paragraph 8

Why Prophets?

If the Festivals are a way to bring Torah into the world, why has Reform been so attracted to the prophets, who often seem to belittle the holy days?

I hate, I despise your festivals,
I take no pleasure in your solemn assemblies
Though you bring Me burnt offerings and grain offerings
I will not accept them.
Though you bring Me choice peace offerings,
I will have no regard for them.

Amos 5:21–22

Why is there a multitude of your sacrifices for Me? says *Adonai*;
I am satiated with burnt offerings of rams, the fat of fed beasts,
The blood of bullocks and sheep and goats I do not desire.
When you appear before My presence this way,
Who asked this of you, to trample My courts?

Isaiah 1:11–12

Why has Reform Judaism always found itself drawn to the prophets? Surely the Torah has no dearth of passages calling for justice, compassion, and the seeking of peace:

When you reap the harvest of your land, do not completely reap the corners of your field or gather the gleanings of your harvest. . . . Leave them for the poor and the stranger. I am *Adonai* your God.

Leviticus 19:9–10

Do not keep the wages of a hired person with you until morning.

Leviticus 19:13

If a stranger abides with you in your land, do not oppress that person; this stranger must be to you as one of your native-born, and you shall love this person as yourself, for you were strangers in Egypt. I am *Adonai* your God, who brought you out of Egypt.

Leviticus 19:34

If one of your countrymen becomes poor among you and sells himself to you, do not make him work as a slave. He is to be treated as a hired worker . . . until the year of the Jubilee. Then he shall go forth from you . . . because the Israelites are My servants whom I brought out of Egypt. . . . Do not rule over him ruthlessly, but hold your God in awe.

Leviticus 25:39–43

If there is a poor person among your kinfolk . . . do not harden your heart or tighten your fist against that person; rather be openhanded and freely lend him whatever he needs.

Deuteronomy 15:7–8

When you approach a city to attack it, make it an offer of peace.

Deuteronomy 20:10

The 1885 Pittsburgh Platform claims that exactly such laws (the "moral" ones) are the only legislation with enduring force. Furthermore, many of them, particularly those related to treatment of the stranger, are tied to the Israelites' experience of redemption from Egypt: Because God redeemed us from the state of strangerhood in Egypt, we are obligated to act as redeemers with all who are, as the Pittsburgh Principles puts it, "in physical, economic and spiritual bondage." The imperative to act justly derives from the very nature of God's covenant with us: *Revelation* instructs us, as a consequence of God's *redeeming* us, to help *redeem* our fellow *creatures.* What could be a stronger imperative than this?

It was the prophets, however, in the Reformers' view, who made the Torah's legislation real. The prophets thundered its injunctions to the people; they based their lives on them, and they suffered because of them. The prophets seemed to nineteenth-century Reform leaders like models of the people the Reformers hoped to be. If the early Reformers viewed the priests as symbols of Israel's mission to bring the nations close to God, they saw the prophets as flesh and blood bearers of that mission. The early Reformers seemed to hope that their generation of Reform Jews would realize God's injunction that as the prophets were called servants of God, the people Israel should become a prophet people who served God:

> But you, Israel My servant,
> Jacob, whom I have chosen . . .
> I, *Adonai*, have called you in righteousness,
> I have seized hold of your hand,
> I will protect you and make you for a covenant of the people
> And for a light of nations,
> To open eyes that are blind
> To bring forth captives from prison
> And to release from the dungeon those who sit in darkness.

Isaiah 41:8, 42:6–7

The prophets were for Reform Jews models of individuals personally moved by God, devoted to moral imperatives at the expense of ritual ones, brilliant, impassioned preachers who understood that for the people to survive the onslaughts of their enemies, they needed to act morally. The 1885 Pittsburgh Platform descriptions of "the indwelling of God in man" were exemplified by the prophetic messages God had placed in the mouths of Isaiah, Jeremiah, and the rest. The prophets were, as the early Reformers wished themselves to be, "God-intoxicated" people. Further, in their attack on religious observance, the prophets seem to say that obedience to the moral law sometimes means to deny the law of ritual:

> Is this the fast that I have chosen,
> A day for a person to humble himself,
> To bend one's head like a reed in a marsh and sprawl on sackcloth
>   and ashes?
> Is this what you call a fast, a day acceptable to *Adonai?*
> Is not this the fast that I have chosen—
> To unlock the shackles of evil,
> To loosen the thongs of the yoke,
> To send forth crushed souls to freedom,
> To tear every yoke in two,
> To tear up loaves for the hungry
> And bring the poor wanderer home?
>
> Isaiah 58:5–7

> Take away from Me the noise of your songs,
> The melody of your lutes I will not hear!
> But let justice roll down like waters,
> And righteousness like a mighty stream!
>
> Amos 5:23–24

Merely to read such poetry is to feel inspired—imagine sitting at the feet of those preachers! In an age when the sermon was the centerpiece of Reform worship, when students were trained at the Hebrew Union College to become powerful orators and at the Jewish Institute of Religion to emulate its charismatic founder Stephen S. Wise, the prophets seemed to represent the image of religious leadership par excellence. Their impact was not only in style; the message that the survival of the people depended on their moral behavior was crucial to a movement that believed our purpose was to be a light to the nations:

> Therefore, because you trample on the poor
> And force them to give you grain.
> Therefore, though you have built stone mansions

You shall not live in them,
Though you have planted lush vineyards you shall not drink their
wine.
For I know how many are your offenses and how great your sins.

Amos 5:11–12

Hate evil, love good,
Maintain justice in the gate;
Perhaps *Adonai*, the God of Hosts, will be gracious to the remnant
of Joseph.

Amos 5:15

Prophetic Messianism

As we know, the prophets' words came true. By attributing the fall of
the First Temple not to the military superiority of the Babylonian con-
querors but to the widespread injustice and callousness of the Israelites,
the prophets were able to interpret a political event in sacred terms.
Because of their faith in God's covenant, however, they believed that the
destruction and exile were only temporary, and a new age would dawn
that would restore Israel to her land and initiate a time of prosperity,
justice, and peace. The prophets believed an anointed (*mashiach*) military ruler, of the seed of David, would bring about such a time, but they
speak much more about the time itself:

And it shall come to pass in the end of days
That the mountain of the house of *Adonai* shall be established as the
top of the mountains,
And shall be exalted above the hills,
And all nations shall flow unto it . . .
And they shall beat their swords into plowshares
And their spears into pruning hooks,
Nation shall not lift up sword against nation
Neither shall they learn war any more.

Isaiah 2:2–4

They shall not hurt nor destroy in all My holy mountain
For the earth shall be full of the knowledge of *Adonai*
As the waters cover the sea.

Isaiah 11:9

The nineteenth-century Reformers did not believe that this vision would be accomplished by the reestablishment of the Israelite monarchy, but they were moved by the vision itself. Indeed, the 1885 Pittsburgh Reformers saw the vision beginning to unfold in their own time:

> We recognize in the modern era of universal culture of heart and intellect the approaching of the realization of Israel's great Messianic hope for the establishment of the kingdom of truth, justice and peace among all men. . . . We acknowledge that the spirit of broad humanity of our age is our ally in the fulfillment of our mission, and, therefore, we extend the hand of fellowship to all who cooperate with us in the establishment of the reign of truth and righteousness among men.

While the Columbus Platform was a little more modest in its reach, it too affirms that social justice is the way to achieve "Israel's great Messianic hope":

> We regard it as our historic task to cooperate with all men in the establishment of the kingdom of God, of universal brotherhood, justice, truth and peace on earth. This is our Messianic goal.

The Centenary Perspective, sobered by the Holocaust and centered on the cause of Jewish survival, shortened the messianic reach even further, while trying to put it into historic perspective:

> Early Reform Jews, newly admitted to general society and seeing in this the evidence of a growing universalism, regularly spoke of Jewish purpose in terms of Jewry's service to humanity. In recent years we have become freshly conscious of the virtues of pluralism and the values of particularism. The Jewish people in its unique way of life validates its own worth while working toward the fulfillment of its messianic expectations.

The 1999 Pittsburgh Principles restored the universal dimensions of Reform messianism, a change that was assisted by its greater distance from the "unspeakable evils" of the twentieth century. However, the Centenary Perspective's emphasis on the values of Jewish particularism had had its effect, as we shall see below, and by 1999 there was a perception that the Reform commitment to universal social justice had weakened and needed to be strengthened. With the word "prophetic" occurring twice in this section, the Pittsburgh Principles reaffirmed the early Reform devotion to the prophets as sounders of alarm for contemporary society and bringers of hope for the future.

Yet scholarship and history have made us more skeptical of the prophets' true contribution than our more optimistic forebears a century ago. Were the prophets really the models in their own time that the early Reformers believed them to be? Yes, God spoke to them directly—even placed words in their mouths so they had no choice but to speak them—but is this how we envision religious people today? This type of relationship is not exactly what we mean by dialogue, which implies the freedom of both parties—God and the human being—to speak from the heart and from the conscience. We are unmoved by those who claim that God told them to do what they have done, for we have always believed that a person speaking in God's name can speak only what we believe has already been revealed in the Torah:

> I will raise up for them a prophet like you from among their kinfolk; I will put My words in his mouth and he will tell them everything I command him. . . . But a prophet who presumes to speak in My name anything that I have not commanded him to say, or a prophet who speaks in the name of other gods, must be put to death.
> Deuteronomy 18:18–20

If this is true, how could the prophets have spoken against sacrifices or other aspects of the sacrificial system as commanded in the Torah? Even though Amos asks, "Did you bring Me sacrifices and offerings for forty years in the desert, O house of Israel?" (Amos 5:25), modern scholarship suggests that Amos may have been referring to a time before the sacrificial laws of Leviticus had been formulated. Most interpreters understand the meaning of "Is this the fast that I have chosen?" (the haftarah for Yom Kippur morning) and "I hate, I despise your religious feasts" as a message condemning the sinful behavior of hypocritical worshipers, expressed in the verse "I cannot abide sin along with solemn assemblies" (Isaiah 1:13). Isaiah was essentially saying, "It is *your* religious feasts, the way you engage in outward ritual while oppressing My people, that God abhors, not the actual religious feasts commanded by

God." And while the prophets clearly were spellbinding speakers, their purpose was often one that all of us would oppose:

> Make the heart of this people fat,
> Make their ears heavy and shut their eyes,
> Lest, seeing with their eyes, hearing with their ears, and understand-
>   ing with their hearts,
> They might turn and be healed.
>
> Isaiah 6:10

The prophets apparently spoke in a way to make people reject their message so that the Israelites would not repent prematurely and escape punishment for their misdeeds. At one point Isaiah mocks them, suggesting that everything they hear just sounds like nonsense syllables: *tzav latzav, kav lakav,* "here a little, there a little" (Isaiah 28:10). These were not the sermons the nineteenth-century Reformers would have chosen, because these texts suggest what they knew was true: that merely raging against people's behavior will not produce change. God indicates to Isaiah that it is too late for change; as free people whose mouths are not taken over by God but are in dialogue with the Holy One, we cannot believe that.

Inspired Preaching, Moral Acting

Given this critique, does anything remain that recommends the prophets to us as models of Reform Jewish practice in the twenty-first century? Two aspects of their message should continue to summon us. The first is the understanding that while redemptive action is what will change society, people need to be roused to action by stirring words. Literate people in the nineteenth century loved to listen to sermons and lectures. They were a major source for both entertainment and enlightenment in a time before film and television. But as the visual media swept away the dominance of the aural media in the latter part of the twentieth century, the literate sermon was one of the casualties. Of course there are still great Jewish preachers in all the movements, but they ply their craft much less frequently, sometimes only on the High Holy Days. If we wish to reinvigorate our commitments to social justice, we need to reinvigorate the prophetic sermon as a means to bring the message of biblical texts alive to people. Stirring sermons can lead people to feel so commanded by the words that they will stride out of the sanctuary to uncover the holiness that hides in the streets, in the failing schools, and in the shattered homes of our communities. It is not only hands that build new homes; hands must be motivated by inspired hearts.

What is the motivation? The second lasting contribution of the prophets is the message that the people's survival depends on their moral behavior. With all the celebration of ritual in the past generation, the Reform Movement has consistently warned, with the Talmud, that our insides must match our outsides, that our behavior to others must match our behavior to God. Having risen in North America from the poverty of the immigrant generation to relative prosperity, Jews need to be ever vigilant in heeding the prophets' call to practice economic and social justice.

In the latter part of the twentieth century, Reform Jews began to describe this call as a mission of *tikkun olam*, the repair of the world. The source of this phrase is found in the *Aleinu* prayer:

> Therefore we hope to You, *Adonai* our God,
> To look soon upon the glory of Your might,
> To cause idols to pass away from the earth and godlets to be totally
>   cut off,
> To repair the world [*l'takein olam*] through the dominion of the
>   Almighty.

What is remarkable about this prayer is the ambiguity regarding the identity of the agent bringing about the dominion of God, a synonym for the messianic age. We hope that we are the ones who will look upon the glory of God's might, but is it not God who will cause the idols to disappear? Do we hope that we or God will "repair the world"? The Reform Movement has treasured the ambiguity, convinced that we have an obligation to work hard in the business of repair, but knowing that without the will of God it will never come to pass.

The *Aleinu*, originally prescribed in the Talmud only for the Rosh HaShanah service, is the oldest source for the phrase *tikkun olam*, but in the seventeenth century, under the influence of the Lurianic kabbalists, it took on another meaning. Isaac Luria understood the creation of light on the first day to mean that God created a light too powerful for material vessels to contain, and so the vessels shattered, sending this primeval light into all the physical corners of the universe. The human task is to repair this shattering—*l'takein olam*, to repair the shattered world, by doing the mitzvot that cause us to interact with both material objects and human beings. Each act of fulfilling one of the mitzvot of the Torah would liberate the light from the object or creature in which it had fallen and put together piece after piece of the original light that had illumined the world. This understanding of the process of *tikkun olam* strengthens both pieces of the ambiguity of the *Aleinu* text and, following the example of Nachshon ben Aminadav, who was the first to step into the Reed Sea that God might split it, reinforces the sense that God waits upon human initiative to repair the world.

Each one of the platforms has stressed the importance of this concept:

> In full accordance with the spirit of Mosaic legislation, which strives to regulate the relation between rich and poor, we deem it our duty to participate in the great task of modern times, to solve, on the basis of justice and righteousness, the problems presented by the contrasts and evils of the present organization of society.
>
> Pittsburgh Platform (1885)

> Judaism seeks the attainment of a just society by the application of its teachings to the economic order, to industry and commerce, and to national and international affairs. It aims at the elimination of man-made misery and suffering, of poverty and degradation, of tyranny and slavery, of social inequality and prejudices, of ill-will and strife. It advocates the promotion of harmonious relations between warring classes on the basis of equity and justice, and the creation of conditions under which human personality may flourish.
>
> Columbus Platform (1937)

Attacking Bosses, Racists, Warmongers—and the USSR

But Reform's commitment to a prophetic *tikkun olam* has not been confined just to lofty statements on paper. As the prophets took the Torah's injunctions to do justly and made them live in the ears of their contemporaries, Reform has in every generation acted to bring peace and justice to the world and to its own communities. When the Torah speaks of assisting the poor neighbor (Leviticus 25:35, Deuteronomy 15:7–8), does it refer to Jews or non-Jews? The Reform Movement has had a clear answer: social justice is to extend to all people. In the nineteenth century, Reform rabbis were on both sides of the abolition question, but as the new century dawned, they became outspoken in favor of the rights of workers in struggles that created the labor movement. While many of the beneficiaries were Jews, of course, the thundering literature reads like a manifesto for the rights of all workers, whatever their faith. As the outlines of Hitler's designs against the Jews became clearer, Reform and other Jewish leaders courageously took on the government of the United States, speaking as forcefully as they felt they could for the rescue of European Jews. Reform rabbis were in the forefront of the civil rights struggle; one Reform lay leader, Kivie Kaplan, helped found the NAACP, and a number of Reform rabbis went to the South to join the Freedom Rides to hasten the end of segregation in one of the most violent eras America had seen.

Those of us who went to the South in those days will never forget watching Martin Luther King Jr. pore over the Book of Psalms in a black church to incorporate appropriate verses into his speeches rallying his followers to risk their lives and their livelihoods to push the struggle forward. We went there not primarily for political motives but out of the religious convictions Reform Judaism had bred in us, as it had in the brave Southern Reform rabbis who stood up for civil rights against often critical and fearful congregations. The black civil rights leaders also were sustained by their faith in the dangerous struggle for political change that would create a more moral society for blacks and whites. We did not go to the South to make ourselves feel better, as some charged at the time. We went because it was right; we went because we knew that our presence would help call attention to the struggle at a time when it was difficult for the civil rights movement to get press on its own.[1]

As the civil rights movement gathered steam, a group in California was beginning to seek rights for its own constituency, the migrant farm workers. Inspired by the same Gandhian principles as Martin Luther King Jr., Cesar Chavez began to organize these workers in the Central Valley and drew to his side Protestant ministers, Catholic priests, and some Reform rabbis. Rabbi Joseph B. Glaser, who at the time was the director of the Northern California office of the Union of American Hebrew Congregations and who later became executive vice president of the CCAR, was particularly involved in this cause. In both roles, Rabbi Glaser mobilized his colleagues and gave a national platform to Chavez and what became the United Farm Workers Union. Jews traveled to the fields, spoke to growers and store owners, and when they refused to budge, boycotted their products. Chavez was a deeply religious man, who would often undertake punishing fasts, as Gandhi did, to deepen the effects of his prayers and his work both on God and on the consciences of the growers and others who were resisting the farm workers. Reform and other synagogues around the country refused to serve boycotted grapes for years, an act that was rooted in the Torah: *Lo taashok et rei-acha*, "You shall not oppress your neighbor" (Leviticus 19:13). Abstaining from boycotted foods was a way to fulfill that mitzvah and remains today as a challenge to Reform Jews in their dietary choices.

The religious community also played a major role in the protest against the cruel war in Vietnam. The great scholar Rabbi Abraham Joshua Heschel was the most prominent national Jewish figure in that struggle, but many Reform Jews were on the front lines as well. Rabbis and others counseled young men terrified at the thought that the draft might force them to kill innocent people in a battle they felt was a civil war that the combatants needed to deal with themselves, and we helped them discover whether they held religious convictions against fighting in such a battle. Synagogues debated whether they should serve as sanctuaries for young men struggling against being drafted. There was a strong religious flavor to the endless rallies called to mobilize the country against the war and against the draft that sent the young to be slaughtered in it— indeed, the word "prophetic" was appropriate to describe the sermons of Rabbi Heschel, the two Father Berrigans, Rabbi Leonard Beerman, Rabbi Balfour Brickner, Rabbi Arnold Jacob Wolf, and many, many others.

The powerful involvement of Jews in the civil rights and Vietnam struggles caused some Jews to ask whether Jewish energies had been misspent on broader human struggles rather than focusing on specific Jewish needs that had no one else to champion. The Centenary Perspective (1976) tried to address this quandary:

Until the recent past our obligations to the Jewish people and to all humanity seemed congruent. At times now these two imperatives appear to conflict. We know of no simple way to resolve such tensions. We must, however, confront them without abandoning either of our commitments. A universal concern for humanity unaccompanied by a devotion to our particular people is self-destructive; a passion for our people without involvement in humankind contradicts what the prophets have meant to us. Judaism calls us simultaneously to universal and particular obligations.

The charge that Jewish activists were more interested in the needs of humanity in general than of Jews in particular was a hurtful one. Intruding into the belief that prevailed in the 1960s and early '70s that Jewish needs paled before those of the wider society came the gradual realization that half a world away, in that great fortress called the Soviet Union, lived Jews beginning to wage their own struggle against the massive power of a totalitarian state. From notes pressed into the palms of visitors and clandestine conversations in Soviet parks, word began to leak out that those Elie Wiesel once called "the Jews of silence" in the Soviet Union were trying to re-create Jewish life there and to make their way to Israel or other countries where they could live as Jews. Rabbis and laypeople from all the movements started traveling to the Soviet Union with a list of Soviet Jews who needed books to pray from and teach to children; later, they brought clothing that people who had been fired from their jobs might sell to support their families. Some of these visitors were followed and spied on; some were detained or thrown out of the country. All joined their Soviet Jewish hosts in prayer services behind closed blinds, made *Kiddush* over vodka, and wept as sweet, brave children showed off their Hebrew and sang songs. This remarkable effort was organized, it was later learned, by the government of the State of Israel to re-create Jewish life in the country and to lay the groundwork for a major emigration to Israel by Soviet Jews. In a few years, an increasing number of Soviet Jews were emboldened to apply for visas to Israel (and some to the United States), most of whom were refused. As a result, they came to be called "refuseniks." These brave Jews, however, did not identify with this name. They dropped the "d" because, they insisted, what was important was not that they had been refused visas, but that they themselves had done the refusing: refusing to bow down to fear of the Soviet state, refusing to obey Soviet laws against religious practice, refusing to go along with a state-approved official Jewish establishment. The refuseniks showed the world that they were Jews of silence no more.

This pattern of visitation and aid was repeated for the Jews of Ethiopia, as middle-class, middle-aged Jews rode donkeys through perilous mountains into impoverished villages, returning home with injured backs and broken hearts. But through the persistence of the Israelis and support from American and other Western Jews and their governments, what seemed like a miracle occurred: the Soviet Jews and the Ethiopian Jews were allowed to leave.

What did these miracles teach us? Was *tikkun olam* the responsibility of God or human beings? All of us who played some small role in the rescue of the Jews of those troubled countries could only look on with wonder—millions of prayers had been answered, heroism and martyrdom had been rewarded. Few of the great number of people involved with these efforts would say that geopolitical considerations alone had brought about these redemptions. To visit the former Soviet Union today and see the vibrant synagogues—many of them Reform—and Hillel foundations, to go to Israel and see how remarkably Ethiopian Jews have integrated themselves, should make any religious person weep. God has not forgotten the promise of redemption.

Where to Pursue Justice Today

Reform Jews have much to be proud of in our struggle for justice in this unhappy world. But veterans of the civil rights, farmworkers, Vietnam, and Soviet and Ethiopian Jewry struggles sometimes look back fondly on these noble campaigns and ask, "Where are the great causes today?" While the threat of war on Iraq evoked some of the largest protests the world has ever seen, they died down once Saddam Hussein was overthrown (though anger at the way the war was pushed through and the chaos that engulfed the country subsequently remained strong for a long time afterward). The imperative for prophetic struggle is less and less to be found within a mass movement in North American society. It is often said that as Reform Jews have embraced more and more traditional practice, our devotion to *tikkun olam* has weakened. I am not convinced of that. Inspired by the heroic work of the URJ's Religious Action Center, and particularly its gutsy director Rabbi David Saperstein, Reform congregations have undertaken a myriad of projects to improve the lot of those in their communities and elsewhere, from building homes for the homeless, to collecting and serving food to the poor, to tutoring children. Nor have these actions been only of a meliorative sort; they have included campaigns to save the environment, to protect women's rights to choose the destinies of their bodies and their lives, and other national issues as well. The Pittsburgh Principles offers an impressive catalog, suggesting that these represent nothing less than a fulfillment of the Deuteronomic call, *Tzedek, tzedek tirdof,* "Justice! Justice you shall pursue!" (Deuteronomy 16:20). The Pittsburgh Principles declares that "we are obligated to pursue *tzedek,* justice and righteousness." Living out this obligation can take many forms:

To narrow the gap between the affluent and the poor. Amos particularly excoriates the wealthy among his people for amassing winter houses and summer houses while selling the poor for a pair of shoes (Amos 8:6). The biblical image of *tzedek,* "justice," is of a balanced society, where no one is excessively wealthy and there are no poor at all. Deuteronomy 15:4 challenges us "There shall be no poor among you!" but ruefully acknowledges a few verses later that because of our unwillingness to redistribute the wealth of society, "The poor shall not cease from the midst of the land" (Deuteronomy 15:11). Leviticus 19 offers a solution, though: give the corners of your field to the poor, and leave the gleanings from your trees and grain for the needy. An elaborate series of *maas'rot*—taxes of one-tenth of income—is established to insure that the sanctuary and its priests are supported, as well as the poor. The English word "philanthropy" blends the Greek words for love and humanity, but the word for Jewish philanthropy is *tzedakah,* meaning "justice." Giving cannot merely flow from love; it needs to stem from a sense of commandedness. We need to give primarily because the poor are *entitled* to the corners of the field, because property belongs not to human owners but to God. Leviticus 25:23 reminds us that *li haaretz,* "the land belongs to Me!"—and not to us. God grants us a tenancy on the land; in the Bible, it returns to its original owner (a stand-in for God) every fifty years at the Jubilee. Between Jubilees, as we have seen, the poor are God's stand-ins, God's agents, in restoring the imbalance of wealth by harvesting our corners—the part that is only partially ours because it abuts the part that belongs to someone else. We bring Torah into the world by making the biblical mitzvot related to the poor part of the reality of our lives today. A movement serious about fulfilling these Torah and prophetic injunctions would examine what the corner of the field might mean to us, how a program of *maaseir*, working toward devoting a tenth of our income to *tzedakah*, might be developed. Groups of Jews (including several rabbis in the HUC-JIR class of 1998) have formed *tzedakah* collectives, giving an agreed-on percentage of their income to a fund that they distribute at year's end. Taxation for Jews should not be merely a political and fiscal issue; the nature of tax cuts and income redistribution is a religious issue rooted in the Torah itself.

To act against discrimination and oppression. The continued reminders to care for the stranger because our Egyptian bondage has let us know the nature of the stranger (Exodus 23:9) are intended as a constant goad to identify the strangers in our midst and investigate whether those individuals are being discriminated against, since (as Jews know well) once society has identified people as "strange," it is much easier to oppress them. Since the events of September 11, 2001, Muslims in the United States have been subjected to intense scrutiny and often shunned. To work on their behalf often takes particular fortitude, because so much of the Jewish community is wary of Muslims as being anti-Israel. Large numbers of people of color in America are still denied the kind of educational opportunities available to other ethnic groups. Are we willing to look beyond those blacks who are admitted to good schools and universities and ask what we can do to broaden opportunity? This effort can begin with our own people: there are congregations of Jewish African Americans in cities like Chicago, New York, and Philadelphia. Will we work together? More and more congregations have members with African American, Latino, and Asian roots—do ours? Do we reach out and get to know each other? Are we willing to work with church groups to build houses, staff homeless shelters, and improve conditions in poor communities in our cities? Are we willing to find out how to influence the legislative process to transform our cities and our states because we are a movement that hears the prophets reminding us that the societies we live in cannot survive unless we all work for justice? Are we ready to confront the meaning of what we say every year at the Pesach seder: *kol dichfin yeitei v'yeichul*, "Let all who are hungry come and eat"? The poor and the hungry are strangers to most of us (though the number of Jewish poor is growing again), and most of us, we must confess, would be uncomfortable inviting the men and women who stand at freeway exits home to our tables. As well as "selling" our *chameitz*, do we also give some of it to food banks, another way of showing our interdependence with non-Jews? Most communities have established Meot Chitim funds to enable all Jews to celebrate Passover, the holiday of freedom, but Reform Jews should see broader implications in this invitation. Many Reform (and other) congregations contribute three percent of their *simchah* bills to MAZON to help them alleviate hunger and the poverty that produces it around the world. To give to MAZON as individuals before Pesach arrives each year can help us make the Haggadah's challenging invitation more of a reality. No one whose poverty forces them to go hungry can be considered free.

To pursue peace. How frustrating this injunction has been! How most of us rejoiced in this century's first year when it briefly seemed as though the struggle between Israel and the Palestinians was almost over, only to have it seemingly set back by the intifada and Israel's unforgiving response. Beyond the hurt and anger of Israelis and Jews all over the world that a proffered peace was slapped down with unrelenting violence, if we are devoted to the pursuit of peace we need to remember that the outlines of peace conceived in the fall of 2000 remain the way in which peace must come to Israel and the Palestinians. Sending suicide bombers and recapturing Palestinian cities cannot blind us to that truth. While achieving it, of course, has proven wretchedly difficult, we can resolve to keep the attention of the Jewish world focused on the compromises—including an end to the settlements—that must be made. In Psalm 34:13–15 we are instructed: "Who is the person who desires life? The one who loves to seek good (all) one's days. Guard your tongue from hurtful speech, your lips from speaking guile; turn from hurting and do good, speak peace and pursue it." Prophetic utterances are found not only in the books of prophets;

this verse is a recipe for the *menschlach* life, beginning with simple acts of kindly speech and progressing to the search for opportunities to make peace. The verse reminds us that while war is usually presented as the only option in a conflict, there are many steps that can be taken to settle disputes peaceably, but like the mediation efforts spurned before the United States waged war on Iraq, we seem always too impatient to try them. What can we ordinary American Jews do in the Middle East? we ask hopelessly. We can start, the Psalmist reminds us, by looking for opportunities to make peace in our families, with our friends, at our work. Strengthened by those experiences, we can reach outward to explore and support opportunities for peacemaking on a larger scale. Absent a nationwide protest against a war, peacemaking often begins in a small arena, and sometimes it can grow.

To welcome the stranger. As we have seen, identifying individuals as strangers makes it easier to oppress them, but often we turn those we believe are oppressing us into strangers as well. One of the ways to work for peace is to get to know the stranger whom we sometimes perceive as the enemy—Palestinians, those people of color who may still inspire uneasiness or fear, black-hatted Orthodox Jews who call themselves *charedim,* "tremblers," who, we convince ourselves, disdain us without even knowing us. Jewish-Muslim dialogues have faltered in recent years, but they are important to rekindle, as are interracial and interfaith projects that move beyond "getting to know you" (as important a first step as that is) to actions that will better our societies. A generation ago Reform Jews who entered these gatherings often found that they were associating with non-Jews whose religious life was very important to them, and we felt awkward because we lacked the vocabulary to describe our faith and our religious experiences. Our greater embrace of Jewish religious language and practice over the past twenty-five to thirty years has changed that, and we should be able to enter into discussions and interfaith projects with a desire to articulate how these activities are part of our religious lives. The language of the prophets is not unknown to Christians and Muslims; the imagery of restoring the light of the world will be a welcome metaphor for all people of faith. As the voices of fundamentalists grow louder in the world, it is crucial that prophetic voices make themselves heard on issues of social justice, equality, and women's rights. To share discussions around a Shabbat table, an evening Ramadan meal, or a Catholic saint's day can remind us all that bridging faith and good works is an important *shiduch* for us all.

To protect the earth's biodiversity and natural resources. Through the Coalition on the Environmental and Jewish Life (COEJL), Reform and other Jewish organizations have created a forceful instrument for joining hands with other environmental groups and putting the weight of Jewish tradition into the uphill fight to protect an environment that the seekers of private gain attempt endlessly to defile. Protecting the environment is not an easy issue. People around the world need food and clothing and shelter and transportation, and it takes our natural resources to provide them. But the ideal of *tzedek* can guide us here as well: preserving a balance of the parts of God's creation to be utilized for human needs and the parts, in all their no longer infinite variety, that must be protected for the future not only of human needs but of all the creatures the Holy One brought into being. We can organize synagogue campaigns to buy hybrid automobiles that use a minimum of gasoline, to utilize devices that save water and electricity, to cut down on meat consumption (thus making more of the world's grain crop available for feeding hungry people instead of animals), and to publicize the real consequences of global warming and excess consumption of all natural resources, punishing government officials who ignore these issues. The charge to Adam and Eve regarding the earth, *l'ovdah ul'shomrah*, "to serve it and protect it" (Genesis 2:15), is as valid as when this verse first made its way into the Torah. Jewish tradition has other conservationist principles as well: *bal tashchit*, the injunction against needless destruction of nature, based on the command not to cut down fruit trees during a war (Deuteronomy 20:19–20); *tzaar baalei chayim*, a concern for the pain of living creatures, considered by the Rabbis as one of the Seven Noachide Laws given to all humanity. To devote time to the cause of protecting the earth is indeed to bring Torah out of the book and into the world.

To redeem those in physical, economic, and spiritual bondage. In a sense, this phrase puts all the previous examples into a clear religious context. It is the language of the covenant, a regard for all of God's Creation, a reminder of the imperatives of God's Revelation in Torah and articulated by the prophets, and a call to step into the sea of human bondage to lend an arm to God's redemptive work. If we are concerned only about the *zachor* part of Shabbat—savoring its holiness—and not the *shamor* part—easing the labor of those in our employ—we are falling prey to Isaiah's attack on "*your* religious feasts." Engaging the stranger, the war-weary, and the oppressed is as much a part of the Reform Jew's religious life as Shabbat, prayer, and kashrut. Integrating the ethical and ritual mitzvot is thus an imperative for Reform Jews: we *must* present a dietary plan that protects other humans and animals as well as nourishes us, and we must look for other ways to develop rituals that will make ethical action a habit of our lives rather than merely a nice thing to do when the synagogue bulletin announces a Mitzvah Day.

One Candle at a Time

What distinguishes the social justice examples outlined in the Pittsburgh Principles from the patterns of Reform social justice in the past is their small scale and relative invisibility. Whereas counseling conscientious objectors was invisible work too, it was part of a very visible national protest. Reform Jews who work in soup kitchens or write letters to members of Congress must in some ways be even more highly motivated to repair the world than previous generations, because there is so little outside encouragement of their efforts and so much doubt as to whether these small actions can really do any good. Even if we were to coalesce around creating major legislation to lessen poverty or preserve a biologically diverse environment, this will be a process demanding much time, persistence, patience, and major compromise. In some ways, the prophetic actions of the early twenty-first century are more in keeping with the kabbalistic idea of *tikkun olam*, taking one material or human vessel at a time—a bill in Congress, a house, a bowl of soup, a single wounded soul—and liberating the light hidden within, restoring that soul to his or her place as a creature of God.

Are these incremental acts of social justice enough to "help bring nearer the messianic age" (*mashiachtzeit* in Yiddish)? One way of answering that question is to see *mashiachtzeit* as the antithesis of the "unspeakable evils" that gutted so much of the twentieth century. If strengthening the forces of *tov* in the world is the best way to tear down the walls of *ra* and chaos, then doing mitzvot—with God and other human beings—is the way to accomplish it. One might even argue that in the (very) long run, it is more effective than our classic models for social action, the great campaigns of the labor movement, civil rights, Vietnam, and Soviet Jewry. Each of those campaigns was directed toward a goal, and one knew, more or less, when the goal had been achieved. But social activists in the twenty-first century know that our work is a long-term campaign, and while each house built and each family redeemed from poverty is a victory, there are myriads of "victories" to be achieved before the messianic goal is reached. Engaging in social justice today is much harder than in the days of the great campaigns, but potentially more lasting. Deuteronomy's realization that the poor will always be with us is a reminder that just as prayer, keeping Shabbat and the Festivals, and kashrut are activities that must endure day after day, year after year, so are the mitzvot comprising social justice. It was easier to give powerful sermons around labor and civil rights and Vietnam, which is why powerful, prophetic preaching is needed even more today. "I hate, I despise your festivals. . . . " Do we celebrate our festivals in a way that will hasten the age of universal justice and peace?

Every day when I drive to the Hebrew Union College, I exit the freeway by an off-ramp where a sad, grizzled man stands. It is not always the same man, but the weary eyes and the lined faces have much in common. Should I reach into my wallet and hand him some dollar bills? Voices crowd in on me: "Don't give him money—give him something to eat; take him to a fast food stand and get him a salad!" "Give him the address of the nearest shelter or food pantry—even better, take him there!" "You're only giving him a couple of dollars?!" Isaiah rebukes me: "Tear up loaves for the hungry, and bring the poor wanderer home!" But I also hear Maimonides' voice: "The minimum rung of *tzedakah* is giving reluctantly when asked"—to offer a few dollars would at least put me on the ladder. And like the black protesters in the South, the Hispanic marchers in the Central Valley, and the refuseniks studying behind closed blinds, this man could take some comfort from my little donation, as car after car whizzes by him, that he is not invisible. While I am agonizing, I see ahead of me a compassionate face in the driver's rearview mirror. The car window rolls down, and a hand with bills reaches out to the man on the off-ramp. "Bless you," I hear the man say quietly.

Blessed be those who let in the light by rolling down a car window. Small amounts of light can grow into a great *tikkun*.

In all these ways and more, Torah gives meaning and purpose to our lives.

THE
REFORM JEW
IN DIALOGUE
WITH THE
JEWISH PEOPLE

12

Ahavat Yisrael and *K'lal Yisrael*:
How a Universal Movement
Fell in Love
with a Diverse Jewish People

We are Israel, a people aspiring to holiness, singled out through our ancient covenant and our unique history among the nations to be witnesses to God's presence. We are linked by that covenant and that history to all Jews in every age and place.

We are committed to the *mitzvah* of *ahavat Yisrael*, love for the Jewish people, and to *k'lal Yisrael*, the entirety of the community of Israel. Recognizing that *kol Yisrael arevim zeh ba-zeh*, all Jews are responsible for one another, we reach out to all Jews across ideological and geographical boundaries.

We embrace religious and cultural pluralism as an expression of the vitality of Jewish communal life in Israel and the Diaspora.

—Statement of Principles, "Israel," paragraphs 1–2

A Religion, Not a People

Of all the issues in Jewish life and thought, Reform has had the most difficult time with matters relating to Jewish peoplehood.

Reform Judaism in North America grew out of a passionate commitment to Judaism and to the belief that the New World promised a more enlightened, strife-free existence for all people. This new form of Judaism seemed a perfect fit for this new land, which unlike the European reality left behind, offered freedom of religion and equality of its citizens. In both Canada and the United States, Jews could be free to practice Judaism as they wished while simultaneously taking full advantage of the freedom and opportunities available to all in the New World. In this new environment, Jews could define their Judaism rather than be defined or limited by it. But alas, Reform was born in strife and often engendered it: in the nineteenth century, more-traditional Jews opposed the changes Reform was advocating, and its leaders engaged the Reformers in heated arguments in the newspapers they created and in well-attended public lectures. While from Cincinnati Isaac Mayer Wise attempted to bring all American Jews under the umbrella of a single American Judaism in the optimistic belief that in this new country, Jews could put past differences behind them, his colleagues on the eastern seaboard—who were either more realistic or more pessimistic than he—believed that a division of Jews into different streams was inevitable and even, for clarity's sake, desirable.

This immersion in controversy may well have contributed to a feeling among many Reform Jews that their allegiance was to Judaism rather than to the Jewish people. The universalistic beliefs of the Reformers fostered by the openness and democratic values of the New World discouraged them from feeling a greater affinity for human beings who were Jewish over other human beings, particularly since Reform Jews held that Jewishness was a religious belief, a matter of individual decision, and not an ethnic trait. How could there be any intrinsic value in the existence of one particular people, even (or especially) if it was one's own? To give preferential treatment to one's own group would seem to deny the universal applicability of the truths that people promulgated.

The 1885 Pittsburgh Platform emphasized only the religious significance of "the Jewish people," with "its mission as the priest of the one God," adding, "We consider ourselves no longer a nation but a religious community."

While the Columbus Platform of 1937 tried to integrate the actual life of the people into the nature of Judaism, asserting that "Judaism is the historical religious experience of the Jewish people," ultimately the Columbus Platform, like the Pittsburgh Platform of 1885, maintains that the people's purpose is primarily, if not solely, as a vessel for the religion: "Judaism is the soul of which Israel is the body. . . . We maintain that it is by its religion and for its religion that the Jewish people has lived."

Without its religion, the Jewish people, like a soulless body, is dead. By "call[ing] upon our fellow Jews" to embrace the principles of the Columbus Platform, the rabbis who adopted it in 1937 suggested that this was the way to resuscitate a people demoralized by the ominous shadow growing ever darker across the seas.

By the time the full implications of those events had dawned on a diminished and shattered people, the perspective of the Reform Movement had changed regarding the body of which "Judaism is the soul." The 1976 Centenary Perspective was promulgated more than thirty years after the Nazis were defeated, but less than a decade after serious reflection on its enormity had begun. It also appeared only three years after the outbreak of the Yom Kippur War, which exposed many Jews to the continued vulnerability of the State of Israel and thus the Jewish people. The Centenary Perspective said solemnly, "We have learned again that the survival of the Jewish people is of highest priority." While the earlier stress on Jewish religion is suggested in the rest of that sentence ("in carrying out our Jewish responsibilities we help move humanity to its messianic fulfillment"), the emphasis on the survival of the Jewish people for its own sake is unmistakable:

> The State of Israel, through its many accomplishments, raised our sense of the Jews as a people to new heights of aspiration and devotion. . . .
> Jews, by birth or conversion, constitute an uncommon union of faith and peoplehood. . . . [W]e are bound together like all ethnic groups by language, land, history, culture and institutions. But the people of Israel is unique because of its involvement with God. . . .

It continues, "Throughout our long history our people has been inseparable from its religion," suggesting a rejection of both the people-faith duality of the Columbus Platform as well as the view that the Jewish people had value only as the carrier of the Jewish religion. In the

Centenary Perspective there is even the sense that affirmation of Jewish peoplehood is an obligation. The Pittsburgh Principles goes further—from obligation to Jews it would move us to love of Jews:

> We are committed to the *mitzvah* of *ahavat Yisrael*, love for the Jewish people, and to *k'lal Yisrael*, the entirety of the community of Israel.

Obligation, as we have seen throughout the Statement of Principles, is defined as heeding the call of mitzvot. Here, though, obligation to the Jewish people is articulated not as survival, as in the Centenary Perspective, but as love. What does it mean to love the Jewish people? Does it also mean to love Jews? All Jews? And why should we love them?

Striving for Holiness

The first paragraph of the Israel section suggests a reason: "We are Israel, a people aspiring to holiness." In earlier drafts of the Pittsburgh Principles, Israel was called "a holy people," but the task force that composed the final document felt it was arrogant to state that Israel has already achieved full holiness.[1] Rather, we adhered to the implications of Leviticus 19:2: *K'doshim tih'yu ki kadosh ani Adonai Eloheichem*, "You shall be holy for I, *Adonai* your God, am holy," emphasizing that the attainment of holiness is a lifelong process. Thus our value is not merely as a passive vessel for the Jewish religion, but in our active commitment to increase the holiness of our actions and our lives. In terms of the soul-body dichotomy between universal truth and a particular people, as aspirants to holiness the Jewish people can show other people how to embody the truths in daily life—as we Jews imbue our lives with holiness, so can others.

But who is this "we"? It is a question we have considered before. Does it empirically mean "every single Jew"? There is no way, short of interviewing every single Jew, to know that. However, the statement does suggest a belief that by being a member of "a people aspiring to holiness," every single Jew should be assumed to be engaged in that task. It suggests that an acknowledgment of our membership in the Jewish people makes each Jew aware that we *should* be aspiring to holiness. Our positive actions should be recognized as attempts to fulfill that aspiration, while our negative actions should be assumed to take place against a backdrop of regret for our shortcomings. After all, a large number of Jews do come to Yom Kippur services; at least once a year we are aware of the gap between our holy aspirations and our ordinary failings.

If that is what being a Jew means, no wonder we are commanded to love Jews! How can we not love a person who is struggling every day to live a holy life, or at the minimum is aware of not living a holy life.

This belief is not the Pittsburgh Principles' only basis for *ahavat Yisrael.* Not only should we view every Jew as struggling with the mitzvah of living a holy life, we are encouraged to see Jews as "singled out . . . to be witnesses to God's presence." What does that mean?

When Isaiah (43:10) hears God proclaiming, *Atem eidai,* "You are My witnesses," God continues, "and [you are] My servant whom I have chosen in order that you may know and believe in Me and understand that I existed before any god was created and there will be nothing after Me." As a people we have been witnesses to God's power by our continued existence, absurd as our survival may seem in the face of constant oppression since our formation. Nothing but God's will can account for this survival, hence the famous midrash about the way the *Sh'ma,* the central statement of Israel's belief in one God, is written in the Torah scroll. An enlarged letter *ayin* concludes the word *Sh'ma* (Hear) and an enlarged letter *dalet* concludes the word *Echad* (One). Together, *ayin* and *dalet* spell *eid,* "witness," suggesting to the Rabbis that when we affirm the reality of God's unique existence, our continued existence bears witness to God's. The Rabbis suggest (Babylonian Talmud, *B'rachot* 6a) that God has a reciprocal verse inscribed in the *t'fillin* that God dons each day: "Who is like Israel, one unique people in the earth!" (I Chronicles 17:21). By stressing that our mere existence bears witness to God's power, we move beyond the indication in the Centenary Perspective that ensuring the survival of the Jewish people is the responsibility of Jews. It is God who has ensured our survival since the promise to Abraham (Genesis 15:5) that we would be as numerous as the uncountable stars in heaven. Survival should not be our concern; the Jewish people's existence *is* a universal truth. Our existence as a Jewish people is evidence—a witness—of God's saving presence in the world. Striving to be holy—imbuing with an awareness of God's presence and mitzvot the ordinary acts of encountering nature, interacting compassionately with other people, eating and speaking and working—is the way we transform our particular existence into a witness of a universal God, a God who helps all people discover aspects of a universal holiness in their own particular existence.

Many Chosen Peoples

This way of living in the world is part of what we have historically understood as the meaning of the "chosen people." The Pittsburgh Principles does not use the word "chosen"—none of the platforms does—but unlike Reconstructionist Judaism, Reform has always embraced it. With all the changes the early Reformers wrought in the prayer book, they never excised from the Shabbat and Festival *Kiddush* or the Torah blessings the praise of God *asher bachar banu mikol haamim,* "who has chosen us from among all the peoples." Yet while the 1999 Pittsburgh Principles may not use the term "chosen people," it does define what the concept means for us today: "singled out through our ancient covenant and our unique history among the nations to be witnesses to God's presence." *Mikol haamim,* "from among all the peoples," here is interpreted to mean not that we were chosen to be better than the (other) peoples, but that our experience *among the peoples* offered us a stage to demonstrate that God desired our eternal existence. Like wise parents who see each of their children as chosen for different destinies, so we believe in a God who declared that Ishmael (father of the Arabs) and Esau (father of the Europeans) would each become a great nation. "Are you not like the Ethiopians to Me?" Amos hears God thunder. "Just as I brought you out of Egypt, did I not bring the Philistines from Caphtor [Crete] and Aram from Kir?" (Amos 9:7). We are not intrinsically superior to the nations; our chosenness lies in our destiny to strive to be holy, in accord with the mitzvot of the Torah, demonstrating that our belief in God makes such a demanding life worthwhile. Merely by continuing to exist as Jews, we bear witness to God's existence. The way in which we live our lives shows others what God means to us—indeed, what God's nature might be.

Yet *ahavat Yisrael* is based on more than a sense of shared mission. What if it were proven that a majority of Jews does not strive to be holy? Would these Jews lose their right to be loved by us? No, the Pittsburgh Principles asserts: the covenant with Abraham and the covenant at Sinai, the five-thousand-year-old history we share through birth or conversion, engender within us a love for all with whom we have shared that history.

We are not always aware of that innate love. We are sometimes harsher on Jews who act wrongly than we are on non-Jews (though sometimes the opposite is also true). Our sharp response to Jewish behaviors can itself be seen as powerful evidence for our *ahavat Yisrael*. These feelings stem both from resentment against Jews who are not striving hard enough to be holy, as well as from a sense of kinship with someone who shares "that covenant and that history." It is analogous to our feelings for cousins who have acted improperly—we condemn them in a way we would not do to those outside the family. How does this apply to converts? The answer is obvious—in the same way that relatives by marriage become family.

What role does *ahavat Yisrael* play in the tension between universal truth and particular people? How do today's Reform Jews reconcile this special love with our classic devotion to the universality of the human race? Are not all human beings created *b'tzelem Elohim*, in the image of God?

The Centenary Perspective sees this question as a tension to be confronted without abandoning either position: "A universal concern for humanity unaccompanied by a devotion to our particular people is self-destructive; a passion for our people without involvement in humankind contradicts what the prophets have meant to us." But as we have seen, it should be possible not just to confront both but to integrate both; this is part of the meaning of "dialogue" as opposed to "autonomy." The very act of entering into dialogue between *ahavat Yisrael* and *ahavat haamim* (love of all peoples) is an act of interrelationship. In every human being is a spark of God; in every human being we get a glimpse of God. Human beings who strive to live up to the Noachide Laws[2] or to the standards of their own religion not only reveal a godly spark, they enable the spark to expand into a flame that makes

God's presence manifest on earth. We need to recognize the human spark in Jews as well, to mitigate our harsh judgment of some Jews by reminding ourselves that as human beings they still bear the spark of God.

Responsibility for All Jews

Sometimes all Jews need a push to remember that *ahavat Yisrael* extends to Jews of movements other than our own. This may help to explain why *ahavat Yisrael* was a difficult concept for the beleaguered Reform Jews of the early years of our movement. Attacks on us by more traditional Jews have not let up; stances taken by Reform Jews that fly in the face of the halachic principles of other Jews have also not abated. When strife between the streams of Judaism roils in Israel, it is echoed in North America, and in the waning years of the twentieth century there was no lack of strife. Orthodox Jews challenged the legitimacy of Reform conversions, even those conforming to the halachah; Reform Jews publicly reaffirmed their quiet nineteenth-century stance that Jewishness should stem from either the father (as in biblical times) or the mother (a Talmudic innovation now the norm among the rest of Jewry); Reform championed the cause of gay and lesbian Jews, and especially of marital or commitment ceremonies between gay or lesbian Jews. The vitriol on both sides rivaled the bruising debates in the warring newspapers of Isaac Mayer Wise and his opponents.

Despite (or because of) this, the Reform rabbis gathered in Pittsburgh in 1999 incorporated into the Statement of Principles an affirmation of intra-Jewish cooperation not found in any of the previous platforms. On the Talmudic principle that *kol Yisrael arevim zeh ba-zeh*, "all Jews are responsible for one another," it affirmed that "we reach out to all Jews across ideological and geographic boundaries."

The principle of *kol Yisrael arevim zeh ba-zeh* is an extreme one. The word *arevim*, here translated "are responsible," literally means "are surety for"—the language of fiscal and moral liability. The Babylonian Talmud (*Sanhedrin* 27b) suggests that every Jew be considered ready to post a moral bond for any other Jew, whether we know that person or not. By including this phrase, the Pittsburgh Principles suggests that a Reform

Jew should, for example, be willing to stand by a Jew in trouble even if that person has been attacking Reform Judaism in print over our stance on patrilineality. If any of us is not ready to assist such a Jew, we need to begin a dialogue with that person to discover our relationship as fellow Jews. The Pittsburgh Principles states, "We reach out"; we need to take the initiative, because as Reform Jews we know we need to embrace *ahavat Yisrael* and *arevut Yisrael*, the sense of responsibility for other Jews.

This approach may sound like the Christian idea of "turning the other cheek" or "loving your enemy" (Matthew 5:38–45), but it's actually quite different. In *Avot D'Rabbi Natan* (23) we read, "Who is the most mighty? Whoever turns an enemy into a friend." The essence of *ahavat Yisrael*, in opposition to the Pittsburgh Platform and Columbus Platform definitions of a Jew, is that whatever one's beliefs or practices, we are enjoined to love all Jews. Whatever they may do (and wrongful deeds of course need to be punished), we are to feel love for them. Some contemporary spokespersons for Orthodox Judaism are careful these days to speak against Reform or Conservative *Judaism*, not Reform or Conservative *Jews*. It is our beliefs and practices that they oppose, not us. But we need to emphasize that our beliefs and practices are part of us, that *ahavat Yisrael* means to love us, warts and all, patrilineality and all.

Are we willing to do the same? Are we ready to unconditionally love our Orthodox neighbors, *m'chitzah* (separate synagogue seating for women and men) and all? What would that mean? The statement "we reach out to all Jews across ideological and geographical boundaries" suggests an answer. When most Ashkenazic Jews with roots in Poland or Russia meet Sephardic Jews with roots in Turkey or Iraq, they are fascinated by their different customs. Few Ashkenazic Jews will eat rice on Pesach because it is simply not in their tradition despite the fact that Sephardic Jews do, and while an Ashkenazic congregation may borrow a Sephardic melody now and then, it is unlikely to borrow the style of a Sephardic service. Ashkenazic Jews seldom feel threatened or criticized by their differences from Sephardic practices, but these feelings often surface in Reform-Orthodox confrontations. Arguments arise over halachic practice and issues of authenticity, not ethnic customs.

If we were able to see our relations with other ideological streams in Judaism as we see our relations with other historical or geographical streams, we might be able to learn how to dialogue rather than threaten each other. Reform has affirmed patrilineality since the late 1800s; we are unlikely to reverse that stand. Similarly, Orthodox Jews are unlikely to abandon separate seating. While there is some porousness in the movements (Orthodox women are being given more halachic authority in some sectors; some Reform Jews are beginning to use a *mikveh*), the basic boundaries of the movements will remain the same, just as Ashkenazic and Sephardic customs will. Let us then reach out to each other and learn about each other, so that we will each become less threatening. Such conversation will help us discover what is lovable in these members of the Jewish people, so we can learn to love not only Jews in the aggregate but individual Jews as well. We cannot engage in this conversation alone, but we can take the initiative. We can begin to search for Orthodox Jews in places where we can share our commitments (in Federation campaigns, community Mitzvah Days, support groups for poor and homeless Jews), and then invite the friends we make to join us in social conversations about beliefs and practices. Rabbis in different movements can also reach out to colleagues they encounter at Boards of Rabbis or Federation meetings. Reform rabbis can also gently remind their Orthodox colleagues that it was their choice to respond to the patrilineal decision with such hostile acts as refusing to marry any Reform Jews without checking into their family histories; less punitive responses would also have been possible. To learn about, acknowledge, and even come to appreciate the different beliefs and practices in the Jewish world will help us model "religious and cultural pluralism as an expression of the vitality of Jewish communal life in Israel and the Diaspora."

Spreading Our Message through K'lal Yisrael

This brings us to the final topic of this chapter, one perhaps even more anxiety-ridden than *ahavat Yisrael*, and that is *k'lal Yisrael*, "the entirety of the community of Israel." When the Reform Movement has taken stands in opposition to the rest of the Jewish world, some Reform Jews have opposed those stands based on a concern about *k'lal Yisrael*, arguing for the integrity of the bonds that link us to the wider Jewish community.

The intrareligious strife that has marked the history of American Judaism has made *k'lal Yisrael* a difficult concept for Reform Jews to embrace. First, this ideal seems to point to an overarching unity of the Jewish people that should transcend the hegemony of each movement, threatening any notion of each movement's "autonomy." In addition, there is a suspicion that to defer to sensitivities of *k'lal Yisrael* is to betray a weakness or a lack of conviction about the authority of Reform. When *k'lal Yisrael* is mentioned, some Reform Jews ask bitterly, "Why should we be concerned with what other Jews think? Are they concerned about our opinion?"

The Pittsburgh Principles clearly rejects these attitudes. Its substitution of "dialogue" for "autonomy" shows how *k'lal Yisrael* is an appropriate piece of twenty-first-century Reform Judaism: We respond to other streams of Judaism not by continuing controversy but through conversation. Our choices need not be either triumphalist or self-abasing, but respectful of a common tradition and a shared history. We also need to commit ourselves to acknowledge that we will probably always see some issues differently and therefore need to work to better understand each other's position and be more responsive to each other's concerns.

Far more than in the past, we need to take into account the effect of our policies on the rest of world Jewry, exploring less confrontative, more embracing methods of taking controversial stands. Had the CCAR in 1985 sat down with Orthodox and Conservative colleagues and asked, "What will be the effect of a public announcement of our patrilineal position?" we might have concluded that a public announcement of this almost hundred-year-old stand was not necessary, or we might have discovered a less divisive way of making the announcement.

There is another, more assertive way to respond to the challenge of *k'lal Yisrael*. Dialogue on controversial issues can not only soften the impact of divisive decisions, it can encourage the making of decisions that alleviate problems not only for Reform Jews, but for all Jews. Concern for *k'lal Yisrael* is appropriate for twenty-first-century Reform Judaism because none of the contemporary streams of Judaism can delude ourselves anymore that we live in isolation from each other. The Orthodox understood more quickly than we how the reaffirmation of patrilineality would affect them. But we have sometimes understood more readily than other streams that while our solutions may differ from theirs, we all share the same issues. If we cannot agree on the answers, at least we need to help open each other's eyes to the problems. If we care about Jews on the margins of our movement, we need to care about Jews on the margins of other movements by encouraging those movements to deal with their marginalized members. It is naive to think that marginalized Jews will all become Reform; if we care about them as individuals, we need to be their advocates to the movements in which they would like to feel at home. We need to push our colleagues in other movements to face our common issues so that the individual Jews touched by these issues may know that their part of the Jewish world embraces them.

Patrilineality is a response to the issue of intermarriage, which has made such devastating inroads on the future of Jewish families. The Talmud considers the child of an intermarriage Jewish only if the mother is Jewish. Reform Judaism asks, Why should we lose the child whose father is the sole Jewish parent, especially since the Bible, with its stress on patriarchy, offers a precedent for accepting that child as wholly Jewish? How will our sister movements deal with the pain of a parent who has tried to raise a son as a Jew, only to find that the young man has fallen in love with a non-Jew, as a result of which the grandchild will be rejected from Jewish institutions because the "wrong" parent was Jewish? Can we help Orthodox and Conservative leaders develop sufficient empathy for that grandparent that if they will not accept the child's Jewishness, they would refer the family to us? If they did so, we could expose the family to Jewish education and observance, which one day could lead the child to desire recognition of his or her Jewishness by the rest of the Jewish world through a formal, halachic conversion. We must try to find ways to persuade our sister movements to work with us in retaining such Jews, for the welfare of the Jewish people as a whole.

When the Reform rabbinate affirmed the religious value of same-gender unions, we were impelled by a similar desire to embrace the Jewish concerns of people whom the majority of the Jewish community has marginalized. We asked how Reform Jews could help to reverse that marginalization. There are gays and lesbians in Orthodox and Conservative synagogues too. Surely by talking more with each other, the movements can figure out how to alleviate the sense of isolation and fear on the part of gay and lesbian Jews and give them more outlets to fulfill their desire to be faithful to the mitzvot that call them. However they may view homosexuality, do our sister movements really want to lose gay and lesbian Jews as they have been losing intermarried families? Does not *ahavat Yisrael* apply to these Jews as well?

Given our differences, to initiate such a dialogue among the different streams of Judaism may be the best way for Reform Jews to model a new sort of pluralism for the Jewish world today. By taking each other's positions seriously and respectfully, by learning with and from each other, we can demonstrate to the Jewish people how vibrant is a Jewry that offers so many different approaches to learning, to observance, and indeed, to existence itself.

Transdenominationalism Is Not the Answer

Increasingly, some Jewish leaders are starting to question the value of all these different approaches. Some of them call on us not only to embrace other Jewish movements but to become "transdenominational," weakening our commitment to our own, or even abandoning it. In periods when Orthodox and Reform Jews throw barbs at each other, when Conservative Jews and black-hatted *charedim* insult each other, it is tempting to cry with Shakespeare's Mercutio, "A plague o' both your houses!" (*Romeo and Juliet,* act 3, scene 1). But this is the same argument that motivates those who forswear religion entirely because it has been the cause of so many wars, denying the life-changing gifts religion brings to its serious adherents, focusing only on the perverse use that some intemperate people make of those gifts. American Jewish life would pale significantly if all the non-Orthodox movements were to merge, for that would deny the special attractions of our own synagogues, our own liturgies, our own camps and public gatherings, our ties to the schools and seminaries of our own movements. For the non-Orthodox movements do differ significantly from each other, as this book and many others have tried to demonstrate, and these differences stem from histories that have helped to mold our unique contributions to Jewish life and our unique interpretations of Jewish ideas. In the struggles each movement undergoes, we are challenged to discover new aspects of God and Torah, and moving new rituals that illumine both for us. If the messianic age will reveal which kinds of Judaism are truly beloved of God, do we not need to support the flowering of a myriad of ideas and practices to make sure that what emerge in the end are really the best?

Having been a Hillel rabbi for thirty-one years, I know the benefits of spending time in an environment where Jews of all stripes mingle, study, and pray within the same walls. But Hillel has been weakest when it has insisted on a single worship service for all students, a single *Birkat HaMazon* (Blessing after Meals), a study series with only one kind of speaker. These environments did not feel transdenominational; rather they felt comfortable for some and alien to others. When synagogues from different movements, often in small communities, are forced to merge lest they both go under financially, everyone is usually unhappy, and while people may continue to attend, they do so because they have no other choice. In larger communities in North America, diverse groups do not have to merge—which often means to submerge—but rather preserve the freedom to visit each other's synagogues and study groups, integrate good ideas with their own, but know that they always have a home. The strongest Hillel Foundations are those that support worship services from all the movements but offer opportunities for students strengthened by their own services to mingle with those from other streams in activities that do not threaten their own religious integrity. We can show our love for other Jews most fervently when we feel loved and supported by movements that feel like home.

Believing that God created a Jewish people to embody God's Torah as a witness to God's other peoples, Reform Jews of the twenty-first century understand that love for that people is a manifestation of our love for God. If we love Jews, we need to feel a responsibility for how the Jewish community relates to the individual Jews in its midst, that we may help all Jews to recognize and live out the invitations to holiness that the Torah extends to us. Patterning our approach to other movements on our dialogue with Jews from different parts of the globe, we can encourage our people to learn about the other streams—and other less formal approaches to Jewish life—in a manner that shows we are not afraid of their influence, nor are we insecure about the value of our own approaches, but are convinced that indeed Torah is the dialogue between "God's ongoing revelation to our people and . . . our people's ongoing relationship with God." To the extent that intra-Jewish squabbling further alienates wavering Jews from Jewish study and practice and indeed from the Jewish community, we shall be striking a blow for the inclusiveness of Jews who prefer their religion to be mutually respectful rather than confrontational. Perhaps in our generation—or at least in our century—we can finally call a truce in the long strife between the movements that has so long blinded us to the values of the different destinies that God has bequeathed to each family of the Children of Israel.

13

Equality and "Full Rights
to Practice Judaism":
Are They Compatible?

We pledge to fulfill Reform Judaism's historic commitment to the complete equality of women and men in Jewish life.

We are an inclusive community, opening doors to Jewish life to people of all ages, to varied kinds of families; to all regardless of their sexual orientation; to *gerim*, those who have converted to Judaism; and to all individuals and families, including the intermarried, who strive to create a Jewish home.
                    —Statement of Principles, "Israel," paragraphs 4–5

Sally Priesand Opens the Door

"Ten adults, male or female, make a minyan," Isaac Mayer Wise proclaimed at the beginning of the Shabbat morning service in his prayer book *Minhag America: The Daily Prayers for American Israelites*, published in 1872. In an 1876 essay called "Women as Members of Congregations,"[1] he argued forcefully that women should be allowed to be members of congregations in their own right. In Europe, Reform had been breaking down the rigid physical separation of women from men by removing the *m'chitzah* (divider between the men's and women's sections) and instituting mixed seating. While neither the

Pittsburgh nor the Columbus Platform differentiates women from men (each reflecting the Enlightenment usage of "man" as a synonym for "human being"), the Centenary Perspective reflects the growing cultural sensitivity to the indignity of this custom. The Centenary Perspective asserts that "substantial numbers have accepted [Reform's] teachings . . . that women should have full rights to practice Judaism." A capstone of this development was HUC president Alfred Gottschalk's 1972 ordination of Sally Priesand, the first woman rabbi in North America; by 2001, over 300 women had been ordained by the Reform Movement. My teacher Eugene Mihaly (*z"l*), professor of midrash at the Cincinnati campus of HUC-JIR, heralded Sally Priesand's ordination in a sermon for her installation at the Stephen Wise Free Synagogue in New York by quoting the midrash comparing Abraham's departure from Haran for the Holy Land to the uncorking of a bottle of perfume. As Abraham's departure from Babylonia inaugurated the spread of God's teachings into the Middle East, so Sally's call to the pulpit of the Free Synagogue signaled the release of the particular insights and talents of women to the leadership of the Jewish world. Since then, women have been invested as cantors and have served as presidents of congregations; indeed women have occupied all the offices that exist within the Reform Jewish world. In 2003 Rabbi Janet Marder was elected president of the Central Conference of American Rabbis, the first woman elected to head a national rabbinic organization. Women have clearly enjoyed equality of responsibility in the Reform Movement.

There is an interesting distinction between the language of the Centenary Perspective and that of the Pittsburgh Principles. While the Pittsburgh Principles speaks of "complete equality of women and men in Jewish life," the Centenary Perspective cites Reform's teaching "that women should have full rights to practice Judaism." The 1976 document does not use the word "equality," implying that there may be areas of Jewish practice in which men and women differ, while the Pittsburgh Principles goes further, suggesting that not only religious practice but everything involved in Jewish life needs to be open equally to men and women. Is there a contradiction between these two statements?

Excluding Everyone: Antidote to Inequality?

In the nineteenth century, the Reform Movement made several efforts to reduce the inequality between men and women, but it sometimes did so by eliminating the areas in which the inequality existed. Women cannot serve as *eidim* (witnesses) before a *beit din*, a Jewish court? Eliminate the *beit din*—and therefore its need for witnesses. Women cannot be counted in a traditional minyan? Eliminate the need for a minyan. The requirement of a *mikveh* (immersion in a ritual pool) puts unequal burdens on a woman during her menstrual cycle? Eliminate the *mikveh*. These approaches to securing equality in the early period of Reform paradoxically lessened the "full rights" of both men and women to practice Judaism. In some ways then, the equality Reform Jewish women have achieved is a shrunken one. In Orthodox Judaism, women cannot be *soferim* (scribes), *shochatim* (kosher slaughterers), *mohalim* (performers of ritual circumcision), members of a *beit din* (a Jewish court), or *eidim* (witnesses). As a growing number of Reform rabbis have reintroduced the *beit din* to approve converts' entry into Judaism, women as well as men can serve as members. Women can be *mohalim* (the feminine form is *mohalot*) if, like men, they are medically certified to do surgical circumcisions and have been trained by the Berit Mila Board of Reform Judaism. But you will not find women—or Reform men—occupying any of the other roles listed above, because they do not exist within the Reform Movement. Reform congregations purchase Torah scrolls and mezuzot written by Orthodox *soferim*. When Reform Jews buy kosher meat, it has been slaughtered by Orthodox *shochatim* and sold in kosher butcher shops run by Orthodox Jews under the direction of Orthodox *mashgichim*, kosher supervisors. If, as the Pittsburgh Principles suggests, Reform Jews are increasingly open to experiencing *k'dushah* in the areas of life governed by these professions, should we not be producing our own professionals, especially since, as we have seen, Reform is expanding the horizons of these fields in directions that, at present, Orthodox professionals would not be willing to go?

Even Reform men's and women's opportunities to serve on a *beit din* are limited. A traditional *beit din* oversees conversions, issues Jewish divorces, and seeks *eidim* to settle civil matters. The Reform Movement's *batei din* exist almost exclusively to certify *gerim* (converts), and we only call on witnesses for the largely pro forma signing of *ketubot*. As a result, the price of some of the equality of women in the Reform Movement has been the contraction of opportunities for both women and men to serve God in these time-honored roles.

Righting the Balance

If we are to maximize the possibilities for equality by allowing the "full rights to practice Judaism" to prevail, should we not consider restoring some of these positions to Reform practice and open them to men and women alike?

Let's begin with the minyan. While most Shabbat services in the Reform Movement are well enough attended that one need not be concerned that there are ten people, alternative Shabbat morning services or, where they exist, daily services may have trouble attracting worshipers.[2] The absence of a minyan means that prayers like *Bar'chu*, the *K'dushah*, and *Kaddish* are not said, the *Amidah* is said silently, and the Torah is not read.[3] The requirement of a minyan is a reminder that each person counts in Jewish worship, and each new person who enters is greeted with great joy. If fewer than ten gather, omitting these prayers reminds us that each person is essential. Without ten, the service feels different, as though one is praying alone in the company of others, but not as a congregation. When the tenth person arrives, inevitably the spirits of the worshipers lift. The custom of the minyan also emphasizes what we tell each bar and bat mitzvah: you now count as an adult in Jewish life.

The *beit din* is another institution that could benefit from expanding men's and women's full rights to practice Judaism. Restoring a *beit din* to the process of conversion has been a major step forward, giving converts the confidence that they are accepted not only by their own rabbi but by others as well, and by extension the whole Jewish community (or at least the Reform Jewish community). It also adds a sense of gravity to the conversion process, sending the message that there are things the community at large, as represented by the *beit din*, expects Jews to know. The new guidelines for conversion, passed overwhelmingly at the

CCAR convention in 2001, strongly recommend that conversion include a *beit din*, immersion in a *mikveh*, and *hatafat dam*, symbolic circumcision. If a *beit din* adds value to conversion, would it not add a serious Jewish spiritual dimension to other areas of life as well?

Divorce is another realm where the equality argument has canceled out the principle of "full rights to practice Judaism."[4] Repelled by the unequal and often humiliating divorce proceedings among traditional Jews in the nineteenth century, the Reformers argued that divorce, which ended a relationship begun under religious auspices, was not a religious act but a civil one. In the United States (unlike in some other countries), divorce has by and large remained a matter for the civil courts. In the hindsight brought on by an age that has sought a greater spiritual dimension to life, it could be argued that removing divorce from the religious realm may have ended a bitter procedure for women but also denied to both men and women the possibility of bringing a marriage begun in a spiritual setting to a close in an equally spiritual one. To deny both men and women the religious experience of that message as they end their marriage is not equality; it is forfeiture of a responsibility by a religious community.

The Reform rabbinate has already gone far to remedy this condition. The CCAR introduced into the 1998 *Rabbi's Manual* a ritual called *Seder P'reidah*, "Ritual of Release." While this ritual does not produce a *get*, a traditional document of divorce, it does offer the couple a religious setting in which to bring their marriage to an end and "release each other . . . from the sacred bonds that held [them] together." While Reform communities in Canada and other countries do provide a *get*, its validity is not recognized by most Orthodox rabbis, nor even by many Conservative rabbis. While the Canadian Reform *get* and the *Seder P'reidah* do offer the personal value of bringing Jewish values to bear on this painful procedure, these solutions do not serve the *get*'s original purpose of freeing the man and the woman to marry again anywhere in the Jewish world without casting a shadow on the status of any future children. The new Reform affirmation of the value of *k'lal Yisrael* has opened the way in some communities for the beginning of discussions with Conservative and Reconstructionist rabbis regarding the establishment of a joint *beit din* whose conversions (and perhaps, eventually, divorces and civil settlements) would thus be recognized by the majority of rabbis in North America. Such an institution has already been established in Los Angeles. Perhaps, as such *batei din* increase, a few Modern Orthodox rabbis might be willing to join.

Reform and Conservative Jewish women have begun to explore ways to find the *k'dushah* present even in the bitterness of divorce through the ancient ritual of the *mikveh*. This is another rite that has suffered in the struggle between the values of equality and full rights of practice. For the Reformers of the 1885 Pittsburgh Platform, "purity" (priestly and otherwise) was one of the areas that they rejected as "not adapted to the views and habits of modern civilization," and so "in our days" it represented an obstruction to "modern spiritual elevation." Nevertheless, as we have noted, an increasing number of women "in our days" are finding the *mikveh* spiritually uplifting. Some of them have friends among a new generation of Orthodox women who have described the power of their own immersions in the waters of a modern, sanitary *mikveh*. Aware of Reform women's positive experience of *mikveh*, some Reform men have begun to enter the waters as well. In this area, for some Reform Jews, equality and the full right to Jewish practice have become one.

Challenges to the harmony of these two principles still remain, however. Should Reform Jews allow their sons to experience *b'rit milah*, the covenant sealed through circumcision? While the early Reformers were willing to accept as converts those adults who were skittish about circumcision, the Reformers insisted upon it for infants. The creation of the Reform *mohalim* program has enabled qualified physicians to create ceremonies that emphasize the *k'dushah* of this mitzvah. A few years earlier, knowledgeable Reform laypeople had begun to devise naming ceremonies for their daughters—sometimes on the eighth day of birth, sometimes later—that would celebrate their daughter's entrance into the *b'rit*, the covenant, as well. While the search for a ritual act as riveting as circumcision has been a challenge in such ceremonies (see chapter 10), here too there has been a blend of equality and the full right to practice.

Every so often, however, some object that these rites are inherently unequal—that whatever rituals are done at a *b'rit bat* cannot match the power of the surgical procedure that marks infant boys' bodies as Jewish for life. Some have proposed the radical solution of making some surgical mark on baby girls, which most Jews oppose as violating the halachah's prohibition against marking the body for purposes other than the mitzvah of *b'rit milah*. Others take the opposite tack, saying that if nothing so dramatic can mark girls' entrance into the covenant, then boys should not have such a dramatic rite either. The great majority of Reform and other liberal rabbis argue that to deny *milah* to Jewish boys is to replicate the nineteenth-century Reform practice of denying certain mitzvot to Reform Jews, but with a much more disastrous effect: an uncircumcised Jewish boy is condemned to be marked as "different" among both Jews and non-Jews, and so is denied the choice of being Jewish, or rejecting it, in his own fashion. God designed boys and girls with different bodies; each needs to be welcomed into the covenant in a manner that befits the child's God-given nature.

There is another aspect to equality that the circumcision debate reveals: equality of opportunity does not necessarily mean equality of expression. To permit women to wear a *kippah* (head covering), a *tallit*, or *t'fillin* is not the same as requiring them to wear these objects. As we have noted, there are women who see all three of these garments as essentially male and so reject them, preferring to create their own spiritual garments in a way that comports with their sense of themselves as women.

Same-Gender Unions, Two-Gender Prayers

The tension between equality of opportunity and equality of expression is also part of the discussion over same-gender unions. For a long time gay and lesbian couples, denied the right of a legally recognized marriage by almost all states in the United States, debated as to whether they wanted to call their unions "marriage" or whether they wanted to develop a ritual unique to gay and lesbian couples. Considering the shaky history of marriage, with all its inequalities, some couples preferred a ceremony of commitment instead. Facing the height of the AIDS epidemic in the 1980s and early 1990s, however, more Jewish gay couples began to favor the commitment to fidelity that marriage represented and wished the ceremonies of *kiddushin* to apply to them as well.

In 1998, torn between members who believed that the Jewish rite of *kiddushin* should be extended to gays and lesbians, those who felt that *kiddushin* was a term specifically for heterosexual couples but wanted to affirm the sanctity of these unions by other kinds of rites, and those who felt uncomfortable about any sort of public rites for gay couples, the CCAR posited two opposing statements representing its position at that time: a resolution by the Task Force on Human Sexuality and a responsum by its Responsa Committee.[5] At its March 2000 convention, the CCAR resolved the issue in the spirit of the Pittsburgh Principles by a near unanimous vote encouraging both rabbis who officiated at same-gender unions as well as those who would not officiate. "Officiation," of course, refers only to a religious ceremony, lacking any legal basis in states that do not permit it.

Another example of the tension between full rights to practice and the equality principle is the issue of gender language in prayer. With few exceptions, Hebrew requires a choice of either masculine or feminine gender, while English is much more nuanced in the use of gender. For example, Hebrew requires either *melech* (king) or *malkah* (queen), whereas English permits genderless words like "ruler," "sovereign," "monarch," or "majesty." Similarly, Hebrew requires either *atah* (masculine) or *at* (feminine); the English "you" is neutral. The Reform Movement, like the Reconstructionist and Renewal Movements, has utilized this neutrality of the English language to create "gender-sensitive" liturgies and to commit itself to gender-sensitive language in all its future liturgical publications. A negative by-product of this otherwise admirable stance is that, in a way, the "right" to express certain aspects of God's nature has been denied to Reform worshipers. In the new edition of *Gates of Repentance*, the High Holy Day *machzor, Avinu Malkeinu* is not translated "Our Father our King" but is merely transliterated as *Avinu Malkeinu*. So far Reform liturgy has by and large resisted speaking of God as "mother," and in so doing we have denied our worshipers the opportunity to relate to God as the ideal mother/father in whose image we may better understand our own mothers and fathers (imperfect, but indispensable for our existence). If God created us in the divine image, male and female, as Genesis 1:26 says, by de-genderizing God-language we eliminate the opportunity to encounter the divine male-female image according to which we were created. Maimonides, who argued that there is no relationship between God's nature and the human terms we use to describe divinity, would be happy, but something has been lost.

One way to recover the relationship of God to our own gender is to use both masculine and feminine language in English, and in Hebrew. *The Open Door*, the new Haggadah published by the CCAR, offers blessings in both the masculine (*Baruch atah . . .*) and the feminine (*B'ruchah at . . .*). Before I began to daven such language in a makeshift siddur some years ago, I was afraid that the language would make me feel.as though I were praying to a feminine deity, but I was wrong. I found myself instead coming in touch with the feminine aspects of God, and thus with my own feminine aspects, of which I am usually unaware. I became more sensitive to the concept of *rechem* (womb) embedded in *rachamim*, the compassionate side of God suggested by the name YHVH.

Though, like most men, I did not identify the masculine forms of prayer (*Baruch atah . . .*) with a masculine God, I can now appreciate that using both genders in prayer may help us reach the divine origins of our own gender and sexuality more than either the exclusive use of the masculine or the *parve*-tude of gender-sensitive English. To use both genders is to provide equality without sacrificing the full rights of practice.

A final example of full rights to practice at odds with equality is the area of women's services that exclude men, the flipside of the concern of the nineteenth-century Reformers that the separation of the sexes was a denial of women's equality. A popular and often moving innovation in Reform and other liberal movements has been Rosh Chodesh celebrations, commemorating the new moon and the dawning of a new month in the Jewish calendar. The Jerusalem Talmud (*Taanit* 1:6) identifies this as a day when women are exempted from certain household duties, and so in the past generation it has become an important opportunity for women to gather and usher in the new month. While men are sometimes invited to these occasions, many women see these as opportunities to bond exclusively with other Jews of their own gender. After millennia in which women were excluded from full participation in such rituals as prayer, the Torah reading, study, and many others, for women to choose to celebrate Jewish acts in groups of other women is to affirm a positive meaning in separate women's gatherings rather than their oppressiveness. Indeed one could argue that these women have discovered a positive meaning of which the tradition may have been unaware when it required their isolation. In a similar vein, there are modern Orthodox women who have worked to transform the women's sections of their synagogues into spaces where they can pray seriously and intently, undisturbed by the sometimes distracting presence of their husbands next to them. Should men not celebrate that women, forced to be separated all these years, have now found positive meaning in this separation?

But if women deserve full rights to practice Judaism, even if they choose to do so in different places from men, the equality principle would grant men the same right. Years of exclusion from male gatherings have made some Jewish women wary of separate men's associations, and some of these have been merely attempts to "copy" Jewish women's gatherings. In Jewish life, however, there is a growing sense that women are more involved than men, and some men, in non-Orthodox circles particularly, have developed an inferiority about their own Jewish competence. Their wives are often more knowledgeable than they, and their children will more often seek out their mothers than their fathers in the search for more information. When men participate in men's prayer or study groups as a way to increase their Jewish knowledge, they seek to right the gender imbalance the same way that women do through Rosh Chodesh celebrations or women's study groups. Part of the increased desire of Reform Jews to feel called by Torah should lead us to celebrate any opportunity to deepen our knowledge and practice in a comfortable atmosphere that will enhance learning, whether with our partners or alone.

The same issue has arisen with the creation of synagogues emphasizing outreach to gays and lesbians. Would it not be better for these Jews to participate in synagogues with a diverse membership? Yet few gay and lesbian Jews have felt comfortable showing affection for their partners in primarily heterosexual synagogues, nor have they been able in those settings to apply "queer theory" to traditional texts and ideas. Gay and lesbian synagogues enable them to do all those things, but ironically, now that "mainstream" synagogues have become more accepting of gay and lesbian Jews, some gay and lesbian synagogues have found it harder to attract members.

There is a particular area, however, in which the conflict between equality and full rights to practice leads us to argue with the tradition rather than merely affirm it. Jewish tradition has not looked favorably upon homosexual unions. Leviticus 18:22 prohibits "lying with a man as with a woman." While there has been some attempt through the ages to limit and reinterpret this passage, it continues to be quoted as justification for opposition to homosexuality. Yet there is a tradition of reinterpreting other troubling passages—for example, the suspected adulteress (*sotah*) and the stubborn and rebellious son—which has resulted in the abolition of punishment for these two types of personages. Unfortunately, unlike the *sotah* and the stubborn and rebellious son, Leviticus 18 still commands the loyalty of large numbers of Jews and so continues to be cited as an obstacle to granting gays and lesbians full rights to Jewish practice. This happens despite the fact that the context of the biblical verse places it in a general condemnation of the long obsolete fertility cults of the idolatrous Canaanite nations. Even Rashi tried to limit its application to a particular kind of sexual intercourse. Why have Jews (including, still, some Reform Jews) who question the authority of so many other biblical passages chosen to adhere to this one?

I fear we have been influenced by the views prevailing in American society. Large numbers of Americans refuse to understand that gays and lesbians have no choice in being attracted to members of the same gender, believing instead that there is something "wrong," even "sinful," about these individuals. This belief has affected many Jews who favor inclusiveness in other areas of life but are not willing to reach out to gay and lesbian Jews. It may also be that, as defined in the "Torah" section of the Pittsburgh Principles, some Reform Jews feel called by the mitzvah of Leviticus 18:22, but one can argue that the call should be directed to their own practice and not that of others. The text does not, after all, adjure the people to persecute those who engage in sexually forbidden practice. Even this text is subject to interpretation: The entire section of sexual misdeeds in Leviticus 18 is bracketed by two important statements. The first, Leviticus 18:5, states, "You shall keep My statutes and My judgments by which, when a person does them, that person shall live," which the Rabbis interpreted to mean that no one should feel compelled to do any mitzvah that would result in his or her death (though sexual crimes, along with murder and public idolatry, did not come under this exception). In addition, the beginning of the next chapter, Leviticus 19, includes the injunction to be holy. Given what we know now of human sexuality, to expect people born with an innate homosexual nature to refrain from sexual activity is to ask them to choke off an essential part of their lives. So long as homosexual relationships, like heterosexual ones, are governed by principles of holiness, Leviticus 18:22 should join the laws of the *sotah* and the stubborn and rebellious son as prohibitions from another age.

This entire discussion about equality reminds us that almost from its inception, the Reform Movement reached out to those who often felt unwelcome in more traditional streams of Judaism. From non-Jews who wished to become Jews but were fearful of circumcision, to today's gay and lesbian Jews who serve as rabbis and cantors in Reform congregations and have their Jewish relationships sanctified in commitment ceremonies or rites of *kiddushin*, the Reform Movement has opened its doors to those who have felt themselves on the margins of the rest of the Jewish world. When in 2003 the Supreme Court overturned its own 1986 anti-homosexual decision (*Bowers v. Hardwick*) on the grounds that "times can blind us to certain truths and later generations can see that laws once thought necessary and proper in fact serve only to oppress," the Reform Movement could feel proud that our stances over the past decade and a half have helped open our generation's eyes.

Effects of Patrilineality

The URJ's Outreach Program, begun in the 1970s, has targeted families in which but one parent is Jewish in the hopes that we might encourage these families to establish Jewish homes and raise the children as Jews. While the impetus behind this has been admirable, the great variety of definitions of "a Jewish home" has often created a mass of families whose definitions might include a Christmas tree, Easter egg hunts, little

Shabbat observance, and even simultaneous attendance at church schools (despite the URJ ruling that children being educated in two religions could not enroll in URJ religious schools). Sometimes non-Jews in a congregation will advocate policies that suggest that there is no difference between synagogue rituals that Jews and non-Jews can enact. To make such distinctions reveals old tensions between "universal" notions of equality in Reform and "particularistic" beliefs that perhaps non-Jews should not have "full rights to practice."

The moment in a bar or bat mitzvah ceremony when parents hand a Torah scroll down to their child symbolizes their desire to pass on their Jewish heritage, whether inherited by birth or chosen through conversion. If the non-Jewish parent has decided not to make Torah part of his or her heritage, how can that parent pass it on? Can a non-Jew be called for an *aliyah* to the Torah when he or she must say a blessing of God "who has chosen us from among all peoples and given us the Torah"? Can a non-Jew be an officer of a synagogue, responsible for directing an institution dedicated to the advancement of a faith that person has not (yet) adopted?

There are multiple ways to examine these questions. When the non-Jewish parent is the mother, who even today often bears the lion's share of buying materials for Jewish home observance, taking the children to religious and Hebrew school, and helping with religious school homework, the restrictions on the public roles she can play in the celebrations to which she has contributed so much often make her feel very "unequal" in a movement committed to inclusiveness. Most Reform synagogues do not permit non-Jews to have an *aliyah* or to be officers of the congregation, and the policy on allowing the non-Jewish parent to receive and hand down the Torah varies between congregations. Some synagogues allow a non-Jewish spouse to accompany the Jewish parent to the *bimah* for an *aliyah* but not say the blessings; others recast the blessing for the non-Jew so it does not include the element of commandedness. These compromises show how our desire to be open equally to all individuals struggling with the pressures of a pluralistic society collides with our need to strengthen our Jewish commitments in a time when the pluralistic society threatens constantly to weaken them. The struggle to maintain Jewish distinctiveness in a congregation with a preponderance of intermarriages has been one of the unexpected, troubling effects of the patrilineal resolution of 1983, and a challenge to our desire to encourage non-Jewish parents in intermarried families in their decision to raise their children as Jews.

There are other groups to whom this section of the Pittsburgh Principles is meant to apply as well. "People of all ages" are of course welcome at all services, but when a service is attended by predominantly seniors, two things happen. Raised in a Reform Judaism with much less Hebrew and traditional observance than are now the norm, some of these members often feel that their commitments are unequally represented in contemporary worship. Some of them wish to turn the clock back to a predominantly English service with music that may even reflect the melodies of the 1940s *Union Hymnal*. On the other hand, when young families make up the bulk of the congregation, it becomes necessary to shorten the service, tell stories rather than give a thought-provoking sermon, and gear the Hebrew to what the average child in that evening's congregation has learned in Hebrew school. Most congregations offer family services or "tot Shabbats" to appeal to the latter group, but these too result in a feeling of exclusion among singles, families with teenagers, or child-free families. Increasingly, larger synagogues have begun to offer simultaneous services for different age groups and different ideologies, although offering a "classical" Reform service just for older members has been slow to catch on, in part because many classical Reformers resist being considered "alternative" rather than mainstream. A growing custom on Friday evenings has been the early Friday evening service, which enables both laypeople and clergy to avoid the family service and spend a leisurely Shabbat meal with their families, another indication of the increased desire by the Reform Movement to balance home and synagogue observance on Shabbat.

Opening the Doors of Disability

A group that is not specifically mentioned in the Pittsburgh Principles, much to the outrage of some, is Jews with varying kinds of disabilities. The task force wrestled with including them, ultimately fearing that continuing to add specific groups would result in an unwieldy list. We had hoped that the phrase "people of all ages" would feel sufficiently inclusive, but this attempt at a general inclusiveness proved once more that equality of opportunity does not mean equality of expression. In fact, the Reform Movement has reached out to Jews with disabilities in a number of ways that have tried to blend the ability to practice fully with issues of equality. More and more of our congregations provide enhanced hearing devices at services, the Reform Movement has assisted deaf Jews who wished to establish their own congregations, and we have welcomed deaf Jews to HUC-JIR and the rabbinate. Many synagogues have rebuilt their facilities to make the *bimah* (pulpit) and other parts of the building accessible to wheelchairs, and still others have opened programs for the physically and developmentally disabled. Speech courses at HUC-JIR have assisted stutterers (including the author of this book) to manage their speaking deficits sufficiently to be able to serve as effective rabbis. As has happened with some of the innovations proposed by Reform Jewish women, some of the improvements created for the disabled have assisted others as well: building a lower, accessible *bimah* has made the entire service more intimate for all worshipers, and the widespread availability of hearing devices has led worshipers embarrassed by their hearing loss to understand the service without calling attention to themselves. After the outcry following the publication of the hefty first edition of *Gates of Prayer*, efforts have been made to print books on thinner paper to make the volumes easier for everyone to hold. Discussions have also begun on the wisdom of continuing to offer the *Nisim B'chol Yom* in its present form, which in both Hebrew and English praises God who "opens the eyes of the blind," where "blind" is used as a metaphor for a lack of understanding. At a service where this was discussed some years ago, a blind woman whose guide dog rested comfortably at her feet expressed pleasure at the fact that her disability was used as a teaching opportunity for people whose eyes could see but whose hearts could not. She saw the metaphor as a reminder to all of us that "sight" comes in many forms.

The teaching that those with physical disabilities may have insights denied to the "able-bodied" is a justification for much of the outreach work of the Reform Movement. Those who conform to the supposed norm have much to learn from those whose lives have taken them in paths closed to Jews in the "mainstream." Women rabbis have taught us a new, more wholesome way of integrating work and family and have modeled relationships based, whenever possible, on networking with colleagues on an equal basis rather than through a hierarchy. We have long known that *gerim* have brought insights and experiences that have deepened the Jewish commitments of those who know them. Gays and lesbians who have battled the prejudice of the heterosexual world share a courage and an insight from their sexual orientation from which their friends have learned much. Elderly Jews and children teach the rest of us lessons that we have either forgotten or have not lived long enough— or hard enough—to learn. Those with disabilities teach us not only about courage, but about humor as well, and both sensitize us to the physical ability we may take for granted and encourage us to acknowledge our own disabilities from which we may have turned aside in denial or embarrassment. Dialogues with the obviously disabled can also help us realize how our own limitations have helped us grow.

One of the *Birchot HaNehenin*, offered when one sees a person with a physical impairment, is a praise of God for *m'shaneh ha-briot*—making varied kinds of creatures. If all human beings are created in the image of God, then people with impairments—and with different genders, ages, sexual orientations, and religious backgrounds—also help us understand what God "looks like." Perhaps that is why it takes at least ten of us, with all our different natures, to understand, each time we gather to pray, how God is present in our midst.

14

The Non-Jew in the Synagogue

We believe that we must not only open doors for those ready to enter our faith, but also to actively encourage those who are seeking a spiritual home to find it in Judaism.

We are committed to strengthening the people Israel by supporting individuals and families in the creation of homes rich in Jewish learning and observance.

—Statement of Principles, "Israel," paragraphs 6–7

"Let Us Shuck Our Insecurities"

On the second of Kislev 5739 (December 2, 1978), Rabbi Alexander Schindler, then president of the Union of American Hebrew Congregations, gave a talk to the UAHC Board of Trustees that would transform the demographics of the Reform Movement for generations to come. Speaking on Shabbat *Toldot*, Rabbi Schindler sought to confront the growing threat of intermarriage in four bold steps: (1) to offer long-term support and encouragement to Jews-by-choice; (2) to reach out to the non-Jewish spouses in intermarriages in order to draw them into Jewish life; (3) to explore the "validity of Jewish lineage through the paternal line"; and (4) to develop an outreach program to the "unchurched" and affirm, through information centers and other means, the values of Judaism for those seeking religious meaning.

The first two of Schindler's proposals became the agenda for the UAHC's Department of Outreach, founded as a result of this talk, and the challenge to reaffirm Reform's historic adoption of what came to be called patrilineal descent became a resolution of the CCAR in 1983. The only part of his proposal that was not made an official policy of the Reform Movement was the last one—until it surfaced on the floor of the 1999 Pittsburgh Convention of the CCAR as an amendment to the draft Statement of Principles and was affirmed on the spot.

Given the Reform Movement's embrace of outreach to Jews who had already converted and to intermarried families, it might seem puzzling that a twenty-year silence should have greeted a proposal to engage non-Jews who might be seeking religious fulfillment. Considering the troubled history of conversion efforts among both Jews and non-Jews, however, the hesitation is understandable. The history of Christian and Muslim persecution of Jewish proselytizers and their converts helped inform this, as well as a concern that our opposition to Christian proselytizing efforts would be undermined if we engaged in the same practices. Thanks to the terrible persecutions Jews have experienced through the ages, many Jews think it would be mad for seemingly comfortable gentiles to voluntarily subject themselves to such dangers. In his address, Schindler challenged all these assumptions:

> Why are we so hesitant? Are we ashamed? Do we really believe that one must be a madman to embrace Judaism? Let us shuck our insecurities; let us recapture our self-esteem; let us, by all means, demonstrate our confidence in the value of our faith.

Schindler was right—we no longer have to fear repercussions from the church, and the years since his address have made it clear that Jews are not the only religious groups to have suffered persecution. Finally, it is clear that our efforts would be very different from the aggressive tactics of Southern Baptists and Jews for Jesus. Some may argue that creating an infrastructure of Jewish information centers in visible areas would create a major financial burden, requiring at least a decade to test their effectiveness. The Reform Movement seems persuaded that it is a better use of resources to reach out to those who have already chosen Judaism and to Gentiles who are married to Jews. Still, if the idea really moved us, we would surely beat the bushes to raise the funds to accomplish it.

And why should the idea not move us? If we find Judaism, and in particular the Reform articulation of it, compelling, why should we not wish to invite non-Jewish seekers to consider it? Part of the prophetic attraction for the early Reform Movement, after all, was the messianic prophecy that non-Jews would come flocking to Judaism:

> And it shall be that all who remain of all the nations that came against Jerusalem shall go up from year to year to worship the Sovereign, *Adonai* of Hosts, and to feast at the Feast of Sukkot.
>
> Zechariah 14:16

> And it shall be from month to month and Shabbat to Shabbat that all flesh shall come to worship before Me, *Adonai* has said.
>
> Isaiah 66:23

Should we not act to facilitate these prophecies by spreading the word among non-Jews?

Esau, Our Twin

It may not have been accidental that Schindler gave his historic talk on the Shabbat of *Toldot*, with its narrative of the troubling encounters of Jacob, the patriarch of the Jewish people, and Esau, whom the Rabbis saw as the symbol first of Rome and then of the church. As Jacob and Esau were intertwined in Rebekah's womb, so the Jew and the non-Jew have been entwined since the period of the Romans. Indeed, a text from the *P'sikta D'Rav Kahana* (*piska* 12:20) argues that the Torah was given in the third month, corresponding to the sign of the Twins (Gemini), as a reminder to the heirs of Jacob's twin Esau that they were welcome to repent of their sins and become Jewish. It is almost as though there is a wistfulness that the Revelation was incomplete without its acceptance by our "other half," Jacob's twin brother. Because the ancestors of Jews who became Christians in the millennia since the church's founding may be said to have stood at Sinai too, in embracing Judaism today some Christians see themselves as returning to their original roots. That a number of Jews-by-choice discover after their conversions that they have Jewish ancestors gives credence to the

Chasidic belief that *gerim* are reclaiming the Jewish *n'shamah*s they inherited from Sinai.

There are other manifestations of the Jacob-Esau connection. An old tradition among Jewish historians explained new Jewish practices as emulations of Christian ones (*wie es christelt sich, so judelt sich es*). The model for many of the early reforms in Judaism can be found in the practices in Protestant churches. On the one hand, it is obvious that any minority culture is influenced by its surroundings, but given the mixed fear and hatred that Jews have felt toward their Christian masters in so many countries, the degree of emulation is remarkable.

A woman preparing for conversion some time ago proposed that we refer to non-Jews as gentiles, lest their identity have meaning only in reference to us—they are only the "non-us." But that is often how we look at gentiles. Most of us today shrink from the Hebrew/Yiddish translation of "Gentiles," *goyim* (literally meaning, like the word "Gentiles" itself, "the nations"), which seems to convey a sense not only of "non-Jews" but "non-persons," and also brings to mind negative images of Christians bred by centuries of persecution. Better "non-Jews," which suggests not so much the opposite of Jews but the other side of Jews, the side of ourselves that is hidden. We know there are Jews who are disappointed when their non-Jewish partners decide to convert, since part of their attraction to the non-Jew may have been this "otherness," through which they thought they might find out something about the hidden, forbidden side of themselves. Descendants of Christians are, like Esau, born with the birthright, the blessing of widespread acceptance, which we, the minority religion, desire. Jacob secured the birthright and the blessing and then ran away. Some Jews believe that to get the birthright they have to stay and marry the holder of it. There are non-Jews who see us as the holders of the birthright and the blessing as well, and in marrying us, some may feel attracted to the exotic side of their majority persona. But as we know, intermarriage creates a Jewish–non-Jewish home, often fraught with conflict even where the practice of the home is Judaism. Isaac, blind to the realities, remarked that "the voice is the voice of Jacob, and [not "but"] the hands are the hands of Esau" (Genesis 27:22), imagining that in one person he could combine both Jacob and Esau. Intermarriage offers a false promise of this dream. A vision of bringing interested non-Jews to Judaism could make Isaac's dream come true.

A Multicultural Faith

The sociologist and demographer Gary Tobin cites Schindler's vision approvingly in his forceful arguments that a serious, sustained drive to attract non-Jews would have a significant impact on the Jewish community as a whole. Tobin asserts that for individuals to "articulate the importance of being Jewish" to non-Jewish seekers would deepen their ideological growth and that those becoming Jewish would bring "enhanced religious depth" to an enlarged Jewish community, increasing Jews' abilities to relate to the ethnic groups of the new Jews-by-choice. Such "proactive conversion" would increase the Jewish population "by hundreds of thousands—and hopefully by millions," thus expanding both the strength of Jewish institutions and our influence in local and national political life.[1]

Urging outreach efforts to non-Jews in various ethnic groups suggests a profound insight into what the Jewish people might look like and accomplish when the twenty-first century draws to a close. Already there are scatterings of Jewish African Americans, Asian Americans, and Hispanics in our synagogues, and as more infertile couples seek to adopt children around the globe, the number of young multiethnic Jews-by-choice will increase as well. Chicago and New York already boast sizable congregations of black Jews, and within a generation we will see rabbis and cantors from a variety of ethnic groups. Not only are these Jews helpful in increasing communication with non-Jews in their ethnic groups of birth, as Tobin argues, but they are expanding the doors of Jewish life to include customs and insights that are their gift to their adopted people. They are helping us live up to our name as an *am olam*, meaning not only an eternal people but also a people from all over the world.

While some of us may thrill at Tobin's projections that outreach to non-Jews will help us expand "hopefully . . . by millions," such figures can frighten even those who applaud the Pittsburgh Principles' call for an active campaign with non-Jewish seekers. Could the Jewish community retain its convictions and practices under such conditions? Would it be Judaism that expands, or a new amalgam of cultures and expectations that over time would break significantly with the Judaism to which these individuals were originally attracted?

While important to consider, these concerns should be seen in perspective. They are a lesson that our efforts should be deliberate and that we should work to integrate new *gerim* gradually. Meanwhile, we have barely begun to reach out to these non-Jews! To worry lest we become too successful could prevent us from doing anything. So what should we do? The first step, to attract the attention of "interested" non-Jews, has already been taken by American society at large, which by the dawn of the new century has made many aspects of Jewish culture visible to urban America, if not the rest of it. Chanukah vies for attention with Christmas, grocery stores teem with Chanukah and Passover products as well as cards for Rosh HaShanah and bar/bat mitzvah. Yiddish words pepper newspaper columns and the daily speech of Jews and non-Jews alike, and some Jewish ethnic foods have become as American as pizza. Television and films have many Jewish characters, who increasingly bring Jewish religious events into the public eye. But like Jews who visit non-Jewish homes around Christmas and enjoy a Christmas tree, non-Jews can passively obtain all sorts of information about Judaism without making a commitment.

Miriam Levy's Theory of Outreach

To build upon this basically positive Jewish background music in American culture, we will need to adopt my mother's theory of party hosting: if you want people to eat your food, you have to carry it to them. The Lubavitch Chasidim have long been proponents of this idea. They make themselves very visible at Jewish public events, bringing *t'fillin* to the multitudes. Lubavitch is not interested in approaching non-Jews though; if we are, we will need to adopt my mother's methods in different ways. The model of the Christian Science Reading Room is an attractive idea. No one is hawking anything there. These inviting libraries just sit among other buildings on the street. But in calling for us "to actively encourage those who are seeking a spiritual home," the Pittsburgh Principles suggests more than building quiet reading rooms. Rather it calls on us to engage in active outreach, even in public settings, to discover and engage non-Jewish seekers. At the same time, we need be no less militant in opposing attempts to proselytize Jews; indeed, we would be offering our own methods of attraction as a model for those Christians who believe their faith compels them to proselytize others.

If we were seriously to act on this principle, we might establish a joint commission of the CCAR and URJ, including Jews-by-choice among rabbis and congregants, as well as others who have had outreach experience with intermarried couples. We would discuss the motivation of these and other Jews-by-choice and explore means, like the Outreach Department's Taste of Judaism program, to stimulate and satisfy those motivations in others. We might set up one or two experimental Jewish information centers in areas of large cities where intellectuals of many faiths gather, perhaps near major universities. The centers could lend and sell Jewish books, as well as videos on Jewish home observance and inspiring synagogue services, and offer live programs of lectures, Jewish music, occasional Shabbat and festival observances, and opportunities for Jewish meditation. (Such centers would surely attract Jews as well.) Outreach workers would follow up with visitors to the centers to welcome them into synagogues, to the homes of observant Reform families, to Introduction to Judaism classes, and to support groups. Interested seekers would put the outreach workers in touch with some of their friends.

Jewish Students Ask for Help

Rabbi Schindler's original motivation in encouraging active approaches to non-Jews was to try to offset the potential loss to the Jewish community of those marrying non-Jewish partners. In the Pittsburgh Principles, however, the purpose appears more intrinsic. It is a means for "supporting individuals and families in the creation of homes rich in Jewish learning and observance." The original inspiration for this sentence was a plea by some Reform Jewish students at the University of Pennsylvania with whom I shared a draft of the Statement of Principles and asked their opinion. They begged me to insert some words of encouragement for young Jews like themselves who were determined to find a Jewish mate, but were struggling to abstain from amorous relations with the ubiquitous non-Jews among whom they studied and lived. Having affirmed the contributions that Jewishly-motivated intermarried families might make, the task force creating the Statement of Principles was unwilling to speak specifically against intermarriage and devised this sentence instead. I do not know whether those students saw themselves reflected in it, but their poignant plea to be included was a reminder that intermarriage is no longer only a deliberate act but often an accidental one as Jews of all backgrounds find themselves falling in love, often unintentionally, with non-Jews because they share a common space or interest. The cry of the Penn students calls out to us to undertake three challenging campaigns at the same time: to strategize with marriageable Jews on how to meet, date, fall in love with, and marry other Jews, maintaining our support as they search out synagogues and work at creating Jewish homes; to strive to increase the pool of Jews in the world through the Jewish information center approach; and to reach out to intermarried households and support them in all the struggles they endure.

We have been most successful with the third initiative. The URJ's Outreach program has provided valuable educational and personal resources to thousands of intermarried families, and their visible presence at Reform synagogues across the country is evidence that it is working.

As successful as outreach has been, it is not without problems. To many Reform Jews, the title of this chapter refers not to bringing non-Jews into the synagogue as Jews-by-choice, but to confronting what parts of synagogue life non-Jews in intermarriages may share. Most Reform rabbis believe it inappropriate for such individuals to say blessings that state that God has given them the mitzvot, a belief that they have not (yet) accepted. They may have excellent reasons (including the fourth commandment of honoring their parents, who might feel rejected by their converting children), but they have not yet chosen to cast their lot with this people, even though they have cast their children's lot with us. An initiative to encourage non-Jewish seekers to commit themselves to Judaism implies a willingness on the part of the synagogue to make distinctions between those who have accepted Judaism (they may say every blessing in the liturgy, like every other Jew) and those who have not (who should not say blessings that cause them to make false statements). This issue has already presented Reform synagogues with a myriad of challenges.

Another problematic area has been our timidity in offering resources to young Jews who wish to marry Jews. For much too long, the URJ was committed to running a college program that had no connection with Hillel, the primary foundation for Jewish college work. As the twentieth century ended and Hillel's visibility and funding grew dramatically, the URJ realized that success for Reform college work lay in cooperation with Hillel and moved the office of Kesher ("Connection"), the Reform college program, into the Hillel International Center's building in Washington, D.C.

Kesher needs all the help it can get. Despite remarkably creative and talented staff members, outreach to Reform college students remains very difficult. Young Reform Jews connect with Judaism primarily through their synagogues, which at their best offer engaging educational and social programs for them as they grow up, and through URJ camps. Neither of these sites is present on campus, and there are few campuses where the numbers and *ruach* (spirit) at Reform services match either their synagogues or the URJ camps. Even Reform students whose homes have been Jewishly observant find it disturbingly easy to fall away from regular Shabbat observance if they do not connect to a Hillel or Kesher group on campus. Students who grow up in kosher homes often find it natural to continue that diet, but they may not engage in other Jewish activities while on campus.

My mother's hostessing theory needs to be applied on campuses as well. Involved Reform students need to take Kesher materials around to the dormitories and Greek houses. They need to hold programs in those places and in public sites, not just at Hillel or in an anonymous building on campus. URJ camps need to supply Kesher activists with lists of songleaders in their regions, who can lead services on campus and otherwise supply the kind of Reform *ruach* that makes camp life so transforming. Groups of rabbis should be encouraged to visit their students on campus together, so they can gather students from varying communities to become aware of each other's existence and have fun and Jewish stimulation in a Reform setting. These rabbis need to meet in Hillel houses to lessen whatever unease may still exist between Reform students and Hillel, for it is through Hillel and its contacts that students will have the greatest opportunity to connect with other Jews.

Hillels that embrace a diverse Jewish population perform another function as well. When students from diverse streams come to know each other and participate in each other's rituals, the sense of distrust and alienation from that which is different breaks down. Gradually, a Reform Jew may come to realize that aspects of kashrut can seem rather attractive; a Conservative Jew may come to see that a guitar at a Shabbat service can be very uplifting; an Orthodox Jew may acknowledge that a commitment to social justice is important for Jews. When a member of Kesher complained several years ago that an early Kesher convention was not kosher, my interest was piqued, since this was not often heard from young Reform Jews in those days. Could this student have learned about kashrut at Hillel? Sure enough, he had. Reform Jewish students active in Hillel have made a decision to live a Reform Jewish life on campus not in isolation but in the company of other Jews—and have taught all of us an important lesson. The commitment to k'lal Yisrael in the Pittsburgh Principles is not theoretical for them; they live it every day. Their commitment has not weakened Reform; by understanding more of the parameters of Judaism than they may have learned growing up, active Reform Jewish students help to broaden the families and synagogues to which they return after graduation, a broadening that has been a significant factor in the transformation of the Reform Movement in the manner the Pittsburgh Principles describes.

When these students fall in love with non-Jews, they are increasingly likely to urge their partners to become Jews-by-choice. Indeed, perhaps it is these college-based Reform Jews whom we should ask to be part of the staff of university-based Jewish information centers, for they have a unique perspective on what it means to be a Reform Jew within k'lal Yisrael, in a community of Jews from diverse backgrounds.

However great the challenges to engage Reform Jews on campus, they pale before the struggle to involve single Jews in Jewish life once they leave the closed and relatively accessible world of the university and disappear into the society at large. Some synagogues program creatively for singles, but much of it is in the form of "meat-market" dances or parties; little of it attempts to draw on the intellectual or religious interests of young Jewish adults. Besides, synagogues are geared primarily to families, and even young adults who come back to their home synagogues often feel that they no longer fit in. Jewish center singles programming has the same problems.

Fortunately, some efforts have been made to address these weaknesses. Rabbis Gary Schoenberg and Laurie Rutenberg have brilliantly modeled the attractiveness of Jewish life for uninvolved Jews in the Portland, Oregon, area, inviting individuals and families into their homes and helping them make connections to synagogues and other Jewish institutions in the city. The name of their program, Gesher, Hebrew for "a bridge," is appropriate. Philanthropist Michael Steinhardt created Makor on the Upper West Side of New York, a remarkable structure whose every floor offers a different "entryway" into Jewish life, from social and musical to intellectual and religious. Makor is probably as nonthreatening and welcoming as any such institution can be, and it is an experiment worth replicating in other cities. Short of that, we need caring rabbis, adult educators, cantors, and programmers to discover where concentrations of young Jews are located and reach out to involve them in appropriate ways. They are a talented, well-educated population that wants both to learn and contribute, and efforts to connect with them will be rewarded. Of course it is easier to prescribe such a program than to effectuate it, given the growth of the number of synagogue members and the absence of growth of synagogue staffs. Laypeople should of course be recruited for these efforts, particularly to offer mentoring for single Jews in their professional fields.

As of this writing, applications to rabbinical schools and some other Jewish professional programs are again on the rise, and in a decade we may find that there are not enough positions for them in the Jewish world. But there is more than enough *need* in the Jewish world. Can we start now to fund positions in synagogues that will be ready when our students are ordained and graduated and that will enable us to do the work of outreach to hungry young Jews for which my interlocutors at Penn cried out?

We fail to fulfill our role as partners with the God who has promised our survival if our answer is anything but yes. We fail to fulfill our prophetic role as a movement that believes the messianic age needs human effort to come into being if we do not say yes to any initiative that will open doors for the message of the Jewish people that God and Torah welcome all human beings seeking light.

15

Between Israel and Diaspora:
Can the Synagogue Shape a Culture?

We are committed to strengthening the people Israel by making the synagogue central to Jewish communal life, so that it may elevate the spiritual, intellectual and cultural quality of our lives.

We are committed to *Medinat Yisrael*, the State of Israel, and rejoice in its accomplishments. We affirm the unique qualities of living in *Eretz Yisrael*, the Land of Israel, and encourage *aliyah*, immigration to Israel.

We are committed to a vision of the State of Israel that promotes full civil, human and religious rights for all its inhabitants and that strives for a lasting peace between Israel and its neighbors.

—Statement of Principles, "Israel," paragraphs 8–10

We affirm that both Israeli and Diaspora Jewry should remain vibrant and interdependent communities. As we urge Jews who reside outside Israel to learn Hebrew as a living language and to make periodic visits to Israel in order to study and deepen their relationship to the Land and its people, so do we affirm that Israeli Jews have much to learn from the religious life of Diaspora Jewish communities.

—Statement of Principles, "Israel," paragraph 12

Making the Synagogue Central

A Force to Change Society

What does it mean to be "central"?

The Pittsburgh Platform of 1885 maintained that the Jewish God-idea was "the central religious truth for the human race." Though they did not use the word, the authors of this document also believed that "the views and habits of modern civilization" (in which "Palestine" seems not to have been included) were central to the religious decisions that Reform Jews made. The Columbus Platform, turning its back on the anti-Zionism of the Pittsburgh Platform, tried to embrace both Herzl's political Zionism and Achad Ha-am's spiritual/cultural Zionism by speaking of Palestine as "not only a haven of refuge for the oppressed but also a center of Jewish cultural and spiritual life." Other than a passing reference to the importance of "creating a Jewish home centered on family devotion," the Centenary Perspective does not use the word "central." The 1999 Pittsburgh Principles expresses a commitment to "making the synagogue central" to Jewish community life.

The different applications of this word in the two Pittsburgh documents and the Columbus Platform suggest a long-simmering tension in the Reform Movement as to what should be the axis around which the Reformer's Judaism should revolve. For the 1885 rabbis, God was clearly the center, but they understood God in terms of the Kantian and Hegelian philosophy of their own time. God and "modern civilization" were thus inextricably tied together; they believed that eighteenth- and nineteenth-century German philosophy, a product of high German culture, led them to the most noble understanding of God that they were convinced was articulated in its highest form by Judaism.

The Columbus Platform speaks of "the doctrine of the One, living God" as the "heart" of Judaism. This may imply the same idea as "centrality," but the metaphor is very different. The heart pumps blood—life—to the entire body, but the body does not revolve around the heart. The Columbus Platform reserves the word "center" not for God, but for the Land of Israel, where Reform Jews are urged to help create "a center of Jewish cultural and spiritual life"—*a* center, not *the* center. Columbus, unlike Pittsburgh, is no longer anti-Zionist, but it is also not Zionist in the traditional meaning of the word, as life in the Land of Israel as *the* center of Jewish existence. Can anything in Reform be considered *the* center? The Pittsburgh Principles answers this affirmatively, proclaiming that what is central—or should be—is the synagogue.

The Pittsburgh Principles envisions the synagogue as central "so that it may elevate the spiritual, intellectual and cultural quality of our lives." This is a much broader calling than the earlier platforms envisaged. The Pittsburgh Platform of 1885 does not speak of synagogues (its authors were calling their houses of worship "temples," in part to affirm that each of these was the only temple to which they had allegiance); the Columbus Platform calls the synagogue "the prime communal agency by which Judaism is fostered and preserved"; the Centenary Perspective calls it "the foundation of Jewish community life." The latter two seem to have been influenced by the work of Mordecai Kaplan (a prime inspiration of the Columbus Platform), who saw the synagogue as a community gathering place, folding its religious and intellectual roles into many other functions.

The meaning of the synagogue's centrality and its mission in the 1999 document may best be understood against the backdrop of the perceived centrality of "the views and habits of modern civilization" in the 1885 Pittsburgh Platform. The Centenary Perspective had already dethroned contemporary culture:

> The widespread threats to freedom, the problems inherent in the explosion of new knowledge and of ever more powerful technologies, and the spiritual emptiness of much of Western culture, have taught us to be less dependent on the values of our society and to reassert what remains perennially valid in Judaism's teaching.

As we have noted before, the decade in which the Centenary Perspective arose had seen a devastating critique of Western—particularly American—political and cultural life. In response to the rise of increased public sexuality and violence in modern culture, a number of

Jewish leaders looked to Jewish life to rescue American Jews from the increasingly degrading influences that surrounded them. The third draft of the Ten Principles for Reform Judaism included a provocative statement that was widely criticized:

> In the worldview of Reform Judaism's founders, modernity was the center, the scale on which we measured what was valuable and enduring in Jewish practice and belief. Looking back at a century which has witnessed some of the greatest gifts and the most awful consequences of modernity, we proclaim that the mitzvot of the Torah are our center, and Judaism is the scale by which we shall judge the modern world.

Some of my colleagues argued that this statement was incorrect, and that while moving away from the 1885 position that modern civilization was the center, we have not replaced it solely with "the mitzvot of the Torah." Rather, they argued, we strive for a balance between the noblest aspects of modern civilization and the noblest aspects of Torah. As this debate raged on, I came to see that the third draft indeed presented too extreme a statement, but rather than giving equal weight to modernity and Judaism, it is preferable to see Torah and modernity in dialogue, critiquing each other. Western civilization can critique Torah in the realm of equality, individual freedom, and creativity; Torah can critique Western civilization through all the mitzvot in which these three qualities are not at issue.

The place where this dialogue needs to occur, the Pittsburgh Principles argues, is the synagogue. As a center, a hub of Jewish life, the synagogue needs to bring the force of Jewish ideas and practice to bear on the events of modern life, particularly their political, artistic, communal, and social justice dimensions. It needs to present Jewish ideas and model Jewish practice in a forceful, compelling way, teaching its members to articulate Jewish concepts and judge their society by them, leading its members to the kind of Jewish practice that will inform their lives with service to God, helping them carry that sense of service out into the world with them.

How does the idea of the synagogue as "the center" affect the role of Jewish federations, Jewish community centers, and adult learning institutions, which have themselves often claimed a place as the center?

Comparing these organizations to the synagogue reminds us that, at its best, the synagogue embraces the whole panoply of Jewish life, while the other Jewish institutions specialize in only one aspect or another. If the synagogue is the center of Jewish life, its teaching and practice will inspire its members to deepen what they know and do through activity in the specialized areas of the Jewish community. In the organizational language of "senders" and "receivers," the synagogue is a sender, whereas the more specialized organizations are receivers. Synagogue members seeking greater cultural or educational depth can search out the adult learning centers that now exist in many cities in North America. The synagogue needs to inspire its members to pound on the doors of Jewish federations, offering to contribute and help others contribute to the needs of Jews in their communities, in Israel, and around the world, and to seek out those Jewish agencies whose constituencies call most passionately to them. Synagogues can elevate their members to inspire graduating high school students to become active in Hillel and the college groups of their movement. Synagogues should also encourage their members to assess which secular areas of the community need support and deploy congregants there as well. If a synagogue has members in the entertainment industry, for example, how can the synagogue motivate them to bring Jewish and ethical values to bear on the shows they produce? How can the synagogue help members in other industries bring such values into their workplaces and boardrooms?

A House of Study, Prayer, and Meeting

Traditionally, a synagogue has served three main purposes: as a *beit midrash*, a house of study; a *beit t'filah*, a house of prayer; and a *beit k'neset*, a house of meeting. Another triad in Jewish thought, which its author Simon the Just believed sustains the world (quoted in *Pirkei Avot* 1:2) is Torah, *avodah* (service), and *g'milut chasadim* (the practice of kind deeds). We move closer to the direction suggested by the Pittsburgh Principles if we explore how the three traditional functions of the synagogue can try to fulfill Simon the Just's three principles.

A *beit midrash* dedicated to Torah does not only offer education to children, adults, and families; it is committed to enabling its members to stand at Sinai to receive the Torah every time they enter the synagogue or the homes in which, inspired by the synagogue, Torah is also taught. Moses, who is called Rabbeinu, "our teacher," communicated Torah in such a way that people believed they were hearing the word of God. Our synagogue teachers need to be inspired by his example to communicate Jewish tradition in a way that will help people answer the question, what does God want me to do? In a Reform context, however, believing that Torah learning is a dialogue with God and Torah, our teachers will help us understand that Torah is a series of questions to us, and our responses are questions to God. "What does God want me to do?" is thus not a dictation from an authoritarian teacher, but an inspiration from an *authoritative* teacher, who can help his or her students participate in this age-old encounter with our texts and our history. In the Yiddish folk song "Oifn Pripitchok," the teacher teaches the *alef-bet* in such a way that the students understand they are learning not just isolated letters, but Torah. When children and adults learn Hebrew, we need to help them understand that they are learning the language in which God carried on a dialogue with the Jewish people. In learning Hebrew, they are learning the love-language between God and ourselves. When we teach history, we need to open our students to the possibility that Jewish history may be, among other things, the working out of God's providential design for the Jewish people. The possibilities for rich Torah learning in the synagogue as *beit midrash* are endless.

A *beit midrash* dedicated to *avodah* will help us understand how Torah learning, in its widest sense, will help us serve God. Such a *beit midrash* will teach us to understand the opening midrash in *B'reishit Rabbah*, that Torah was God's blueprint for the entire universe. Thus it will not shrink from seeing itself in the image of Philo, Maimonides, Hermann Cohen, Shimshon Raphael Hirsch, and the German Reformers who believed that the highest creations of Western culture reveal aspects of Torah by showing how the noblest human minds serve God through their craft. Such a *beit midrash* will encourage learners to study *Julius Caesar,* the *Henry* plays, and Greek tragedies and compare them with the ideas of monarchy found in the Books of Judges, Samuel, and Kings, and in Maimonides' *Sefer HaM'lachim* in his *Mishneh Torah.* Its learners will study the Song of Songs and explore how it was utilized by Hebrew and Western poets as well as novelists like Toni Morrison. They will study images of the Garden of Eden in biblical and rabbinic texts and in Milton's *Paradise Lost*. They will study the Book of Psalms, Handel's *Chandos Anthems*, Stravinsky's *Symphony of Psalms*, and Leonard Bernstein's *Chichester Psalms*. They will study the Song at the Sea, Handel's *Israel in Egypt*, and Jeffrey Katzenberg's film *The Prince of Egypt*. Such a *beit midrash* will remind Jews that we have influenced Western culture in ways beyond Yiddish phrases and Jewish cuisine. Even more important, it will remind us that we are not the only ones who have seen Torah as a Revelation from God. Through reading and listening to the philosophy, literature, devotional music, and poetry through which descendants of our twin Esau have interpreted our tradition in their service of God, we may be inspired to return to Jewish texts and ask how they help us to serve God too.

A *beit midrash* committed to *g'milut chasadim* will seek the foundations in Torah for actions based on compassion, justice, and peace. Inspired teachers will enable the lessons from *Parashat Mishpatim* (Exodus 22–24) and *Parashat K'doshim* (Leviticus 19) to leap off the page and cry out "Do not stand idly by!" When our country asks whether it should go to war, our teachers will pull out the great chapter 20 of Deuteronomy, its midrashim, and its mishnah in Tractate *Sotah*. They will show us the great sermon on peace in the midrash to *Parashat Naso* (the Priestly Blessing in Numbers 6:24–26) and then ask their students: How does this apply to the current situation? Into which of the rabbinic definitions of war does this war fit that we are being asked to fight? Would Moses have approved it as well?

A *beit t'filah* devoted to Torah will probe the relationships between Torah and prayer. Its rabbis will ask why the Torah is read after the offering of the *Amidah*, which during the week includes petitionary prayers for health, prosperity, justice, repentance, and other gifts. While we do not offer these petitions on Shabbat (Shabbat is to be experienced as though all these requests had been granted), we do offer them on two other days when the Torah is read—Mondays and Thursdays. It is as though, after pouring out our hearts that God might grant us these hopes, we sit back in our seats and listen for a response. That response comes in the reading of the week's Torah portion. A *beit t'filah* grounded in Torah will show us how to listen to the Torah reading as a response to our prayers and will help its members understand where in the text that response may be found. Such a *beit t'filah* will also recognize that to hear that response, Shabbat services alone, with an *Amidah* shorn of these petitions, are not sufficient; the American Reform Movement, like Reform synagogues in Toronto, needs to start offering at least one daily prayer session a week.

A Reform *beit t'filah* will also encourage its members to study the siddur itself, including understanding its development from a material system of drawing near (*hitkarvut*) to God through the *korban*, the sacrifice, to the spiritual system of prayer. What are the origins of the structure and content of the *Union Prayer Book*, *Gates of Prayer*, and *Mishkan T'filah?* How did the various generations of editors of these siddurim make their decisions on what to include, exclude, and change from the traditional siddur? What changes would today's worshipers make? One of the changes a number of Reform synagogues have made stems from the realization that smaller, "alternative" minyanim may allow more members to take leadership roles in a service that may offer more or less Hebrew, different kinds of music, or more varied styles of Torah reading and *parashah* discussion than the "main" service.

Our *beit t'filah* needs to be devoted to *g'milut chasadim* as well. Merely to engage in projects of social justice can easily degenerate into a series of secular activities. Doing good is important, surely, but a synagogue community needs to do mitzvot, doing good as a response to the requests of God. A synagogue that engages in social action needs to study and practice the religious dimensions of doing justly, and prayer is one way to discover that. To begin a project of feeding the homeless with a meal at which *Motzi* and *Birkat HaMazon* are offered, to gather one's congregation together at the start of a peace march (particularly if it takes place on Shabbat) and offer prayers appropriate for the time of day, puts both the Jews and non-Jews present in a mood to see the spiritual dimension of what might otherwise pass as merely a political or charitable activity. Acts of *g'milut chasadim*, are, after all, acts in imitation of the God who fed the hungry in the wilderness, clothed the naked in Eden, and freed the captives from Egypt. When a synagogue engages in *g'milut chasadim*, it is appropriate to acknowledge through prayer that God is our guide.

Finally, a synagogue that is conscious of its role as a *beit k'neset*, a house of meeting, will ask itself: how can everything we do encourage members to meet each other—and members to meet non-members, Jews to meet non-Jews? By "meet," what is meant is not merely to wear name tags or shake hands, but to strive for Martin Buber's ideal that true meeting is to stand in relation with a total person. The leader of Torah study should encourage the students in a *beit midrash* to come to know each other through the texts with which they wrestle, just as Jacob and the angel came to know each other's identity in their wrestle by the waters. The waters of Torah should bring forth similar self-revelations, not like 1960s-style "encounter groups," but as a group encouraged to see themselves reflected in the texts, bringing their own experience, along with the insights of past ages, to understanding the text. *Avodah*—the service of prayer and observance—should also encourage meeting. The seating should be arranged so that worshipers can hear each other pray and see each other wrestle with the meanings of prayers and the search for the presence of God. Time should be allotted in the service for worshipers to study a prayer text together, to share their feelings about a prayer text, and to see the image of the God to whom they pray in the persons of the people praying with them. Acts of *g'milut chasadim* should enable participants to share discussions of their motivations and struggles in deciding to do these actions, as well as to spend time getting to know the people with whom they are sharing food, time at the bedside, energy in building a house, or passion in working for peace in the world. Acts of social justice fulfill the prophetic command to act as servants of God. We must get acquainted with those who are serving with us, that we may more profoundly understand what serving God can mean.

There is a more practical dimension to the *beit k'neset* as well. A synagogue offering a variety of study groups, alternative minyanim, and social justice projects may come to believe that the place is becoming too fractionalized. To prevent such a perception, the synagogue might consider a radical restructuring of its board of directors, asking each study group, minyan, social justice project, and the school to select a member of the board, which could grow into a council representing the various vibrant communities within the synagogue. This council would be an enabling body, setting goals, apportioning funds, continually evaluating the manner in which the synagogue was carrying out its mission. By reporting on its work at each meeting and carrying back to each community's members the work of other groups within the synagogue and encouraging them to join other groups as well, the council would exemplify a synagogue in which its constituent parts and their members are committed to gathering together and meeting each other.

The "Holy Vessels" of the Synagogue

How does such a "representative" synagogue integrate its rabbi(s) and cantor(s), educators, and other professionals? The first step is that the synagogue does not merely see them as "professionals." Synagogue members should strive to relate to them as *k'lei kodesh*, vessels for the sharing of the holiness sought by each member of the synagogue. Rabbi Paul J. Menitoff, as executive vice president of the CCAR, urged us not to "hire" or "employ" our *k'lei kodesh*, but rather to "engage" them, "make covenants" with them. Rabbi Eric Yoffie, president of the URJ, has urged that we sign not a "contract" with these professionals, but a *b'rit kodesh*, a holy covenant. The synagogue has expectations of its *k'lei kodesh*, as they have for the members; it is a mutual relationship that requires ongoing dialogue to ensure that the *k'lei kodesh* are nurtured as well as the members are and that both the *k'lei kodesh* and the members are fulfilling their expectations. It is a relationship that affirms the *k'dushah* of the personal lives of both members and *k'lei kodesh* and is determined to protect that sanctity. These are not usually the ways the relationship between laity and professionals is articulated, but a synagogue that seeks to become central to the lives of both members and *k'lei kodesh* will see itself in a partnership, whose members pour forth their desire to learn and their time, talents, and generosity into the *keilim*, who in turn pour out their own time, learning, and love of teaching and service into the members. In such a synagogue, everyone aspires to be *k'lei kodesh*, giving and receiving, receiving and giving. Dialogue in a great synagogue can be a pouring forth of *k'dushah* from one to another to another, in all the diverse streams God daily pours into us.

In her book *A Congregation of Learners* (UAHC Press, 1995), Dr. Isa Aron calls for a synagogue in which learning permeates the entire congregation, in much the way I have suggested that the synagogue needs to be a true *beit midrash*. But I would argue that the Reform synagogue also needs to become a congregation of worshipers and a congregation gathering as a community, a congregation whose every activity is permeated by Torah, *avodah*, and *g'milut chasadim*. This kind of synagogue becomes the center not only for its own members, but for the larger community as well.

There are those who would say that "the center" can never be a building, even a synagogue, but that one's center needs to reside within oneself, in one's own *n'shamah*. In this understanding, the synagogue is a metaphor for the need to transform oneself into a *beit midrash*, where Torah pours from us into every aspect of our daily lives, informing everything we read and see and hear; a *beit t'filah*, where prayer is so ingrained in our being that the sight of a sunset or a rainbow or a wise person spontaneously evokes one of the *Birchot HaNehenin*, and where we instinctively gravitate to a place of prayer each morning, afternoon, and evening; and a *beit k'neset*, where compassion for others created in God's image leads us to instinctive acts of love and justice whenever our paths cross that of another human being. A synagogue that inspires this kind of personal transformation will surely elevate the spiritual, intellectual, and cultural quality of our lives.

A World with Two Centers

The Diaspora's Gift to Israel

If the synagogue is central to Reform Jewish life, what does this say about Israel, which according to the classical Zionist position is the proper center of Jewish life?

It is frequently stated that the Columbus Platform of 1937 overturned the 1885 Pittsburgh Platform's rejection of a return to Zion. In a way, though, the Pittsburgh Platform is inconsistent in saying that "we . . . expect neither a return to Palestine . . . nor the restoration of any of the laws concerning the Jewish state" while also affirming that "we consider ourselves no longer a nation, but a religious community." If Judaism is (only) a religion to be practiced in any country, why did the nineteenth-century Reformers turn their backs on Jewish life in Eretz Yisrael? The view that Jews should be able to practice Judaism in any country they inhabit has not been the rationale for Reform's support of Jewish life in *Eretz Yisrael*. It has been much more affirmative than that.

When the CCAR adopted "Reform Judaism and Zionism: A Centenary Platform" in 1997, it called the State of Israel "the spiritual and cultural focal point of world Jewry." The Pittsburgh Principles, adopted two years later, uses different language, more in keeping with the thrust of Reform policy toward *Eretz Yisrael* from the time of the Columbus Platform. On the one hand, the Pittsburgh Principles does not see the State of Israel as just another state in which Jews have a right to live. But it also does not see Israel as the center of Reform Jewish life. In a sense it sees Israel as equivalent to all the states of the Diaspora in which Jews reside and calls for a reciprocal relationship between the State of Israel and the Diaspora:

> As we urge Jews who reside outside Israel to learn Hebrew as a living language and to make periodic visits to Israel in order to study and deepen their relationship to the Land and its people, so do we affirm that Israeli Jews have much to learn from the religious life of Diaspora Jewish communities.

In some ways, this statement affirms the principle enunciated in 1957 by Shimon Rawidowicz in "Jerusalem and Babylon"[1] asserting that the Jewish world is an ellipse with two centers, in Israel and the Diaspora. While classical Zionists would certainly reject the notion that Israel is just one of many countries in which Jews live, they would also deride some of the language of the 1999 Pittsburgh Principles as preposterous: how can the Diaspora have anything to teach those who live at the center?

The Pittsburgh Principles itself suggests an answer: as the synagogue is the center of Diaspora life, so should it be the central gift the Diaspora can make to Israel. The synagogue is the primary (though not the only) place where Diaspora Jews learn Hebrew. Though it is usually the Hebrew of the Bible and siddur, those texts form the basis of a knowledge of the language for most Diaspora Jews. Even this "synagogue Hebrew" can encourage young Jews to want to speak and read modern Hebrew. Year-abroad programs and youth programs of the URJ, Hillel, and other movements have brought record numbers of young Jews into the life of the State of Israel. These young Jews have been in the forefront of the cross-pollination of American and Israeli religious life, bringing the melodies and *minhagim* from Israel back to North America, which in turn enrich American synagogue offerings, which in turn become models for Reform and other rabbis in Israel to introduce in their own synagogues. The innovations in worship, the insights into turning synagogues into "congregations of learners," and many other aspects of American synagogue life have helped transform the Israeli religious and educational scene.

So it has always been. The prayer and study communities conducted by the prophets and priests during the Babylonian exile developed into the *maamadot*, gatherings of communities in *Eretz Yisrael* during the Second Temple period when those communities' priests and Levites would go up to the Temple to do their service. Following the destruction of the Second Temple, these developed into full-fledged synagogues in *Eretz Yisrael* and Babylonia and seeded themselves in Jewish communities throughout the Diaspora. Each country developed its own *minhag*, customs, and after the expulsion from Spain, the particular culture of Sephardic synagogues also took root around the world. Medieval *paitanim*, liturgical poets, and kabbalistic scholars in Safed added to the worship in synagogues. Later, in the eighteenth century, Kabbalah helped create the Chasidic *shtieblach* in eastern Europe that had so profound an effect on eastern European and North American synagogues. When those Chasidim who could do so fled Nazi Europe to *Eretz Yisrael*, the movement took firm root in the *yishuv* and the Jewish state as well. Reform synagogues migrated from Germany to North America, where the Conservative and Reconstructionist Movements founded their own houses of worship, and by the 1950s these movements were starting to export their brand of worship to Israel as well. To this day, some of the most vibrant synagogues in the world—of all the movements—are those that have brought American Reform, Conservative, and modern Orthodox models to the State of

Israel, where they have flourished and taken on new forms in the atmosphere of a land awash in *k'dushah*.

For the Reform Movement, it is the synagogue and its *k'lei kodesh* who have begun to spark a revolution in the Jewish state. Until the Reform and Conservative Movements began to spread their influence in Israel, the state had hardened into two opposing camps: *datiyim* and *chiloniyim*, the Orthodox (including the *charedim*, the anti-Zionist ultra-Orthodox "tremblers") and the secularists. The Israeli Reform Movement, there called the Israel Movement for Progressive Judaism, has tried to bridge the gap, reaching into the "secular" community to find Jews longing for a spiritual dimension to their lives. These are Israeli Jews who want to learn Torah not as a nationalistic book but as a reflection of God's relationship with the Jewish people. While Reform synagogues have multiplied and grown (with a few in Jerusalem and Tel Aviv becoming quite sizable), the greatest influence of Reform has been its contributions to the celebration of life cycle events. Thousands of Israelis have asked Reform rabbis to preside when their children become bar or bat mitzvah, to perform their weddings, and to work with them on conversion. The interest in Reform weddings in particular has been remarkable. Because of the power of the state to control marriages, those who desire a Reform marriage have had to fly out of the country (usually to nearby Cyprus) for a legal ceremony and then return for a Reform religious service. Reform educators have made their way into government schools through the innovative TALI program and have enlisted parental support to teach Jewish subjects neither from a secular nor an Orthodox viewpoint, but a liberal Jewish one. For a long time the Israeli Reform Movement was dismissed as a Diaspora import, but since the Hebrew Union College began ordaining Israelis in 1980, a significant number of homegrown Israeli Reform rabbis, cantors, and educators are beginning to enter Israeli society. As part of an intensified effort begun by HUC president David Ellenson to integrate Diaspora and Israeli concerns, the college's year-in-Israel program continued uninterrupted through the worst years of the Second Intifada, and Israeli faculty members and rabbinic students are being helped to spend some time in North America as part of their work.

The Issue of Aliyah

This historic and contemporary flow between *Eretz Yisrael* and the Diaspora is echoed in the Pittsburgh Principles and distinguishes it significantly from the thrust of the 1997 Reform Zionist platform. By insisting on reciprocal language rather than the language of the center, the Pittsburgh Principles suggests that while Reform Jews are of course free to affirm a belief in Israel as "the spiritual and cultural focal point of world Jewry," as expressed in the Reform Zionist platform, it is not a universal affirmation of the Reform Movement. Both documents support *aliyah*, for example, but for very different reasons.

According to the Reform Zionist platform:

> While affirming the authenticity and necessity of a creative and vibrant Diaspora Jewry, we encourage *aliyah* [immigration] to Israel in pursuance of the precept of *yishuv Eretz Yisrael* [settling the Land of Israel]. While Jews can live Torah-centered lives in the Diaspora, only in *Medinat Yisrael* do they bear the primary responsibility for the governance of society, and thus may realize the full potential of their individual and communal religious strivings.

The Pittsburgh Principles states:

> We affirm the unique qualities of living in *Eretz Yisrael*, the Land of Israel, and encourage *aliyah,* immigration to Israel.

There was considerable debate on the floor of the Pittsburgh convention regarding the phrase "encourage *aliyah*." Many rabbis seemed to have forgotten that two years before they had endorsed this same language in the platform on Reform Zionism and argued forcefully that it seemed to affirm a preference for life in Israel rather than the Diaspora. Some preferred the verb "support" over "encourage." "Support" suggested to them that if one wanted to make *aliyah*, we would support them, while "encourage" seemed to suggest that the Reform Movement was taking the initiative, completely reversing its century-and-a-half privileging of the Diaspora and turning the Diaspora and its educational system into but a feeder for immigration to Israel. For a while it seemed that any mention of *aliyah* was about to fall victim to the struggle between an Israel-centered and a two-centers philosophy. Then Rabbi Margaret Meyer, whose son had made *aliyah* some years before, argued movingly that she merely wanted her CCAR to stand behind the family's decision to "encourage" him, turning the tide to retain the original wording. The two-centers position was subsequently strengthened by the adoption of Rabbi Herbert Bronstein's motion for the reciprocal language ("As we urge Jews who reside outside Israel . . . so do we affirm that Israeli Jews . . .").

But the difference between the Reform Zionism platform and the Pittsburgh Principles on the rationale for *aliyah* is illuminating. The Zionist platform argues that *aliyah* permits Jews full participation in the governance of a Jewish state, and this fact "may realize the full potential of their individual and communal strivings." The Pittsburgh Principles merely speaks about "the unique qualities of living in *Eretz Yisrael*," without affirming the political Zionist idea of *hagshamah*, "fulfillment" of Jewish life. By affirming the synagogue as the center of Jewish life, the Pittsburgh Principles makes a very different statement: Jewish life needs to be centered around a religious and educational institution, not a political one.

A Force to Change Israel

On the other hand, contrary to the Reform Zionist document, the Pittsburgh Principles suggests that we can influence politics in Israel even though we may not live there:

> We are committed to a vision of the State of Israel that promotes full civil, human and religious rights for all its inhabitants and that strives for a lasting peace between Israel and its neighbors.

While the Pittsburgh Principles urges us to work for that vision from the Diaspora, the platform on Reform Zionism helps us understand what that vision should be:

> We believe that the eternal covenant established at Sinai ordained a unique religious purpose for *Am Yisrael*. *Medinat Yisrael*, the Jewish state, is therefore unlike all other states. Its obligation is to strive towards the attainment of the Jewish people's highest moral ideals to be a *mamlechet kohanim* [a kingdom of priests], a *goy kadosh* [a holy people], and *l'or goyim* [a light unto the nations]. . . . Ultimately, *Medinat Yisrael* will be judged not on its military might but on its character.

Taken together, the Pittsburgh Principles and the Reform Zionist platform envision a Jewish state governed by Torah as understood in a liberal Jewish perspective. "Full civil and human rights," interpreted in the light of CCAR and RAC resolutions, should be understood as referring to the rights of Israeli Arabs to be given full rights of citizenship,[2] while "full . . . religious rights" should be understood as guarantees of the rights of non-Orthodox Jewish groups to have the same access to government funds as Orthodox groups, even if that means the government stops giving funds to religious schools and organizations. It means eliminating the obstacles the religious establishment periodically imposes against building Reform synagogues or including Reform and Conservative rabbis in positions of authority. Similarly, it means either allowing Reform and Conservative rabbis to register marriages, as Orthodox rabbis do, or eliminating religious marriage altogether. The Reform Movement, in and outside of Israel, has been ambivalent about which of these courses it prefers. A state in which marriage and divorce are secular functions, as in the United States, provides a level playing field for all, but it prevents Jewish ideals and practices from playing a role in the governance of the state. Would secular marriage and divorce lessen the Jewish character of the State of Israel? Is the only way to end the Orthodox monopoly on status issues to completely eliminate religion from these decisions? Should it not be possible, or at least desirable, to provide for a pluralistic system of marriage, divorce, and conversion in which Reform and Conservative rabbis could officiate at ceremonies officially sanctioned by the Jewish state?

Another difference between the platform on Reform Zionism and the Pittsburgh Principles appears in the two documents' treatment of the issue of peace between Israel and the Palestinians and Israel and her Arab neighbors. The Reform Zionist platform speaks of peace as a far-off messianic vision:

> While that day of redemption remains but a distant yearning, we express the fervent hope that *Medinat Yisrael*, living in peace with its neighbors, will hasten the redemption of *Am Yisrael*, and the fulfillment of our messianic dream of universal peace under the sovereignty of God.

The Pittsburgh Principles, however, speaks of a state that works for peace in the present—"that strives for a lasting peace between Israel and its neighbors." Reform organizations were among the strongest supporters of the Oslo peace process in the 1990s and were among the most disillusioned when Yasser Arafat backed away from the generous offer presented by the government of Ehud Barak in 2000. Reform rabbis have been among the strongest supporters of Rabbis for Human Rights, an organization that has exposed Israeli military and government excesses in the occupation of the territories and brought Jews from around the world to meet Palestinians whose human rights have been abused accidentally or purposefully by Israel. In light of the Second Intifada, which followed the breakdown of the 2000 and 2001 negotiations, many Reform Jews have followed the drift of the rest of the Jewish world away from hoping and working for a peace settlement to a deep suspicion of Palestinian intentions and a backing away from the hope that a peaceful settlement can be achieved. Though the Pittsburgh Principles was passed in a heady time of hopes for peace, despair that a settlement can be achieved is contrary to our vision of a Jewish state "that strives for a lasting peace." The operative word is "strives," which means continued work, searching, struggling, strategizing, negotiating, and meeting failure with a determination to begin again. To "strive for a lasting peace" means to support defensive measures to try to ensure security, but it does not mean supporting brutal measures of occupation that are justified in the name of security. Striving for a lasting peace means enlisting in the fight against despair based on the knowledge of what a final settlement might look like, as envisioned in the post–Camp David discussions in Taba in January 2001: an end to Palestinian violence, a demilitarized Palestinian state on most of the West Bank and in Gaza, dismantling most of the Israeli settlements in Gaza and the West Bank, ceding sovereignty over parts of Arab East Jerusalem, Palestinian renunciation of the right of refugees to return to Israel, and unimpeded passage for Palestinians between Gaza and the West Bank. Since we know what peace will mean, we can be hopeful that with continued pressure, the time will come when it can be implemented.

If the Pittsburgh Principles encourages Diaspora Jews to weigh in from abroad on the debate about Israeli policy, then as American Jews we must ask whether we have done all we can. In the peace process particularly, the United States has played a major role for decades, with Democratic presidents generally inserting themselves more actively to try to bring the parties together and Republican presidents generally preferring to let the parties determine the peace timetable for themselves. But if we are to realize our vision of an Israel striving for peace, we in the United States cannot sit idly by. There are always American Jews (and increasingly evangelical Christians) who decry any attempt to pressure Israel, but if too many Israelis have despaired of striving for peace, Reform Jews have an obligation to use whatever influence we have to encourage them. Peace cannot be merely a messianic dream. The midrash argues that peace should be valued above all else, since the Rabbis point out that on several occasions the Torah even allows for the distortion of truth or the profaning of God's name in order to bring about peace between one human being and another (Joseph and his brothers, a suspected adulteress and her husband). Here is a clear example how the lessons taught in text study in the synagogue can be mobilized to send us out into the political arena to help realize our visions for the Jewish state.

Nor should we consider such activity only "political" in nature. The stalemate in the peace process has severely hampered the *hagshamah*, the fulfillment, of the vision of interpenetration of the best features of Israel and Diaspora, even the fulfillment of a vision of the synagogue as the centerpiece for the enrichment of Diaspora and Israeli religious and educational life. The Second Intifada decimated the number of American Jews willing to go to Israel on year-abroad or summer programs, a development that has weakened the exposure to modern Hebrew speech and literature as a vehicle for understanding Israeli life from the inside. It has discouraged the young American Jews who have often been the primary instruments of exchange between American and Israeli spiritual life.

In the days when Oslo was working, dovish American Jews would often cross into the West Bank and meet with Palestinians, in search of aspects of Palestinian culture that they could integrate into American Jewish consciousness, particularly poetry and literature. That source also dried up during the Second Intifada. In the previous chapter we spoke of Jacob and Esau as twin sides of Western culture. We speak of Isaac and

Ishmael, Jew and Arab, in a similar vein. They are not twins, but half-brothers—cultures that have lived side by side for millennia in the divers roles of good neighbors, benign masters, and cruel oppressors. While life in the Western Diaspora has made Jews aware of the Jacob-Esau interrelationship, it is the State of Israel that has made us aware of our shadow life with Arabs. Our languages are from the same family, our religions are much closer than Judaism and Christianity, yet we know Latin and even Greek much better than we know Arabic, and we are much better informed about Christianity than we are about Islam. Though Ishmael is but a half-brother, he is intrinsically much more like us than Esau is like Jacob. (The Rabbis see the verb *m'TZaCHeiK* in Genesis 21:9, usually translated "making sport," to mean "pretending to be *YiTZCHaK* [Isaac]"). Paradoxically, the creation of the State of Israel simultaneously created for us the reality of Ishmael as the "other side" of our being as Zionists. The creation of the State of Israel has made dovish Jews—and Reform Jews are a high percentage of those—desirous of finding out more about the people with whom we have been struggling for the same piece of land, with whom we must, selfishly, make peace if the full potential of Zionism and a moral Jewish state are to be realized. Peace for us cannot be seen as merely a political desideratum. If Reform Jewish life is properly lived between the poles of Israel and Diaspora, peace is crucial for the full flowering of a spiritual, intellectual, and cultural life informed by the fulfilled cultures of both communities.

A Center Made of Stones

I began writing this chapter as I sat in Jerusalem on a terrace of the house that Nelson Glueck built on the grounds of the Hebrew Union College when he was still its president. The house is built of thick Jerusalem stones, each one different, some with glints of rose, others of brown, still others of black dirt, each one leaving some of its dust on your hands when you finish caressing it. In the gardens behind me, children in the nursery school that the College operates are squealing with the delight of being able to run and shout in the clear blue Jerusalem air, and in the classrooms below me, the future rabbis, cantors, and educators of the Reform Movement are learning and singing together, arguing, and dreaming of the kind of world they want to help create when they leave this city and return to the Diaspora to begin to serve their people and their God. Nelson Glueck was the first Zionist to head the Hebrew Union College, and it was his selection that made Stephen S. Wise content to merge the Jewish Institute of Religion he had founded into the older institution. When Dr. Glueck built this house, it was one of the few pieces of Jewish property that could see into the Old City in the years before the Six-Day War. The gardens teem with palm trees, the plant of righteousness and justice, and olive trees, the symbol, since Noah's time, of peace. Adjacent are Bet Shmuel, the movement's youth hostel, and Bet Shimshon, the center for the World Union for Progressive Judaism. This section of Jerusalem, so close to the Old City but part of a thriving Jewish West Jerusalem, is a tribute to the determination of the Reform and Progressive Movements not only to remain in Jerusalem, but to affect it, and the country beyond. We want to be a force for godliness and Torah here, for uplifting the Jewish spirit beyond the towers of the Old City and the high-rises on the Mediterranean to bring God into the lives of everyone whose feet tread this ancient soil. We want to be a force for peace here, to elevate Israelis' gazes from the bloodstained ground they daily walk and to be able to believe in their dreams that Jews and Palestinians who walk this same ground may share parts of this land together. We want to believe that present enemies may grow and prosper together, may worship God as Elohim or Allah and believe that the God behind the names loves them both, as God must love this land they share, so poignantly has the Holy One watered it with tears from the beginning until this day. It is not enough for us that secular Israelis might become religious. We must also enable them to believe that a religious life will help them reach out to the stranger, to the enemy, and to lose the face of the enemy that the stranger sees in us.

As the earth tips away from the sun, different colors emerge from the stones on this terrace. Are not human beings at least as compassionate as stones, to be able like them to live side by side in our differences? *Shaalu sh'lom Y'rushalayim*—in all the synagogues where Reform Jews pray, we pray that in the near future peace will come to this city whose dust will never leave our hands.

16

The Progressive Way
in a Strife-Torn World

We are committed to promoting and strengthening Progressive Judaism in Israel, which will enrich the spiritual life of the Jewish state and its people.

We are committed to furthering Progressive Judaism throughout the world as a meaningful religious way of life for the Jewish people.

—Statement of Principles, "Israel," paragraphs 11, 13[1]

Return to Europe

Despite the destruction of central and eastern European Jewry in the Second World War, Jews have refused to accede to Hitler's dream of a Europe *Judenrein*, cleansed of Jews. Our belief, as the Pittsburgh Principles states, that despite the attempt to eradicate European Jewry, "the partnership of God and humanity will ultimately prevail," is shown most dramatically in the postwar return of Jews to Europe, the birthplace of the Reform Movement. While Orthodoxy had reasserted itself in the years after the war as the dominant European religious community, Reform and Conservative communities have gradually strengthened their presence there. The Liberal and Reform Movements in Great Britain survived the war and in the years following increased the number of their synagogues. They jointly founded a rabbinical school in London, the Leo Baeck College, named for the great leader of German Jewry who endured Theresienstadt and went on to lead the World Union of Progressive Judaism until his death. The rabbi of the Paris Union Libérale Israélite, Louis-Germain Lévy, emerged from hiding after the war and rebuilt his synagogue, which had been heavily damaged by the Nazis. New Progressive synagogues sprang up in Germany, the Netherlands, Belgium, and Switzerland. European Jewry, and European Progressive Jewry, was once again on the rise.[2] Reform also continued to grow in South America, Australia, and South Africa, though the chaotic death throes of apartheid led many Jews to flee to Israel or the United States in fear of its consequences.

The most remarkable developments, however, took place after the fall of the Soviet Union in 1989. Reform Jews, like many in other movements, had been strong supporters of the refuseniks for almost twenty years, with rabbis and cantors teaching the secret communities gathered behind locked doors and drawn shades. Clergy and congregants brought siddurim, *tallitot*, Bibles, and educational materials, primarily to strengthen the Jewish commitment of Soviet Jews so that when the government allowed it, they would be motivated to make *aliyah*. But everyone knew, including the Israeli government, which secretly funded these visits, that a majority of the three million Jews in the Soviet Union would never go en masse to Israel. Thus the visitations were also intended to help create a Jewish life for those Soviet Jews who would remain. It is generally accepted that the refuseniks' struggle was one of the factors that contributed to the undermining of the entire Communist regime, so that when Mikhail Gorbachev relinquished power, the Soviet government and the entire structure of the Union of Soviet Socialist Republics collapsed, as did its hold on the Eastern European nations of the Warsaw Pact. The careful, steady work of creating a Jewish infrastructure during the refusenik period succeeded. Synagogues, Hillel foundations, and other Jewish organizations began to flourish in the newly independent states of the old Soviet Union, with the result that as of this writing one hundred Reform synagogues and organizations exist there. The World Union, now led dynamically by Rabbi Uri Regev, has opened an Institute for Modern Jewish Studies

(*Machon*) in Moscow, which sends out the graduates of its two-year pararabbinic school to serve its vibrant congregations. Despite these successes, however, many problems still remain. The Russian Orthodox Church is still hostile to other religious groups, though Judaism is listed as a legal religion by the Russian government. Inside the Jewish community, Lubavitch, which had done courageous work supporting the refuseniks in the Soviet period, maneuvered to secure the Chief Rabbinate in Russia, preventing government support from flowing to Reform synagogues—a new chapter in an old story in Europe and Israel. But the worldwide Progressive Movement has not been deterred by either of these obstacles. Rabbi Joel Oseran, associate director of the World Union, has done noble work in making frequent visits to the nascent synagogues there, bringing resources and enthusiastic support to this remarkable community.

The fall of the Soviet Union had an impact on Progressive communities in the rest of Europe as well. A number of Soviet Jews migrated to Germany when the Berlin Wall fell, swelling the number of Jews in that country. Thirteen liberal synagogues now exist in Germany, and a liberal rabbinical school, Geiger College, has been created in Potsdam, a suburb of Berlin, by Rabbi Walter Jacob, rabbi emeritus of Rodeph Shalom in Pittsburgh, who was born in Berlin, and whose grandfather Benno was a major Jewish scholar in Germany before the Second World War. The school is directed by Rabbi Walter Homolka, who studied at the Leo Baeck College and was ordained by Rabbi Jacob.

While the spread of liberal Judaism in Europe has been part of a wider phenomenon of the re-Judaization of Europe, the phenomenon has special poignancy for Reform Jews. Reform was born in Germany, and nineteenth-century German philosophy was a major inspiration for the hopeful, messianic thrust of early Reform. The Pittsburgh Platform of 1885, while written in the United States, continued the theological reflection of the German Reform Synods and was heavily influenced by German idealist philosophy. As we have seen, the destruction of German and European Jewry both destroyed the communities in which Reform had taken root and affected the descendants of the German Jewish émigrés who had created Reform on this continent. It also threatened some of the confidence that gave early Reform in America its panache.

Reform's rootedness in German optimism helped it win wide acceptance in the optimistic, messianic world that was the America of Manifest Destiny. Were the early Reformers misled in their confidence? Were they wrong?

Though the Holocaust seemed to sound the death knell to any hopeful reading of European Jewry's future, the return of Jewish life, and especially Reform Jewish life, to Europe compels us to take a second look. On one level, this return is not so unique; Jews have often returned to the countries from which they were driven out. European Jews were not only driven out though—they were murdered and gassed. Their physical destruction was a cornerstone of the policies of the Nazi Party. But *t'chiyat hameitim* is an old Jewish belief, even if the German Reformers rejected it. Just as the dry bones of Ezekiel's vision rose to renewed life, as we read in the haftarah for the intermediate Shabbat during Pesach, the dry bones live again in Germany, Russia, and the rest of Europe. The return of Reform Judaism to a reborn Europe reminds us that we need to exercise broad vision when we try to discern the pattern of God's will in history. It reminds us that when we pray for redemption, we need to be patient as we listen for God's response. Many factors effected the freeing of Jews in the Soviet Union—the policies of Ronald Reagan and Mikhail Gorbachev were only part of the puzzle. I firmly believe that our prayers and actions made a contribution too. The Progressive Movement in Judaism has said: we did not seek only the economic and political liberation of Soviet Jews, we sought their religious liberation as well. Liberal Judaism can contribute to the personal spiritual lives of Russian and Ukrainian Jews, and it can also contribute to the commitment of Jews to a democratic future for their troubled countries.

The return of Reform Judaism to Europe is, in many ways, a powerful "thank you" to the original sources of Reform, which created and inspired us. German Jews (Reform and others) clung for too long to their optimism that they might continue to thrive in Nazi Germany. That the Progressive Movement has returned to that country is in some ways a tribute to those Jews, as though to say, "We understand your optimism. We have been chastened by the price you paid for it, but we refuse to betray it." Before the Nazis, Jewish religion, scholarship, and culture flourished abundantly on German soil, and the products of the German spirit enshrined in nineteenth-century Reform messianism can stir us still. As Reform Jews, we should be able to see our return to Europe not only as a sociological or political act but also a religious one, reclaiming something of the divine in German culture that so nourished generations of Jews who flourished there. We can lend our spirits and our shoulders to the rebuilding of a democratic and responsible German culture.

We face new challenges in European countries that have seen a resurgence of anti-Semitism, either by neo-Nazis or anti-Israel Muslims. Shall we fight for our rights to live undisturbed in those countries? Shall we use whatever influence we have to punish our attackers? Shall we hold out a vision for a diverse and democratic Europe, joining with whatever allies we may find, in the face of these attacks? Israeli leaders speak out forcefully to governments whose Jewish communities are threatened; should not Jews in North America enlist the commitment of our governments to make sure that European nations protect our brothers and sisters? And is it not in the Jewish community's interest to prod the U.S. government particularly to develop a respectful partnership with its allies so that such American diplomatic interventions will receive a hospitable reception? And if, God forbid, the time should come again when the demonic forces rout the democratic ones, shall we help Jews turn their backs on their European hosts before they are entrapped once again? The answers to all these questions must be yes. We must be guided on the one hand by our traditional Reform optimism, taking risks to further the developing culture of post–Cold War Europe, and on the other hand by a realistic appraisal of the course of the battle between the forces of light and the forces of darkness.

American Reform: Help or Hindrance to World Progressives?

Well in advance of such calamitous occurrences, we need to strengthen our own credibility as a partner with liberal Jewish communities around the world. We need to recognize that relations between North American and European Reform have played out with both mutual regard and one-sided insensitivity. While American liturgical publications have helped inspire European ones, the British prayer books of the Union of Liberal and Progressive Synagogues in the 1960s helped create the North American *Gates* series. When the late Rabbi Chaim Stern was serving in Great Britain, he and Rabbi John Rayner wrote *Service of the Heart* and *Gate of Repentance*; the CCAR contracted with him to use the British publications as the basis for *Gates of Prayer* and *Gates of Repentance*. Another positive example of interdependence came about when the Executive Board of the CCAR met in London in December 1997 with rabbis of World Union congregations in Israel, Europe, and elsewhere to discuss mission statements and platforms. Heretofore, the CCAR had not been very engaged in discussions about a proposed new statement of principles. But as its board was about to consider the first draft of the Ten Principles, its members were very interested in seeing what colleagues in Europe had done. Much of that meeting was spent discussing the British mission statement, a draft of a French statement, and an Israeli statement. When the CCAR members saw that their work was part of a development throughout the rest of the Liberal Jewish world, they began to see the importance of a new North American state-ment. In the CCAR board meeting that followed the joint sessions with World Union colleagues, the first draft of the Pittsburgh Principles was considered thoroughly and thoughtfully. The discussion of the North American Principles began in London and, a year and a half later, took its place in a worldwide Progressive dialogue about what Judaism could be in the twenty-first century.

The influence of the European communities on the Pittsburgh Principles is, unfortunately, an exception to a relationship in which too often North American Reform is oblivious to developments in the rest of the world. As noted earlier, one particularly poignant example is the American Reform position on patrilineal descent. When the patrilineal discussions were taking place in the CCAR in the mid-1980s, not only were there no attempts to discuss their impact with representatives of other streams of Judaism, but we did not even reach out to Progressive Jews in Israel and around the world. American Reform Jews did not properly understand the effect patrilineal descent would have on world Liberal Jewry. Because Liberal Jews are a minority of the Jewish com-munity outside North America, they are much more vulnerable to verbal attack than American Reform Jews. They fear that these attacks undermine their credibility with their own members as well as with those who might be drawn into the movement. It is hard for Liberal and Reform Jews around the world to distance themselves from American Reform positions, and they do not like to do so, because they see themselves as linked to us in a worldwide movement. We in America have not always been so sensitive, often arguing that because we are the largest Reform Movement, we should not have to compromise our positions with those of the smaller Progressive Movements in Europe, Israel, and elsewhere. This attitude seems uncomfortably similar to the unilateral positions taken several times by the American government at the turn of the twenty-first century. It is uncomfortable to be reminded that positions we take as Reform Jews are sometimes influenced by positions endemic to the American general culture after the Cold War.

Awareness of these tensions with other Progressive Jews was in part responsible for the inclusion of a commitment to *k'lal Yisrael* in the 1999 Pittsburgh Principles. One of the issues that roiled us in London in 1998 was the question of officiation at same-gender marriages, a bit of unfinished business on the CCAR agenda from the many attempts of the CCAR to include gay and lesbian Jews fully into the life of American Jewry. While the Israeli Reform rabbinate has quietly affirmed to itself that its members would officiate at these services when asked, they were not ready to go public with these affirmations, and they pleaded with their American colleagues not to hamper the growth that the Israeli Progressive Movement had been enjoying by a public declaration. In the end, the leadership of the CCAR agreed and decided to declare that the position of the CCAR was represented in statements developed by two CCAR committees, one that affirmed and the other that opposed such marriages. Two years later, after a concerted effort to educate colleagues about the nature of these ceremonies and of the couples who had been married in them, the CCAR passed a resolution supporting both those who did officiate and those who did not. Thanks to a great deal of sensitive work by then president Rabbi Charles A. Kroloff, the resolution passed with fewer than ten rabbis voting against it. Most of the Israeli rabbis present voted for the resolution. The leadership of the CCAR also promised to begin discussions with leadership from the other American movements about the implications of this vote for them and their homosexual populations. Perhaps this process represents a new trend in working together with Progressive colleagues.

One of the delicate issues at work between American and Israeli Progressive Jews is the fact that what the Israeli Progressive Movement needs most from us is people and money. A significant Reform Jewish *aliyah* and significant underwriting of Israeli Reform *k'lei kodesh* and institutions could transform the Israeli Reform Movement and Israeli religious life. Israeli rabbis make periodic fund-raising trips to the United States, and American congregations partner with Israeli communities. On the other hand, the terrorism of the Second Intifada has kept many American Jews from going to Israel to see the progress of Israeli Reform firsthand, and so some of the ardor kindled by personal observation of the movement's growth in the late 1990s has cooled. Meanwhile, the Israeli rabbis, exhausted by all the time they spend on their transatlantic missions, occasionally wonder quietly why more traffic does not go the other way. No doubt it will again, if American pressure on Israel and the Palestinians can restore a greater sense of mutual security and hope for a settlement. Still, as Israeli Reform has become more vibrant and compelling, the leaders of American Reform have increasingly involved Israeli colleagues in North American projects. A representative of the Israeli Reform rabbis attends every board meeting of the CCAR; the editor of *Avodah She-balev*, the Israeli Reform siddur, sat on the editorial committee of *Mishkan T'filah*, the new North American Reform siddur; the dean and director of the rabbinical school of HUC in Jerusalem have spent significant time at American campuses of HUC, and reciprocal visits have also taken place; American colleagues and rabbis have taught in Jerusalem; the provost, deans, directors of schools, and heads of faculty at the four HUC campuses meet monthly by videoconference. Once seen almost as charity events, the fund-raising campaigns for Israeli Reform institutions in the United States now feel more like rallies for successful family members. Supporting Israeli Reform feels less and less like assistance for a minority movement and more like a campaign for Israeli society as a whole.

This perception, that support for Progressive Judaism is support of a progressive nation, is crucial if we are to realize the Pittsburgh

Principles' commitment to worldwide Reform. When American Jews enlist in the campaign to strengthen Progressive Judaism around the world, our vision needs to be a broad one. On one level, it is similar to our vision of Reform in North America—to create a vibrant, profound, inclusive experience of Jewish learning and practice that can transform us into knowledgeable, compassionate, spiritual human beings able to respond to the will of God and to repair a battered world. Most of us work at this vast task one synagogue at a time, one study group and prayer and observance at a time, but when the inevitable frustrations with synagogue politics or the constraints of schedule or budgets cause us to despair, holding onto the larger vision can help keep us going. The Progressive mission has its best chance in the United States, but a movement that began in Europe can never lose sight of its obligations to strengthen Progressive Judaism in countries other than our own. A movement that has been so transformed by the encounter with Israel has at least as powerful an obligation to expand the Progressive Movement there as well.

Yet if we are sincere in our desire to give back to Israel and other countries something of what they have enabled us to do here, we must be motivated by more compelling motives than merely gratitude or the desire to help them survive. In some ways it is easier to see our relationship with the Israeli Progressive Movement as transformative compared to the relationship with Reform in other countries. The Israeli Reformers can help transform the State of Israel by opening the beauties of Judaism to a greater percentage of the population. Reform can offer more Israelis the right to marry, to educate themselves and their children, and to be buried in a manner befitting their beliefs; to celebrate in language and in deed the equality of participation by all women and men without regard to sexual orientation; and to create a powerful alternative to the forces of fundamentalism and resistance to accommodation with the Palestinians. To say that only a significant North American Reform *aliyah* will accomplish this is to underestimate the effect on the next generation of vibrant, inviting Reform synagogues and schools. Twenty and more years ago, critics were saying that concentrating on building synagogues was not in keeping with the Israeli mentality. But fifty years of working at those synagogues, combined with a growing cadre of effective rabbis and lay leaders, has produced Israeli Reform synagogues that have both drawn loyal congregations and become forces in their cities. The partnership between American and Israeli congregations needs to be strengthened by all the institutions in the movement. The Reform presence in the Israeli TALI schools has also helped spread the message of a Progressive way of life that informs Jewish practice in the home and synagogue and breeds liberal commitments for justice and peace in the society at large. Some of these civic qualities have been sorely tested by the shattering of hope in the Second Intifada, but once the inevitable search for peace resumes on both sides, these civic commitments will again rise to the surface of Israeli Reform consciousness. American Jews who have remained steadfast in their devotion to a peaceful settlement can strengthen this part of the Progressive cause in Israel as well.

It is harder to support the Progressive way in other countries as much more than a struggle for survival. Even in Great Britain, where the Liberal and Reform Movements are relatively robust, it seems unlikely that in a country with an Orthodox chief rabbi the Progressive Movements can ever rise to the status even of loyal opposition. But to say that is, I believe, to fall victim to myopia. The most important secular developments in Europe are toward unity, toward seeing the continent—including Britain—as a united entity, and despite the periodic fractures in that unity, the desire to make it a reality remains very strong. If North American Reform is to assist in the growth of Progressive Judaism in Europe, perhaps we too need to look at the movement as an instrument of wider European progressivism. How can the movement harness its rabbis and its lay leaders in the cause of a European union that will protect Jews from the growth of anti-Semitism of recent years, project a more progressive view of Israel in the face of hardening anti-Zionism on the continent, and at the same time enlist Progressive Jews in the cause of European union? How can Progressive Jewish communities contribute to that union? How can the movement to erase the borders that have been so poisonous in the past help enlist Jews in its cause? Just as Israeli Reform Jews came to understand that they could not only press for greater benefits for the movement but also had to confront the wider issues confronting Israeli society, so American Jews might take a lesson from the concern about American unilateralism surrounding the war in Iraq and engage our European colleagues in discussions about how Progressive Judaism might further both European union and a bridging of the American-European divide.

Can Reform Be a Force in Europe?

It may, of course, be completely unrealistic to envision the small European Progressive Movement as a force to impact the countries of Europe. Many questions arise. If American Reform Judaism, with our significant numbers, was unable to cobble together a coherent position either to oppose the war in Iraq or to approve of it, how can we expect a much smaller and more fragmented movement in Europe to weigh in on the side of internationalism? Besides, is European union "good for the Jews"? The stronger Europe becomes, it may well tend to take an ever harsher position vis-à-vis Israel. On the other hand, it may well be in Israel's ultimate interest for others to push a peace process if her government and that of the Palestinians are paralyzed. The Progressive way in Israel has been that a peace settlement with a Palestinian state is good for Israel; resolutions from the CCAR and the URJ over the years have taken the same position. It would surely be in Israel's interest if Progressive Judaism backed European Union support for a peace process, alongside the United States, provided of course that they supported Israel's security within viable borders.

Involvement by European Progressive Jews in wider continental issues may well work to the movement's advantage. To encourage European assistance in the peace process may make the movement more visible and win to its side those enlightened European Jews who oppose the hawkishness of much of the Jewish establishment. While such a stance may also earn Reform more enemies on the Jewish right, early American Reform and contemporary Israeli Reform have understood that taking principled positions can increase a small movement's visibility and cause potential allies to take notice.

While European democracy is solid, democracy in other lands where the Reform Movement has taken hold is not. In the Former Soviet

Union, South Africa, and South American states, the Progressive Movement can work for the betterment of the nation by lending what weight it has to the democratizing forces in the country. In these lands and in Australia, where democracy is strong but the Liberal Jewish Movement is not, there is an urgent need for rabbis, educators, and cantors to help meet the growing needs of the Liberal Movement. The URJ and the Hebrew Union College need to band together to ease the way for new rabbis, educators, and cantors to take positions that can strengthen the movement, enabling existing synagogues to meet their members' needs, creating new synagogues, and reaching out to those who are not members—including the intermarried—to cast their lot with Progressive expressions of Judaism. Salary enhancements, assistance in paying off loans, and increased eligibility for American positions for those who return to North America are all important kinds of support. When the economy is down, it is of course difficult to develop this support, but the Pittsburgh Principles does not say that our commitments to world Progressive Jewry are operable only during a booming economy. We can never leave off nurturing the deep roots of messianic optimism bred in us by our European past.

We are Israel, a people aspiring to holiness, singled out through our ancient covenant and our unique history among the nations to be witnesses to God's presence. To witness God's presence in France, in South Africa, in Russia means not only to show other Jews that God is with them, but to show the citizens among whom they live that God is working to redeem their peoples as well as ours. Our vision needs to encompass not only individuals; ultimately it can affect all the nations of the world.

> In all these ways and more, Israel gives meaning and purpose to our lives.

17

A Closing Prayer

Baruch she-amar v'hayah haolam.
Praised be the One through whose word all things came to be.
May our words find expression in holy actions.
May they raise us up to a life of meaning devoted to God's service
And to the redemption of our world.

Baruch she-amar v'hayah haolam, "Praised be the One through whose word all things came to be," is the opening sentence of the prayer that introduces the psalms of *Shacharit* (Morning Service), reflecting, of course, the descriptions in Genesis 1 of God's creating the world through words. The Pittsburgh Principles is filled with words, human words, taught to us by the God who used words to create that grand expanse of earth and sky we live between. Reflecting the Statement of Principles' evocation of covenant "as reflected in our varied understandings of Creation, Revelation and Redemption," this concluding prayer asks that the words of the Pittsburgh Principles will lift us to fulfill the promise of all three elements of the covenant. If God's words brought a world into being, a world alive with the presence of God's holiness, "may our words find expression in holy actions." May the words in this document and in this book push us out the doors of our homes to pray, to study, to better our neighbor's lot, to wash a bit of the dirt away from the world, to polish the mirrors in which we may see the *tzelem Elohim* in our neighbors' faces, in strangers' faces, and even in the faces of the doers of wickedness. May these words surround the cups of wine on our table, the *lulav* and *etrog* in our sukkot, the words of confession and deeds of *t'shuvah* as we begin the new year, and the Hebrew book from which our children lick honey as they head off to school.

But as we walk the ways revealed to us by the mitzvot, let us feel not only the dirt beneath our feet, but the wind as well. May the mitzvot lift us off the ground, raising us up with the vision to see God's world entire, to see how every puzzling piece of life can fit together, how joy and tragedy and laughter and bitter tears fit together, creating meaning out of isolated pieces, meaning that reassures us that with all that demeans us in the world, we can merit our heritage as a people of priests and prophets, serving God, serving God's creatures, raising up those who are bowed down in the dust so they can know the dust as dry ground between the roaring walls of water, rising up to walk, to run, to cry out, every one, "I too can be redeemed!"

In all these ways and more, we too may walk with meaning and purpose into the vision of holiness that can be our lives.

Declaration of Principles:
The Pittsburgh Platform (1885)

In view of the wide divergence of opinion, of conflicting ideas in Judaism to-day, we, the representatives of Reform Judaism in America, in continuation of the work begun at [the] Philadelphia [conference], in 1869, unite upon the following principles:

First. We recognize in every religion an attempt to grasp the Infinite, and in every mode, source or book of revelation, held sacred in any religious system, the consciousness of the indwelling of God in man. We hold that Judaism presents the highest conception of the God-idea as taught in our Holy Scriptures and developed and spiritualized by the Jewish teachers, in accordance with the moral and philosophical progress of their respective ages. We maintain that Judaism preserved and defended, midst continual struggles and trials and under enforced isolation, this God-idea as the central religious truth for the human race.

Second. We recognize in the Bible the record of the consecration of the Jewish people to its mission as priest of the one God, and value it as the most potent instrument of religious and moral instruction. We hold that the modern discoveries of scientific researches in the domains of nature and history are not antagonistic to the doctrines of Judaism, the Bible reflecting the primitive ideas of its own age, and at times clothing its conception of Divine Providence and justice dealing with man in miraculous narratives.

Third. We recognize in the Mosaic legislation a system of training the Jewish people for its mission during its national life in Palestine, and to-day we accept as binding only the moral laws, and maintain only such ceremonies as elevate and sanctify our lives, but reject all such as are not adapted to the views and habits of modern civilization.

Fourth. We hold that all such Mosaic and rabbinical laws as regulate diet, priestly purity and dress originated in ages and under the influence of ideas altogether foreign to our present mental and spiritual state. They fail to impress the modern Jew with a spirit of priestly holiness; their observance in our days is apt rather to obstruct than to further modern spiritual elevation.

Fifth. We recognize in the modern era of universal culture of heart and intellect the approaching of the realization of Israel's great Messianic hope for the establishment of the kingdom of truth, justice and peace among all men. We consider ourselves no longer a nation, but a religious community, and, therefore, expect neither a return to Palestine, nor a sacrificial worship under the sons of Aaron, nor the restoration of any of the laws concerning the Jewish state.

Sixth. We recognize in Judaism a progressive religion, ever striving to be in accord with the postulates of reason. We are convinced of the utmost necessity of preserving the historical identity with our great past. Christianity and Islam being daughter religions of Judaism, we appreciate their providential mission to aid in the spreading of monotheistic and moral truth. We acknowledge that the spirit of broad humanity of our age is our ally in the fulfillment of our mission, and, therefore, we extend the hand of fellowship to all who cooperate with us in the establishment of the reign of truth and righteousness among men.

Seventh. We reassert the doctrine of Judaism that the soul of man is immortal, grounding this belief on the divine nature of the human spirit, which forever finds bliss in righteousness and misery in wickedness. We reject, as ideas not rooted in Judaism, the beliefs both in bodily resurrection and in Gehenna and Eden (Hell and Paradise) as abodes for everlasting punishment and reward.

Eighth. In full accordance with the spirit of Mosaic legislation, which strives to regulate the relation between the rich and poor, we deem it our duty to participate in the great task of modern times, to solve, on the basis of justice and righteousness, the problems presented by the contrasts and evils of the present organization of society.

The Guiding Principles of Reform Judaism: The Columbus Platform (1937)

In view of the changes that have taken place in the modern world and the consequent need of stating anew the teachings of Reform Judaism, the Central Conference of American Rabbis makes the following declaration of principles. It presents them not as a fixed creed but as a guide for the progressive elements of Jewry.

A. Judaism and Its Foundations

1. *Nature of Judaism.* Judaism is the historical religious experience of the Jewish people. Though growing out of Jewish life, its message is universal, aiming at the union and perfection of mankind under the sovereignty of God. Reform Judaism recognizes the principle of progressive development in religion and consciously applies this principle to spiritual as well as to cultural and social life.

   Judaism welcomes all truth, whether written in the pages of scripture or deciphered from the records of nature. The new discoveries of science, while replacing the older scientific views underlying our sacred literature, do not conflict with the essential spirit of religion as manifested in the consecration of man's will, heart and mind to the service of God and of humanity.

2. *God.* The heart of Judaism and its chief contribution to religion is the doctrine of the One, living God, who rules the world through law and love. In Him all existence has its creative source and mankind its ideal of conduct. Though transcending time and space, He is the indwelling Presence of the world. We worship Him as the Lord of the universe and as our merciful Father.

3. *Man.* Judaism affirms that man is created in the Divine image. His spirit is immortal. He is an active co-worker with God. As a child of God, he is endowed with moral freedom and is charged with the responsibility of overcoming evil and striving after ideal ends.

4. *Torah.* God reveals Himself not only in the majesty, beauty and orderliness of nature, but also in the vision and moral striving of the human spirit. Revelation is a continuous process, confined to no one group and to no one age. Yet the people of Israel, through its prophets and sages, achieved unique insight in the realm of religious truth. The Torah, both written and oral, enshrines Israel's ever-growing consciousness of God and of the moral law. It preserves the historical precedents, sanctions and norms of Jewish life, and seeks to mould it in the patterns of goodness and of holiness. Being products of historical processes, certain of its laws have lost their binding force with the passing of the conditions that called them forth. But as a depository of permanent spiritual ideals, the Torah remains the dynamic source of the life of Israel. Each age has the obligation to adapt the teachings of the Torah to its basic needs in consonance with the genius of Judaism.

5. *Israel.* Judaism is the soul of which Israel is the body. Living in all parts of the world, Israel has been held together by the ties of a common history, and above all, by the heritage of faith. Though we recognize in the group loyalty of Jews who have become estranged from our religious tradition, a bond which still unites them with us, we maintain that it is by its religion and for its religion that the Jewish people has lived. The non-Jew who accepts our faith is welcomed as a full member of the Jewish community.

In all lands where our people live, they assume and seek to share loyally the full duties and responsibilities of citizenship and to create seats of Jewish knowledge and religion. In the rehabilitation of Palestine, the land hallowed by memories and hopes, we behold the promise of renewed life for many of our brethren. We affirm the obligation of all Jewry to aid in its upbuilding as a Jewish homeland by endeavoring to make it not only a haven of refuge for the oppressed but also a center of Jewish culture and spiritual life.

Throughout the ages it has been Israel's mission to witness to the Divine in the face of every form of paganism and materialism. We regard it as our historic task to cooperate with all men in the establishment of the kingdom of God, of universal brotherhood, justice, truth and peace on earth. This is our Messianic goal.

B. Ethics

6. *Ethics and Religion.* In Judaism religion and morality blend into an indissoluble unity. Seeking God means to strive after holiness, righteousness and goodness. The love of God is incomplete without the love of one's fellowmen. Judaism emphasizes the kinship of the human race, the sanctity and worth of human life and personality and the right of the individual to freedom and to the pursuit of his chosen vocation. Justice to all, irrespective of race, sect or class, is the inalienable right and the inescapable obligation of all. The state and organized government exist in order to further these ends.

7. *Social Justice.* Judaism seeks the attainment of a just society by the application of its teachings to the economic order, to industry and commerce, and to national and international affairs. It aims at the elimination of man-made misery and suffering, of poverty and degradation, of tyranny and slavery, of social inequality and prejudice, of ill-will and strife. It advocates the promotion of harmonious relations between warring classes on the basis of equity and justice, and the creation of conditions under which human personality may flourish. It pleads for the safeguarding of childhood

against exploitation. It champions the cause of all who work and of their right to an adequate standard of living, as prior to the rights of property. Judaism emphasizes the duty of charity, and strives for a social order which will protect men against the material disabilities of old age, sickness and unemployment.

8. *Peace.* Judaism, from the days of the prophets, has proclaimed to mankind the ideal of universal peace. The spiritual and physical disarmament of all nations has been one of its essential teachings. It abhors all violence and relies upon moral education, love and sympathy to secure human progress. It regards justice as the foundation of the well-being of nations and the condition of enduring peace. It urges organized international action for disarmament, collective security and world peace.

C. Religious Practice

9. *The Religious Life.* Jewish life is marked by consecration to these ideals of Judaism. It calls for faithful participation in the life of the Jewish community as it finds expression in home, synagog and school and in all other agencies that enrich Jewish life and promote its welfare.

The Home has been and must continue to be a stronghold of Jewish life, hallowed by the spirit of love and reverence, by moral discipline and religious observance and worship.

The Synagog is the oldest and most democratic institution in Jewish life. It is the prime communal agency by which Judaism is fostered and preserved. It links the Jews of each community and unites them with all Israel.

The perpetuation of Judaism as a living force depends upon religious knowledge and upon the Education of each new generation in our rich cultural and spiritual heritage.

Prayer is the voice of religion, the language of faith and aspiration. It directs man's heart and mind Godward, voices the needs and hopes of the community, and reaches out after goals which invest life with supreme value. To deepen the spiritual life of our

people, we must cultivate the traditional habit of communion with God through prayer in both home and synagog.

Judaism as a way of life requires in addition to its moral and spiritual demands, the preservation of the Sabbath, festivals and Holy Days, the retention and development of such customs, symbols and ceremonies as possess inspirational value, the cultivation of distinctive forms of religious art and music and the use of Hebrew, together with the vernacular, in our worship and instruction.

These timeless aims and ideals of our faith we present anew to a confused and troubled world. We call upon our fellow Jews to rededicate themselves to them, and, in harmony with all men, hopefully and courageously to continue Israel's eternal quest after God and His kingdom.

Reform Judaism:
A Centenary Perspective (1976)

The Central Conference of American Rabbis has on special occasions described the spiritual state of Reform Judaism. The centenaries of the founding of the Union of American Hebrew Congregations and the Hebrew Union College–Jewish Institute of Religion seem an appropriate time for another such effort. We therefore record our sense of the unity of our movement today.

One Hundred Years: What We Have Taught

We celebrate the role of Reform Judaism in North America, the growth of our movement on this free ground, the great contributions of our membership to the dreams and achievements of this society. We also feel great satisfaction at how much of our pioneering conception of Judaism has been accepted by the Household of Israel. It now seems self-evident to most Jews: that our tradition should interact with modern culture; that its forms ought to reflect a contemporary esthetic; that its scholarship needs to be conducted by modern, critical methods; and that change has been and must continue to be a fundamental reality in Jewish life. Moreover, though some still disagree, substantial numbers have also accepted our teachings: that the ethics of universalism implicit in traditional Judaism must be an explicit part of our Jewish duty; that women should have full rights to practice Judaism; and that Jewish obligation begins with the informed will of every individual. Most modern Jews, within their various religious movements, are embracing Reform Jewish perspectives. We see this past century as having confirmed the essential wisdom of our movement.

One Hundred Years: What We Have Learned

Obviously, much else has changed in the past century. We continue to probe the extraordinary events of the past generation, seeking to understand their meaning and to incorporate their significance in our lives. The Holocaust shattered our easy optimism about humanity and its inevitable progress. The State of Israel, through its many accomplishments, raised our sense of the Jews as a people to new heights of aspiration and devotion. The widespread threats to freedom, the problems inherent in the explosion of new knowledge and of ever more powerful technologies, and the spiritual emptiness of much of Western culture, have taught us to be less dependent on the values of our society and to reassert what remains perennially valid in Judaism's teaching. We have learned again that the survival of the Jewish people is of highest priority and that in carrying out our Jewish responsibilities we help move humanity toward its messianic fulfillment.

Diversity Within Unity, the Hallmark of Reform

Reform Jews respond to change in various ways according to the Reform principle of the autonomy of the individual. However, Reform Judaism does more than tolerate diversity; it engenders it. In our uncertain historical situation we must expect to have far greater diversity than previous generations knew. How we shall live with diversity without stifling dissent and without paralyzing our ability to take positive action will test our character and our principles. We stand open to any position thoughtfully and conscientiously advocated in the spirit of Reform Jewish beliefs. While we may differ in our interpretation and application of the ideas enunciated here, we accept such differences as precious and see in them Judaism's best hope for confronting whatever the future holds for us. Yet in all our diversity we perceive a certain unity and we shall not allow our differences in some particulars to obscure what binds us together.

I. God

The affirmation of God has always been essential to our people's will to survive. In our struggle through the centuries to preserve our faith we have experienced and conceived of God in many ways. The trials of our own time and the challenges of modern culture have made steady belief and clear understanding difficult for some. Nevertheless, we ground our lives, personally and communally, on God's reality and remain open to new experiences and conceptions of the Divine. Amid the mystery we call life, we affirm that human beings, created in God's image, share in God's eternality despite the mystery we call death.

II. The People Israel

The Jewish people and Judaism defy precise definition because both are in the process of becoming. Jews, by birth or conversion, constitute an uncommon union of faith and peoplehood. Born as Hebrews in the ancient Near East, we are bound together like all ethnic groups by language, land, history, culture and institutions. But the people of Israel is unique because of its involvement with God and its resulting perception of the human condition. Throughout our long history our people has been inseparable from its religion with its messianic hope that humanity will be redeemed.

III. Torah

Torah results from the relationship between God and the Jewish people. The records of our earliest confrontations are uniquely important to us. Lawgivers and prophets, historians and poets gave us a heritage whose study is a religious imperative and whose practice is our chief means to holiness. Rabbis and teachers, philosophers and mystics, gifted Jews in every age amplified the Torah tradition. For millennia, the creation of Torah has not ceased and Jewish creativity in our time is adding to the chain of tradition.

IV. Our Obligations: Religious Practice

Judaism emphasizes action rather than creed as the primary expression of a religious life, the means by which we strive to achieve universal justice and peace. Reform Judaism shares this emphasis on duty and obligation. Our founders stressed that the Jew's ethical responsibilities, personal and social, are enjoined by God. The past century has taught us that the claims made upon us may begin with our ethical obligations but they extend to many other aspects of Jewish living, including: creating a Jewish home centered on family devotion; life-long study; private prayer and public worship; daily religious observance; keeping the Sabbath and the holy days; celebrating the major events of life; involvement with the synagogues and community; and other activities which promote the survival of the Jewish people and enhance its existence. Within each area of Jewish observance Reform Jews are called upon to confront the claims of Jewish tradition, however differently perceived, and to exercise their individual autonomy, choosing and creating on the basis of commitment and knowledge.

V. Our Obligations: The State of Israel and the Diaspora

We are privileged to live in an extraordinary time, one in which a third Jewish commonwealth has been established in our people's ancient homeland. We are bound to that land and to the newly reborn State of Israel by innumerable religious and ethnic ties. We have been enriched by its culture and ennobled by its indomitable spirit. We see it providing unique opportunities for Jewish self-expression. We have both a stake and a responsibility in building the State of Israel, assuring its security, and defining its Jewish character. We encourage *aliyah* for those who wish to find maximum personal fulfillment in the cause of Zion. We demand that Reform Judaism be unconditionally legitimized in the State of Israel.

At the same time that we consider the State of Israel vital to the welfare of Judaism everywhere, we reaffirm the mandate of our tradition to create strong Jewish communities wherever we live. A genuine Jewish life is possible in any land, each community developing its own particular character and determining its Jewish responsibilities. The foundation of Jewish community life is the synagogue. It leads us beyond itself to cooperate with other Jews, to share their concerns, and to assume leadership in communal affairs. We are therefore committed to the full democratization of the Jewish community and to its hallowing in terms of Jewish values.

The State of Israel and the diaspora, in fruitful dialogue, can show how a people transcends nationalism even as it affirms it, thereby setting an example for humanity which remains largely concerned with dangerously parochial goals.

VI. Our Obligations: Survival and Service

Early Reform Jews, newly admitted to general society and seeing in this the evidence of a growing universalism, regularly spoke of Jewish purpose in terms of Jewry's service to humanity. In recent years we have become freshly conscious of the virtues of pluralism and the values of particularism. The Jewish people in its unique way of life validates its own worth while working toward the fulfillment of its messianic expectations.

Until the recent past our obligations to the Jewish people and to all humanity seemed congruent. At times now these two imperatives appear to conflict. We know of no simple way to resolve such tensions. We must, however, confront them without abandoning either of our commitments. A universal concern for humanity unaccompanied by a devotion to our particular people is self-destructive; a passion for our people without involvement in humankind contradicts what the prophets have meant to us. Judaism calls us simultaneously to universal and particular obligations.

VII. Hope: Our Jewish Obligation

Previous generations of Reform Jews had unbounded confidence in humanity's potential for good. We have lived through terrible tragedy and been compelled to reappropriate our tradition's realism about the human capacity for evil. Yet our people has always refused to despair. The survivors of the Holocaust, on being granted life, seized it, nurtured it, and, rising above catastrophe, showed humankind that the human spirit is indomitable. The State of Israel, established and maintained by the Jewish will to live, demonstrates what a united people can accomplish in history. The existence of the Jew is an argument against despair; Jewish survival is warrant for human hope.

We remain God's witness that history is not meaningless. We affirm that with God's help people are not powerless to affect their destiny. We dedicate ourselves, as did the generations of Jews who went before us, to work and wait for that day when "They shall not hurt or destroy in all My holy mountain for the earth shall be full of the knowledge of the Lord as the waters cover the sea."

Reform Judaism and Zionism:
A Centenary Platform (1997)

Preamble

In recognition of the centenary of the first World Zionist Congress (August 29, 1897), the Central Conference of American Rabbis hereby issues its first platform dedicated exclusively to the relationship between Reform Judaism and Zionism.

In 1885 the framers of the Pittsburgh Platform of Reform Judaism declared that they no longer expected Jews to return to a national homeland in Palestine. The Platform's authors proclaimed: "We consider ourselves no longer a nation, but a religious community, and, therefore, expect neither a return to Palestine . . . nor the restoration of any of the laws concerning the Jewish state."

By 1937 the CCAR had reversed its stand on Jewish peoplehood, and declared in its "Columbus Platform" that "Judaism is the soul of which Israel [the people] is the body." The document further states: "We affirm the obligation of all Jewry to aid in its [Palestine's] up-building as a Jewish homeland by endeavoring to make it not only a haven of refuge for the oppressed but also a center of Jewish culture and spiritual life." This affirmation of Jewish peoplehood was accompanied by a reaffirmation of Reform Judaism's universal message: "We regard it as our historic task to cooperate with all men in the establishment of the kingdom of God, of universal brotherhood, justice, truth and peace on earth. This is our Messianic goal."

The CCAR returned again to the question of Zionism in 1976, asserting in its "Centenary Perspective": "We are bound to . . . the newly reborn State of Israel by innumerable religious and ethnic ties. . . . We have both a stake and a responsibility in building the State of Israel, assuring its security and defining its Jewish character." The "Centenary Perspective" also affirmed the legitimacy of the Diaspora and the historic universalism of Reform Judaism: "The State of Israel and the Diaspora, in fruitful dialogue, can show how a people transcends nationalism even as it affirms it, thereby setting an example for humanity, which remains largely concerned with dangerously parochial goals." Here again, the CCAR embraced Zionism as a means of fulfilling its universal vision and its opposition to narrow nationalism.

A century after Theodor Herzl called for the creation of a modern Jewish state and nearly fifty years since the State of Israel joined the family of modern nations, the fundamental issues addressed in the previous CCAR pronouncements continue to challenge us, making this a fitting time to re-examine and redefine the ideological and spiritual bonds that connect *Am Yisrael* [the People of Israel] to *Eretz Yisrael* [the Land of Israel] and to *Medinat Yisrael* [the State of Israel]. The CCAR affirms through this Platform those principles which will guide Reform Judaism into the 21st century.

I. Judaism: A Religion and a People

The restoration of *Am Yisrael* to its ancestral homeland after nearly two thousand years of statelessness and powerlessness represents an historic triumph of the Jewish people, providing a physical refuge, the possibility of religious and cultural renewal on its own soil, and the realization of God's promise to Abraham: "to your offspring I assign this land." From that distant moment until today, the intense love between *Am Yisrael* and *Eretz Yisrael* has not subsided.

We believe that the eternal covenant established at Sinai ordained a unique religious purpose for *Am Yisrael*. *Medinat Yisrael*, the Jewish

State, is therefore unlike all other states. Its obligation is to strive towards the attainment of the Jewish people's highest moral ideals to be a *mamlechet kohanim* [a kingdom of priests], a *goy kadosh* [a holy people], and *l'or goyim* [a light unto the nations].

II. From Degradation to Sovereignty

During two millennia of dispersion and persecution, *Am Yisrael* never abandoned hope for the rebirth of a national home in *Eretz Yisrael*. The *Shoah* [Holocaust] intensified our resolve to affirm life and pursue the Zionist dream of a return to *Eretz Yisrael*. Even as we mourned for the loss of one-third of our people, we witnessed the miraculous rebirth of *Medinat Yisrael*, the Jewish people's supreme creation in our age.

Centuries of Jewish persecution, culminating in the *Shoah*, demonstrated the risks of powerlessness. We, therefore, affirm *Am Yisrael's* reassertion of national sovereignty, but we urge that it be used to create the kind of society in which full civil, human, and religious rights exist for all its citizens. Ultimately, *Medinat Yisrael* will be judged not on its military might but on its character.

While we view *Eretz Yisrael* as sacred, the sanctity of Jewish life takes precedence over the sanctity of Jewish land.

III. Our Relationship to the State of Israel

Even as *Medinat Yisrael* serves uniquely as the spiritual and cultural focal point of world Jewry, Israeli and Diaspora Jewry are inter-dependent, responsible for one another, and partners in the shaping of Jewish destiny. Each *kehilla* [Jewish community], though autonomous and self-regulating, shares responsibility for the fate of Jews everywhere. By deepening the social, spiritual, and intellectual relationship among the *kehillot* worldwide, we can revitalize Judaism both in Israel and the Diaspora.

IV. Our Obligations to Israel

To help promote the security of *Medinat Yisrael* and ensure the welfare of its citizens, we pledge continued political support and financial assistance.

Recognizing that knowledge of Hebrew is indispensable both in the study of Judaism and in fostering solidarity between Israeli and Diaspora Jews, we commit ourselves to intensifying Hebrew instruction in all Reform institutions. Hebrew, the language of our sacred texts and prayers, is a symbol of the revitalization of *Am Yisrael*.

To enhance appreciation of Jewish peoplehood and promote a deeper understanding of Israel, we resolve to implement educational programs and religious practices that reflect and reinforce the bond between Reform Judaism and Zionism.

To deepen awareness of Israel and strengthen Jewish identity, we call upon all Reform Jews, adults and youths, to study in, and make regular visits to, Israel.

While affirming the authenticity and necessity of a creative and vibrant Diaspora Jewry, we encourage *aliyah* [immigration] to Israel in pursuance of the precept of *yishuv Eretz Yisrael* [settling the Land of Israel]. While Jews can live Torah-centered lives in the Diaspora, only in *Medinat Yisrael* do they bear the primary responsibility for the governance of society, and thus may realize the full potential of their individual and communal religious strivings.

Confident that Reform Judaism's synthesis of tradition and modernity and its historic commitment to *tikkun olam* [repairing the world] can make a unique and positive contribution to the Jewish state, we resolve to intensify our efforts to inform and educate Israelis about the values of Reform Judaism. We call upon Reform Jews everywhere to dedicate their energies and resources to the strengthening of an indigenous Progressive Judaism in *Medinat Yisrael*.

V. Israel's Obligations to the Diaspora

Medinat Yisrael exists not only for the benefit of its citizens but also to defend the physical security and spiritual integrity of the Jewish people. Realizing that *Am Yisrael* consists of a coalition of different, sometimes conflicting, religious interpretations, the Jewish people will be best served when *Medinat Yisrael* is constituted as a pluralistic, democratic society. Therefore we seek a Jewish state in which no religious interpretation of Judaism takes legal precedence over another.

VI. Redemption

We believe that the renewal and perpetuation of Jewish national life in *Eretz Yisrael* is a necessary condition for the realization of the physical and spiritual redemption of the Jewish people and of all humanity. While that day of redemption remains but a distant yearning, we express the fervent hope that *Medinat Yisrael*, living in peace with its neighbors, will hasten the redemption of *Am Yisrael*, and the fulfillment of our messianic dream of universal peace under the sovereignty of God.

The achievements of modern Zionism in the creation of the State of Israel, in reviving the Hebrew language, in absorbing millions of immigrants, in transforming desolate wastes into blooming forests and fields, in generating a thriving new economy and society, are an unparalleled triumph of the Jewish spirit.

We stand firm in our love of Zion. We resolve to work for the day when waves of Jewish pride and confidence will infuse every Jewish heart, in fulfillment of the promise: When God restores the fortunes of Zion we shall be like dreamers. Our mouths will fill with laughter and our tongues with songs of joy. Then shall they say among the nations God has done great things for them.

Twelve Questions for Focus Groups
on a New "Principles of Reform Judaism"

1. The rabbis meeting in Pittsburgh and Columbus called their documents "Principles." If a new set of "Principles for Reform Judaism" should be adopted, what topics should be covered?

2. It has been suggested that the section on "God" should discuss the implications of God's role as sovereign over our lives (*ol malchut shamayim*). What implications for Reform Jews do you see in this role? What other aspects of God should be included here as important for Reform Jews?

3. It has been argued that in a democratic society it is a given that Jews have the autonomous right to choose what beliefs and practices will inform their lives, but for Reform Jews the hard question is the role of Torah and mitzvot in their lives. What do you see that role to be?

4. In some sense, as an article of belief or as a metaphor which Reform has adopted since it instituted Confirmation on Shavuot, all Jews stood at Sinai. To affirm this suggests that *the entire Torah heard at Sinai is open to Reform Jews as to all other Jews*. It follows from this that the Reform Movement should help its members respond (whether positively, negatively, ambiguously, creatively) to as much as possible of what we heard there, as well as what subsequent ages—including our own—can hear as guidance for

their/our own time. How do you feel about these views? How might you modify them?

5. From Pittsburgh to our own day, a commitment to the mitzvot of social justice has been a cardinal principle of Reform Judaism. How would you articulate this principle, and those mitzvot, today?

6. Given our affirmation of Zionist principles in the Platform on Zionism adopted in Miami, what should a new Statement of Principles say about the State of Israel? About Israel and the Diaspora?

7. What, if anything, should a new Statement of Principles say about our relations with other movements in Judaism, and with the Jewish people as a whole? What, if anything, should it say about our relations with non-Jews, and with Christian and Muslim institutions?

8. Much of the motivation for reform in the nineteenth century stemmed from the conviction that a new age of freedom and universal respect had dawned which should guide new formulations of relevant Jewish doctrine and practice. In the twilight of the twentieth century we often believe that Judaism needs to rescue us from the cruel, demeaning aspects of much of our age. How, if at all, should we articulate the need for Judaism to be a transforming force in society?

9. Should the Principles articulate some other specific theological issues (e.g., the afterlife, the nature of prayer, etc.)? What issues and what should we say about them?

10. Should the Principles say anything about the way in which we should formulate policy in the twenty-first century regarding issues that may put us at odds with the halachah or the majority of the Jewish community, as was the case with patrilineality?

11. It has been suggested that this Statement of Principles should be no longer than the Pittsburgh Platform, which was about fifty-two lines (which might enable it to be included as a page in the new prayer book), supplemented by a specific plan for implementation and by essays, and even books, of commentary. How do you feel about this?

12. What other questions should we be asking? What other suggestions do you have?

APPENDIX 6

Ten Principles for Reform Judaism: Third Draft

Preamble: Who Are We Reform Jews?

Much has changed in the Jewish world since the Central Conference of American Rabbis issued its Centenary Perspective 100 years after the founding of the Union of American Hebrew Congregations and the Hebrew Union College. Then as now we have been a movement of varying beliefs and practices, strengthened by our diversity yet increasingly in search of common themes that can deepen the religious life of the Reform community. We do not attempt to legislate a code of belief or conduct for Reform Jews, nor presume to advocate a single mode of religious expression for all. As Reform Jews we are open to the entirety of our tradition, commanded to engage in the study and practice that will embody that tradition in a manner appropriate to our different situations.

As rabbis dedicated to a Reform Judaism that can transform through holiness the lives of individuals, the Jewish people and ultimately humanity, the CCAR offers these responses to those who seek to know: *Who Are We Reform Jews—where are we going, what can we believe and what can we practice*—at a significant moment in Western history, the dawn of a new century.

Toward God
First: Created by the Holy One, We Are Seekers After God

Reform Judaism embraces the story of the Jewish people which tells of three great encounters with God: Creation, our redemption from Egypt, and our standing together at Sinai. These encounters, re-enacted throughout the Jewish year, lead us to seek our own relationships with God, however different our beliefs, experiences and questions may be. Based on traditional liturgies and our movement's creativity, we pledge to create texts and worship environments that will enable us as individuals and communities to drink deeply from the Fountain from which our lives spring, and regularly to praise, thank, celebrate, petition, sing to, argue with and cry out to the *Ribono shel Olam*, the Great One who presides over all time and all space.

Second: Having Stood at Sinai, We Respond to the Call
*   of Mitzvot Amid Modernity*

Standing at Sinai, the Jewish people heard God reveal the Torah. Through study, we become aware of God's mitzvot, commandments, that call to us even though we live in a modern society. In the worldview of Reform Judaism's founders, modernity was the center, the scale on which we measured what was valuable and enduring in Jewish practice and belief. Looking back at a century which has witnessed some of the greatest gifts and the most awful consequences of modernity, we proclaim that the mitzvot of the Torah are our center, and Judaism is the scale by which we shall judge the modern world.

Though all the mitzvot are open to us as to all Jews, the Reform movement believes that changing times affect the way we understand the mitzvot. We respond to the call of Torah in two ways: out of the ever-growing body of interpretation by *Kenesset Yisrael*, the eternal community of the Jewish people, and out of our individual understanding of what is holy in our own time. Study, prayer and reflection on our actions will help us offer informed responses to the Torah's call to do God's will in our days. Such responses will help us transform a life too often lived exclusively in a state of *chol*, ordinariness, into a life filled with *kedushah*, with holiness. We want to deepen the Jewish content of our lives not only to enrich our own existence, but to enhance the quality of the communities and the lands in which we live. Reform Judaism calls us to help transform our culture and our world.

Third: We Were Redeemed from Egypt to Help Repair the World

Central to the mission of Reform Judaism from its inception has been a belief that God has called us to the prophetic task of *tikun olam*, increasing the spiritual dimensions of our material existence in ways that can repair our shattered world. In our learning, in our daily striving to increase the holiness of our existence, in the private and public spheres of our lives, we pledge to work for the cause of the poor and oppressed as the Torah commands us, and for the protection of the earth and all the creatures God vouchsafed to us. Mindful of our own redemption from Egypt, we commit ourselves to help redeem the new century in modernity, striving to transform it into a realization of Israel's great messianic hope for the establishment of truth and justice, for moral and spiritual discipline, compassion and integrity, and at long last, a world repaired, a world at peace.

Toward Torah
Fourth: We Are Committed to Shabbat, Which Elevates Our Work and Frees Us From It

As a model for a life lived in *kedushah*, we commit ourselves to observance of the mitzvot of Shabbat, which our tradition has seen as *mey-eyn olam ha-ba*, a foretaste of the world to come, a world transformed. Standing at the climax of the week, Shabbat and its holiness inspire us to bring the highest moral values to our weekday labor and our interactions with other human beings. Shabbat also liberates us from the obligations which our work places upon us that we may focus on our obligations to God.

Shabbat offers us the opportunity to participate in the sanctity of our synagogue community and to sanctify our homes through *shamor*, the mitzvot of refraining from ordinary weekday acts, as well as *zachor*, the mitzvot of welcoming the special Shabbat rituals into our lives.

Fifth: We Are Committed to Learning and Seasonal Celebration

An informed response to the call of the mitzvot requires a disciplined commitment at every stage of our lives to learn Torah in the widest sense—biblical, rabbinic, medieval and modern texts, history, literature, philosophy, art, music and dance; and by encouraging our children and our friends to learn and interpret these with us.

Because Torah needs to be studied in an environment of *kedushah*, we commit ourselves to steer the course of our lives by creative celebration of the seasonal festivals and the other commemorative days of our calendar, delighting in the special foods and observing the somber fasts that nourish our modern souls. We will celebrate the seasons of our personal lives as well, through traditional and creative rites of entrance into the *brit*, God's covenant, for girls and boys, at stages in children's maturation, at marriage, at other milestones in the adult life cycle, at creative ceremonies of commitment to those closest to us, at times of healing, and when faced with death. Conscious always of our mortality, we are committed to filling our days with the joy of living as Jews.

Sixth: We Are Open to Expanding the Mitzvot of Reform Jewish Practice

As we strive to admit a greater degree of holiness into our own lives and those of our communities, we commit ourselves to some mitzvot that have long been hallmarks of Reform Judaism, and, in the spirit of standing at Sinai with all other Jews, we know we may feel called to other mitzvot new to Reform Jewish observance. We also respect the Jewish beliefs of the past, and are open to explore how they may be applied to each new generation's search. As part of Reform Judaism's classic belief in ongoing revelation, we know that what may seem outdated in one age may be redemptive in another.

Thus we renew our classic devotion to *chinuch*, to Jewish education, some of us sending our children to Jewish day schools, others to supplementary schools, but all striving to participate actively in our children's Jewish schooling. We renew our commitment to *tzedakah*, to setting aside a portion of our earnings to provide justice for those in need, and to engage in regular acts of *gemilut chasadim*, showing by our caring presence our love for those in pain.

In the presence of God we may each feel called to respond in different ways: some by offering traditional or spontaneous blessings, others by covering our heads, still others by wearing the tallit or tefillin for prayer. Some will look for ways to reveal holiness in our encounters with the world around us, others to transform our homes into a *mikdash me-at*, a holy place in miniature. Some of us may observe practices of *kashrut*, to extend the sense of *kedushah* into the acts surrounding food and into a concern for the way food is raised and brought to our tables. Others may wish to utilize the *mikvah* or other kinds of spiritual immersion not only for conversion but for periodic experiences of purification. Some of us may discover rituals now unknown which in the spirit of Jewish tradition and Reform creativity will bring us closer to God, to Torah, and to our people.

In the spirit of early Reform Judaism, we too hope to fulfill our mission as an *or la-goyim*, a light to the nations we live among, by creating communities of learning, celebration, moral rectitude and respect for diversity.

Toward Israel, People and Land
Seventh: We Are Members of a Holy People, From Whom We Learn,
  Whom We Can Teach

Seeking to draw from the wisdom of *am kadosh*, the people to whom God imparted a particular measure of holiness, we wish to strengthen our ties with Jews from all the movements in Judaism. Reminded that we all once stood together at Sinai, we seek to work together in mutual respect, aware of our many serious differences, trying to understand the motivations that lead to our divergence. While our solutions may radically differ, we all face common problems. If we can only listen to each other, we can learn much.

Perhaps our greatest common concern is the consequences of the successful integration of Jews into our society. While this often seems an invitation to assimilation, our Reform commitment to let Judaism help transform society leads us to see this integration as a challenge to expand individuals' knowledge and practice of Jewish tradition. Because of Reform Judaism's openness to Jews from patrilineal and other untraditional backgrounds, we believe that by filling the minds, hearts and souls of seeking Jews, we can assist Jewish life on this continent to fulfill its great potential.

We are cheered that by the opening of the 21st century Jewish life has been reborn across Europe. We pledge to help provide Progressive congregations around the world with rabbinic service, to share insights with each other, and to respect our common membership in *Kenesset Yisrael*. We promise to be vigilant in helping Jews around the world protect ourselves against renewals of anti-Semitism and other forms of discrimination.

Eighth: Members of a Holy People, We Are Rooted in a Holy Land

After 2000 years of statelessness and powerlessness, the restoration of *Am Yisrael*, the people of Israel, to its ancestral homeland in *Eretz Yisrael*, the Land of Israel, represents an historic triumph of the Jewish people and of modern Zionism, which created *Medinat Yisrael*, the State of Israel. We wish to help create a State which promotes full civil, human and religious rights for all its citizens, and in which no religious interpretation of Judaism takes legal precedence over another. We wish to help the State work unceasingly for a mutual atmosphere of peace, justice and security with Palestinians and other Arab neighbors.

While Israeli and Diaspora Jewry are both creative and vibrant communities, independent yet responsible for one another, we encourage Reform Jews to make *aliyah*, immigration to Israel, in fulfillment of the precept of *yishuv Eretz Yisrael*, settling the Land of Israel, in a manner consistent with our Reform commitments. We call upon Reform Jews everywhere to dedicate their energies and resources to strengthening an indigenous Progressive Judaism that can help transform *Medinat Yisrael*. (*Adapted from* Reform Judaism and Zionism: A Centenary Platform)

Ninth: Members of a Holy People, We Are Heirs to a Holy Tongue

Seeking holiness, we echo our people's belief that God endowed the Hebrew language with a particular measure of *kedushah*. Hebrew binds us to Jews in every land, and especially to our brothers and sisters in the State of Israel. We shall strive to read it, to let it help articulate our prayer and inform our study, to speak it. The more Hebrew we use in our prayer and our study, the more we shall share in the holiness of our people's heritage.

Tenth: We Are Committed to the Equality of All the People of God

We have all benefited from the growing fulfillment of Reform's historic promise of equality between women and men. Jewish women and men alike have been strengthened from the admission of women to the rabbinate, the cantorate and other positions of Jewish religious leadership. Listening to women's voices in our tradition has taught us all a new language to encounter faces of God once hidden from us, new ways to encounter God's presence in our lives, new ways to relate to each other and conduct our institutions. We shall encourage Jews in all the movements to learn from these voices as well. We all commit ourselves to honor the different contributions men and women can make to our movement and to ensure that the women and men who lead us, whether professionals or laypeople, are able to fulfill their calling with appropriate recognition and respect.

We affirm that all people, regardless of gender, age, belief, physical condition, or sexual orientation, are all created in the image of the Holy One. In whatever ways we can, we shall strive to help all the children of God and all the peoples of God fulfill their divine potential to contribute to a world transformed, the world of our people's storied dream.

Ken y'hi ratzon. May this be God's will.

Notes

Chapter 1

1. See Michael A. Meyer, *Response to Modernity: A History of the Reform Movement in Judaism* (New York: Oxford University Press, 1998), p. 319.

2. "Report of the Committee on Patrilineal Descent on the Status of Children of Mixed Marriages," adopted by the CCAR at its 94th Annual Convention, Los Angeles, CA, March 15, 1983.

3. In a generous and loving act of historical continuity, Dr. Borowitz assigned the twelve questions to his theology class at the New York School of HUC-JIR, asking these future leaders of the Reform Movement to develop their own answers, which he passed on to me, and which I incorporated wherever feasible into the early drafts of the Pittsburgh Principles.

4. The rabbis were Harry Danziger from Memphis, several years later elected president of the CCAR; Lewis Kamrass from Cincinnati; Charles Kroloff from Westfield, New Jersey, my successor as president of the CCAR; Shimeon Maslin from Philadelphia, immediate past president of the CCAR; Paul Menitoff, executive vice president of the CCAR; Daniel Polish from Poughkeepsie, New York; Michael Stroh from Toronto; and me. The HUC faculty members were Dr. Michael Meyer of the Cincinnati campus, author of *Response to Modernity: A History of the Reform Movement in Judaism* and *The Reform Judaism Reader*, and Dr. Carol Balin, assistant professor of American Jewish history at the New York School. The rabbinical student was Leah Cohen of the Cincinnati campus, as of this writing a rabbi in Georgetown, Connecticut. The laypeople were Judge David Davidson, then chair of the Joint Commission on Social Action; George Markley, co-chair of the Joint Commission on Religious Living; and Dolores Wilkenfeld, a former president of Women of Reform Judaism and a member of the board of the World Union for Progressive Judaism.

5. Almost literally twenty-five hours. Dr. Balin woke up at 3 A.M. with an idea for the conclusion and wrote it out before dawn.

6. Lance J. Sussman and Robert M. Seltzer, "Pittsburgh II and the Crisis of Confidence in the Reform Rabbinate," *CCAR Journal*, Winter 2000, p. 28.

7. Ibid., p. 31.

8. Ibid.

9. Ibid., p. 26.

Chapter 2

1. Immanuel Kant, *Foundations of the Metaphysics of Morals*, trans. Lewis White Beck, Library of Liberal Arts (Englewood Cliffs, NJ: Prentice-Hall, 1997), p. 25.

2. Eugene Borowitz, *Reform Judaism Today*, bk. 2, (New York: Behrman House, 1977), pp. 40–41.

3. Because this name eventually was permitted to be pronounced only by the High Priest on Yom Kippur, its exact pronunciation became lost, and so when the letters appeared in the Torah, it was early ordained that they should be pronounced as *Adonai*, from the word *adon*, meaning "Lord." That the exact name of God is unknowable is indicative of the fact that, while God is real, God's nature is unknowable.

4. See the well-known Talmudic story of Rabbi Eliezer confronting the majority of the rabbis in the case of the Oven of Achnai (Babylonian Talmud, *Bava M'tzia* 59b).

5. The particle *im*, often rendered as "*if* you hearken . . . , *then* you will become a treasure," can also be understood as connoting an oath: "I adjure you."

6. Reform views of revelation will be discussed in greater detail under "The Reform Jew in Dialogue with Torah."

Chapter 5

1. Mark Washofsky, *Jewish Living: A Guide to Contemporary Reform Practice* (New York: UAHC Press, 2001), p. 97.

2. Leo Baeck, *This People Israel* (New York: Holt, Rinehart and Winston, 1965), p. 169.

Chapter 6

1. Eugene Borowitz, *Reform Judaism Today*, bk. 2, p. 44.

2. *Encyclopaedia Judaica*, vol. 15, p. 180.

3. Kaufmann Kohler, *Jewish Theology* (New York: KTAV, 1968), pp. 296–97.

4. *Gates of Understanding* (New York: CCAR Press, 1977), p. 218.

Chapter 7

1. *Jewish Encyclopedia* (1902), vol. 4, p. 220.

2. See *Mishnah Sanhedrin* 8:4 and Babylonian Talmud, *Sanhedrin* 71a.

3. See Galatians 3:19.

Chapter 8

1. Meyer, *Response to Modernity*, pp. 96–97, 137.

2. Ibid., p. 230.

3. Over the years a friendly struggle has developed between some HUC students and some Hebrew faculty members. The students return from Israel with limited flu-

ency in conversation and wish their classes to be taught in Hebrew so they can hone their speaking skills, while the Hebrew scholars want the classes taught in English so students can understand the nuances of their Hebrew texts.

4. A small but dedicated group of Hebraists in the Reform rabbinate have consistently opposed the inclusion of transliteration in Reform siddurim out of the belief that the siddur is a text for learning Hebrew and transliteration will impede that learning. The overwhelming majority of their colleagues—and, judged anecdotally, of laypeople as well—has been drawn to the prayer role of the siddur rather than the study role, supporting the widespread transliteration in *Mishkan T'filah*. As an act of compromise, the CCAR Board of Trustees voted to publish an edition of the volume without transliteration, for those who wish to use it for educational purposes.

5. In 2001, the CCAR's Hebrew Literacy Task Force surveyed attitudes toward Hebrew among CCAR members. It found that 70% thought that Hebrew should be a higher priority than it is, and that 91% offered an adult Hebrew program, compared to 64% in 1975. A full description of the survey results can be found in Jeffrey Wildstein, "Hebrew in the Reform Movement," *CCAR Journal*, Winter 2005, pp. 82–91.

Chapter 9

1. Some defenders of the Pittsburgh Platform of 1885 note that one of the reasons for rejecting diet, purity, and dress was that "their observance in our days is apt rather to obstruct than to further modern spiritual elevation," perhaps leaving a loophole for accepting them in later days when spiritual value could be found. That a later age might find spiritual value in them was so antithetical to the Pittsburghers' view of the course of Western civilization that one might speculate that in an age that found dress, purity, and diet elevating, the Pittsburghers might despair that Reform even had a place. Those who adhere to the 1885 view today often take the position that Reform's mandate is to return to the worldview of the late nineteenth century, but this is a belief totally at odds with the Pittsburghers' Hegelian conviction that each new age is an improvement on the one before.

2. The content of all these volumes, as well as the many volumes of *t'shuvot* (responsa) published by the CCAR Responsa Committee have now been incorporated into a significant volume of normative contemporary Reform observance by Rabbi Mark Washofsky, a professor of Talmud at HUC-JIR, called *Jewish Living: A Guide to Contemporary Reform Practice* (New York: UAHC Press, 2001).

3. David Ellenson, "Autonomy and Norms in Reform Judaism," *CCAR Journal*, Spring 1999, p. 25.

4. Another source of the mitzvah of study is Deuteronomy 17:18, in which the monarch was commanded to write a *sefer Torah*. As monarchs became occupied with other tasks, this mitzvah was altered in two important ways: to allow the monarch to assign another, more skilled individual to write it, so the monarch could study it; and then to extend the obligation to study it to every individual.

5. Reform congregations in Toronto are an exception to this.

6. *T'fillin* are wound on one's weaker arm (the left for right-handers, the right for lefties) to demonstrate this connection.

7. For a fuller discussion of the history of *t'fillin* and other traditional garb in the Reform Movement, see Washofsky, *Jewish Living*, pp. 6–15.

8. Other forbidden elements of kashrut include the mixing of milk and meat, the eating of blood, the eating of the *gid hanasheh* that runs through the animal's loins, and the requirement of *sh'chitah*, special rules for animal slaughter.

9. Over the next decade the CCAR will be releasing a Guide to Dietary Practices in the Reform Movement, which will make suggestions similar to the ones mentioned above. See also a symposium on Reform dietary practice in *CCAR Journal*, Winter 2004, pp. 3–71.

10. Meyer, *Response to Modernity*, pp. 138, 292.

11. Rachel Adler, "*Tum'ah* and *Toharah*: Ends and Beginnings," *Response*, Summer 1973, no. 18:119–20. Because the common understanding of *tum'ah* has long been used to impose restrictive prohibitions on women's participation in Orthodox Jewish religious and communal life, Dr. Adler renounced her original uplifting interpretation of *mikveh* in 1993. Because her original essay played a major role in the spiritual rediscovery of *mikveh*, I believe it still deserves to be quoted.

Chapter 10

1. Redemption is the theme of the afternoon *Minchah* service, which has become an increasingly popular time for Reform bar and bat mitzvah observances. Here the feminine evening and masculine morning are brought together in the mingling of twilight and the approach of Elijah the Prophet's promise of the messianic coming.

2. Washofsky, *Jewish Living*, p. 84.

3. See ibid., pp. 93–96, 388–89.

4. These brief descriptions of the seven lower *s'firot*, the kabbalistic manifestations of the nature of God named here in parentheses, hardly do them justice. For a nuanced, scholarly introduction to these concepts, see Arthur Green, *A Guide to the Zohar* (Stanford, CA: Stanford University Press, 2004), pp. 28–59. For some applications of the doctrine in the realm of personal behavior, see Laibl Wolf, *Practical Kabbalah: A Guide to Jewish Wisdom for Everyday Life* (New York: Three Rivers Press, 1999), pp. 113–220.

5. Other people, of course, have been given their own revelations into the seasons. For Christians, winter brings the hope of Jesus's birth for light in the dark times of the year; spring offers the emergence of Jesus from the tomb of death to offer atonement to Christian sinners.

6. One can of course argue that selling one's *chameitz* to a gentile emphasizes our interdependence with our neighbors; without the non-Jew's agreeing to "buy" our *chameitz*, the only way we could remove it from our possession would be to destroy it all, thus violating mitzvot against needless waste.

7. Sue Levi Elwell, ed., *The Open Door: A Passover Haggadah* (New York: CCAR Press, 2002), pp. xviii–xix. See also Susannah Heschel, "Orange on the Seder Plate," in *The Women's Passover Companion*, ed. Sharon Cohen Anisfeld, Tara Mohr, and Catherine Spector (Woodstock, VT: Jewish Lights Publishing, 2003).

8. It was God, after all, who told Abraham and Sarah to name their child Yitzchak, "The One Who Laughs," and the Rabbis speak of God laughing just as they speak of God weeping. Sometimes, of course, it is hard to tell the difference.

9. See Lewis M. Barth, *Berit Mila in the Reform Context* (Secaucus, NJ: Carol Publishing Group for the Berit Milah Board of Reform Judaism, 1990).

10. See Rachel Adler, *Engendering Judaism*, pp. 169–207.

Chapter 11

1. See James Dao, "Forty Years Later, Civil Rights Makes Page One," *The New York Times,* July 13, 2004, p. 1.

Chapter 12

1. Yeshayah Leibowitz argues that Korach's demagoguery was demonstrated by his saying, "All the congregation *is* holy" (Numbers 16:3). See *Etz Hayim* (New York and Philadelphia: Rabbinical Assembly and Jewish Publication Society, 2001), p. 861.

2. Laws for the nations that the Rabbis believed were first given to Adam and Eve and renewed with the sons of Noah for all humanity: avoidance of blasphemy, idolatry, murder, adultery, stealing, and cruelty to animals; and an injunction to establish a legal system (*B'reishit Rabbah* 16:6).

Chapter 13

1. Published in *Selected Writings of Isaac Mayer Wise,* ed. David Philipson and Louis Grossman (repr., New York: Arno Press, 1969).

2. The limitation of a minyan to ten is generally thought to derive from the verse in the story in Numbers in which the faithless scouts, who returned with the counsel that the people should not try to occupy the Promised Land, are called an *eidah raah* (Numbers 14:27), usually translated as a "wicked congregation." While there were twelve scouts, two of them (Joshua and Caleb) urged the people to take the land, leaving ten who were the "wicked congregation," suggesting to the Rabbis that at least ten people—not righteous people, not leaders, but even ten wicked people—were needed before there could be a congregation. The number is also associated with Abraham's refusal to bargain for the rescue of Sodom if fewer than ten righteous people could be found in it (Genesis 18:32), a notion somewhat at odds with the rabbinic willingness to accept even ten wicked people as enough for a congregation. The Rabbis argued that because prayer itself was one of the affirmative mitzvot that had to be done at a set time, women should be excused from the obligation, originally lest they have to choose between a demanding infant and a commanding God. A later generation of sages ruled that because women were not obligated as men were, they could not participate in prayer on the same basis as men, neither to be counted in a minyan nor to engage in any of the public roles of the service. The Reform Movement eventually argued that women's obligations were the same as men's.

3. The rationale for this is that all these prayers imply a community. *Barchu* consists of a call by the leader to praise God, to which the community responds, "*Baruch!*" And in Leviticus 22:32 we read of God that "I will be sanctified [*nikdashti*] amidst the Children of Israel," which the Rabbis connect to Numbers 16:21, where "amidst" is equated with "congregation," signifying that God's *k'dushah* cannot be extolled without a congregation. Hence the main praises of God's *k'dushah*—the *K'dushah* and the *Kaddish*—cannot be said by fewer than ten.

4. For a thoughtful, concise treatment of the issue of divorce in Reform Judaism, see Washofsky, *Jewish Living,* pp. 168–76.

5. Discussed in ibid., pp. 323ff.

Chapter 14

1. Gary A. Tobin, *Opening the Gates: How Proactive Conversion Can Revitalize the Jewish Community* (San Francisco: Jossey-Bass, 1999), chap. 7.

Chapter 15

1. The last chapter appeared in English in the Spring 1969 issue of *Judaism*, published by the American Jewish Congress, vol. 18, no. 2, pp. 131–142, translated by Frank Talmadge.

2. In June 1984, completing a year-long program of study and "open dialogue," the CCAR adopted a resolution stating that "the legitimate demands of security for Israel can—and must—be reconciled with the dignity, the human rights, and the right of self-determination of Palestinian Arabs. . . . Our commitment to pluralism in Israel, as elsewhere, is multi-dimensional. We reject attitudes which ignore the religious, cultural, and ethnic rights and concerns of *Edot Hamizrach* [Jewish communities from Arab countries], Israeli Arabs, Ethiopian Jewry, as well as of Reform and Conservative Jewry" ("On Israel," adopted by the CCAR at the 95th Annual Convention of the Central Conference of American Rabbis, Grossingers, New York, June 18–21, 1984). On March 26, 2003, as the Second Intifada was raging, the CCAR Board "affirm[ed] Judaism's deep religious commitment to the prophetic teaching of liberty, justice and peace. The realization of these principles is a prerequisite for harmonious co-existence. This is of particular importance at this time when Israeli Arabs' and Palestinian rights are so adversely affected by the current violent conflict. We are deeply pained by the growing poverty and hunger within the Palestinian community. The current dire situation of Palestinians is largely a byproduct of Palestinian terror, but the long lasting occupation has contributed to the Palestinians' plight. We call on Palestinians as well as Israeli leadership to address this immediately. . . . We call upon the government and Jewish citizens of Israel to do all in their power to ameliorate the social, economic and educational situation of Israel's Arab citizens."

Chapter 16

1. In the official Pittsburgh Principles document, these two affirmations of our commitment to Progressive Judaism around the world are separated by the paragraph on the interdependence of Israel and the Diaspora. The two have been combined here to provide an opportunity to speak about North American Reform's commitment to Progressive Judaism around the world.

2. Based on Meyer, *Response to Modernity*, pp. 339, 346–48.